THE ECOLOGY OF THE NEW ECONOMY

SUSTAINABLE TRANSFORMATION OF GLOBAL INFORMATION, COMMUNICATIONS AND ELECTRONICS INDUSTRIES

Edited by Jacob Park and Nigel Roome

The Ecology of the New Economy

SUSTAINABLE TRANSFORMATION OF GLOBAL INFORMATION, COMMUNICATIONS AND ELECTRONICS INDUSTRIES

CONTRIBUTING EDITORS
JACOB PARK AND NIGEL ROOME

Greenleaf
PUBLISHING
2002

Published by Greenleaf Publishing Limited
Aizlewood's Mill
Nursery Street
Sheffield S3 8GG
UK

Printed and bound, using acid-free paper from managed forests, by
Bookcraft, Midsomer Norton, UK.

British Library Cataloguing in Publication Data:
  Ecology of the new economy : sustainable transformation of
     global information, communications and electronics
     industries
  1. High technology industries   2. Social responsibility of
  business
  I. Park, Jacob   II. Roome, Nigel, 1953–
  658.5'14

  ISBN 1874719470

CONTENTS

FOREWORD

Jonathan Lash

President, World Resources Institute, USA

There is evidence of an amazing global epidemic of green competition and global accountability. Few in the environmental community, private sector or government ten years ago anticipated the onset of this epidemic. Yet today it seems evident that competition is a powerful force for sustainability. How did this startling about-face occur? A key factor has been the rapid evolution of information and communications technologies and their availability to more and more of the world's people.

The globalisation debate, in WTO meetings or on the streets of Seattle, typically focuses on emergence and facilitation of global markets. While global markets for goods, labour and capital accelerate depletion of natural resources and environmental degradation, we do well to remember there are other, equally powerful waves of global change that can empower other values in the marketplace. First, there is the globalisation of information, powered by the advance and proliferation of information and communications technologies. We live in the age of CNN, cell phones and the Internet, all of which put more and fresher information in the hands of more people than ever. Information is power, and people increasingly use it to hold accountable governments and companies who conceal, pollute, cheat or just ignore social expectations. The international flow of information, images and ideas overwhelms the significance of borders as barriers, diminishing the capacity of governments to control events. And so we have a new era of information regulation, pioneered by the Toxics Release Inventory in the US and rapidly spreading to the most unexpected places. So what a surprise, and a breath of fresh air, it is to see the giant reader-board in Shanghai with real-time data on four primary air pollutants: even the Chinese government sees that the best way to clear the air is to put information in the hands of the people

Another wave of change, overlapping with the globalisation of markets and of information, is the rise of civil society. While the rise of global markets is powered by about 20,000 multinational corporations, the UN estimates there are now several million non-governmental organisations active throughout the world, each of whom needs only Web access to achieve global reach. This reach does not guarantee a global audience, but it creates the opportunity of connection with low transaction costs, making it a powerful vehicle for building ad hoc communities of common purpose that amplify voices. These ad hoc alliances, built around purpose and action rather than jurisdiction or entitlement, appear increasingly to be how things get done in the world—not by mandate. Governments and companies that ignore these voices find themselves subject to retribution that is sudden, non-negotiable, not necessarily fair and not subject to appeal.

And so today we find a growing list of industries where social and environmental stewardship have muscled their way out of the compliance box and now set the strategic agenda. BP and Shell compete to provide alternative and renewable energy sources. Ford, Honda, GM and Toyota race electric, hybrid and fuel-cell vehicles to market, and not just in California. Interface, Collins & Aikman and Milliken compete to be the greenest in the floor-covering industry. Home Depot and Lowe's one-up each other with pledges to stock only sustainably harvested wood products. Only some of this occurred because CEOs suddenly developed a passion for social responsibility: green competition is much more powerful. We need to better understand how the rise of the global information, communications and electronics industries has created this competitive dynamic, because we do not know how to sustain it, nor spread it to other industries. Although there are grounds for optimism, grimmer scenarios are equally arresting. We need to understand better how information and communications technologies can help us vector the three great waves of globalisation—markets, information and civil society—to a sustainable path. This book will help point the way.

INTRODUCTION
Atom to bits: e-sustainability in the global economy

Jacob Park
University of Maryland, USA

Nigel Roome
Erasmus University Rotterdam,
the Netherlands

The two revolutions

Information, communications, computing and electronic (ICCE) technologies are developing rapidly and assuming a more prominent role in the global economy. They are impacting the industrialised countries, the developing world and the rapidly industrialising economies. At the same time, the international community is confronting critical challenges of environmental sustainability around such issues as global climate change, industrial pollution, and intensive patterns of material consumption. Many companies, from traditional manufacturing to e-commerce, are adopting ICCE solutions and applications as part of their business growth and development.

Yet the implications for sustainable development arising from the adoption of these new technologies and systems are far from certain. The advance of ICCE has been so rapid that we do not yet know, for instance, under what circumstances tangible gains or losses will arise for sustainable development from these technologies, or the degree to which ICCE technologies serve as substitutes or complements to existing technologies and socio-technical systems. In terms of the companies that are in ICCE technology-related industries, it is far from clear whether and to what extent sustainable development is viewed as a strategic business priority.

What we do know is that the intersection of these two global trends raises a number of new and complex issues of major importance to the providers and users of ICCE technologies and to society at large. This book is in part an attempt to understand some of these issues and discuss appropriate responses. It has the modest goal of provoking greater interest in the examination of ICCE technologies and their impacts on society and the global environment while beginning to establish an intellectual foundation for future research in this field. The goal of this introductory chapter is to set the broad context within which the debate about the environmental sustainability of technologies, in general, and ICCE technologies, in particular, can be framed. It maps out critical public policy and business issues that link the themes of sustainability, ICCE technologies and globalisation, and then concludes by highlighting and discussing some of the key analytical and conceptual issues contained in this book.

Technology and human development

Technology and technological innovation represent human knowledge and ingenuity embedded in material form. Technology is so central to human development that dominant technologies are used to specify epochs in the history of our development—the Stone Age, Bronze Age, Steam Age, Industrial Revolution and Information Age. However, we have become increasingly aware—particularly in the past 50 years—that our systems and patterns of production and consumption have significant impacts on the resource endowments and services of the natural and physical world. Electricity, steam engines and automobiles represent important symbols of technological innovation and human ingenuity that have proven to be less than neutral in their impact on the natural environment. Moreover, social and institutional systems have developed around these technologies to shape our understanding of development and provoke a set of economic, social and environmental issues.

The US National Academy of Engineering's list of the most important engineering achievements of the 20th century, including electrification (no. 1), the automobile (no. 2) and the aeroplane (no. 3), reflect monumental technological achievements and human progress. These technologies and the systems of which they are part often generate far-reaching environmental impacts, which were not anticipated and sometimes still remain unrecognised. New technologies often create societies' need for them, rather than the other way around. Invention can sometimes be the mother of necessity (Diamond 1997).

In recent years, growing concerns about the degradation of environmental resources have led to calls for more sustainable forms of development (Agenda 21 1992; WCED 1987). Given the contribution of technology to development, it is not surprising that any move towards sustainable development needs to have a strong technological underpinning. The Brundtland Report stated that sustainable development involves 'a process of change in which the exploitation of resources, the direction of investments, *the orientation of technological development*, and institutional change are all in harmony and enhance both current and future potential to meet human needs and aspirations' (WCED 1987: 46 [our italics]). A recent report of the World Business Council for Sustainable Development observes that 'technology has consistently provided the opportunities from which we have been able to make and sell better goods and services and to do so more cleanly and more safely' (Brown *et al.* 2000: 1).

However, transforming the orientation of technology is not simple or straightforward. The first reason is that technology is often a double-edged sword, capable of both improving and degrading environmental quality. For example, technological advances in electronics—propelled by economic, regulatory and environmental pressures—have resulted in a 70%–80% decline in the vehicular emissions of volatile organic compounds and carbon monoxide per mile travelled in the US (Austin and Macauley 2001: 24). However, these technological advances became necessary in effect to mitigate the environmental damage caused by the unsustainable growth in the use of automobiles, which the US National Academy of Engineering regards as the second most important engineering achievement of the 20th century.

The second reason is that technologies do not exist in isolation. They are linked to other technologies, embedded in socio-technical systems, and connected to networks of actors that depend on those technologies and systems. The process of transformation to more sustainable forms of development therefore involves not simply change in technologies but also changes in these socio-technical systems and, ultimately, in the relationships and position of actors in the networks that span these systems. The automobile provides another good illustration of this point. The internal combustion engine provides the power train for much of our current stock of personal transport. It influences automobile production and design, the broader system of transport and transport infrastructure, the design of houses, and the layout of towns and cities—including the planning, location and design of retailing outlets as well as the movement and sale of oil products, the nature of leisure activities and lifestyles, and many other aspects of contemporary life.

In terms of actor networks, the internal combustion engine provides a focus of technical, managerial and organisational competence. It determines the relative economic positioning of actors (institutional and individual) involved in automobile manufacturing, petroleum production, transport engineering and construction, town planning, and the design and development of shopping malls and leisure facilities—from McDonald's to sports stadiums. Technological innovations (e.g. fuel cells or the Smart car) have the potential to alter the position and interaction of many of these actors and their associated socio-technical systems and networks. The technological innovations required to reformulate our notions of mobility in ways that reduce our dependence on the automobile, for instance, encounter even greater social and institutional rigidities and technological lock-ins. These would include the capital stranded in the transport infrastructure, the redundancy of knowledge that provides the basis for competence across the whole array of automobile/transport/urban designers, suppliers and users, and the altered economic position and power of various actors.

Technology development also creates more subtle social effects. It provides us with new ideas, metaphors and concepts based on the language that emerges with technology. In this way technology impacts the way we think about and envisage our world. Everyday examples include 'spaceship Earth', 'wind farm', 'factory', 'laboratory' and the 'information superhighway', even the 'network society', which has brought with it a far greater attention to networks between individuals, organisations, places and levels of government. Technology shapes both our physical and metaphysical world and contributes to the meaning and value of our lives. Technologies and their associated socio-technical systems are intimately bound to our economic system, our understanding of human progress, our experience of development, and our understanding of the natural world. Indeed, technology, society and environment are so interwoven that it is not meaningful to discuss one in isolation from the other. Yet few commentators and practitioners take the step to envisage the interplay between technology, society and environment within the framework of one system.

Globalisation, sustainable development and ICCE technologies

In an increasingly complex and interdependent world, it has become ever more impor-tant to address technologies and their related systems within the context of the socio-technical systems and actor networks. This raises the issue of the extent to which ICCE technologies are different from other types of technology. How far are ICCE technologies 'unique' and 'different' in terms of their patterns of innovation and diffusion? What are the new sustainable development dimensions of ICCE technologies and how do they differ from a wide range of energy and manufacturing technologies, many of which have important implications for managing corporate environmental issues? Compared to relatively mature technologies, ICCE technologies stand out in four important ways.

First, at the most conceptual level, ICCE technologies reflect and drive economic and financial globalisation. They are the basis for greater economic, social and environmen-tal interdependence and complexity. Moreover, ICCE technologies contribute to the rapidly emerging globalisation of human activities, especially markets and the economic systems, as well as new patterns of global trade, production and consumption. They contribute to the global connection of cultures and the emergence of new communities of interest that transcend the traditions of place and national identity. In other words, they contribute to 'broad definition globalisation' (Roome 1998a: 173-75), by which we mean the increasingly connected economic, financial, social, cultural and environmental aspects of the contemporary world and the emergence of new sets of actors who are set to gain or lose from the changes that are being put in place or that are anticipated. In this way they alter how we relate to one another and to our environmental context. However, they also alter how we see and understand the world. This point is not trivial as it echoes and probably extends the insight provided by Marshall McLuhan that the introduction of a new medium of communication (e.g. print, television or, in this case, ICCE technolo-gies) involves a major shift in the mental posture of the medium's users, irrespective of what is actually communicated (Marchand 1998: 257).

Second, mature systems such as automobile-based mobility systems—unlike ICCE technologies—are changing at best in a slow, incremental fashion (e.g. the internal com-bustion engine has not changed significantly in over a hundred years). The broad envi-ronmental, economic and social axes of automobiles, transport and society are relatively clear, although they still prove extremely difficult to change. ICCE technologies and systems are still evolving, but we do not yet know the shape of the socio-technical systems that will develop around them or the nature of the actor networks that will emerge. This will only become clearer as the rate of technological change begins to slow and more stable patterns emerge. Consequently, we have a much less clear picture of the broad environmental, social and economic axes of these technologies, their associated socio-technical systems, and how those effects are distributed across actor networks.

Compounding this ambiguity is the speed at which many ICCE technologies are developing and transforming. Imagine what the world might be like if personal income or environmental productivity followed the regularity of Moore's Law (named after Intel Corp.'s co-founder Gordon Moore), which postulates that the power of a memory chip doubles every two years. More than a hundred years after the introduction of the auto-mobile we are still living in the age of the internal combustion engine. Yet in the case of

ICCE technologies one would be hard pressed to 'predict' what the world is going to look like in just five years let alone in a century. Are we still in the personal computer era dominated by the Wintel (Windows–Intel) monopoly or are we slowly gravitating toward what some computer scientists call the age of 'distributed or networking computing'? What advances can we expect or anticipate in the case of personal digital assistants and mobile communication devices such as cell phones and pagers or as ICCE technologies become ubiquitous?

Third, ICCE technologies are transforming the operations and business strategies of companies and industry groups, and, as a consequence, may have important implications for organisations in terms of environmental management and policy issues. One striking feature of the intersection between environmental sustainability, ICCE technologies and corporations is that contested opinions, uncertain outcomes, irresolvable positions and vested interests overshadow the discourse about ICCE. For example, there are those who argue that, because ICCE technologies speed up transactions, provide more perfect information and are less materially intensive than other forms of communication and information, they are likely to yield more concrete environmental benefits. Others argue that these technologies are not so light as is claimed and that the quantity of data and the problem of distinguishing between information and disinformation undermine the potential for accessing better information.

While our knowledge on a wide range of environment–ICCE technology issues may be limited, anything that fundamentally affects the way business operates can obviously have significant environmental implications. Because the shift towards e-commerce can impact the environment—while impacting a large number of companies in a number of industries—in a variety of ways, the long-term environmental impacts of ICCE technologies on corporations could be much larger than anticipated (Rejeski 1999). This is why research and analysis of the sustainability–ICCE technology linkage is fraught with so much difficulty and why it is arguably so different from traditional technology R&D analysis. Only a systemic and systematic analysis will help sharpen our understanding of the intersection between ICCE technologies and the environment and permit a response that can steer e-commerce and the e-economy toward environmentally beneficial outcomes (White 2000).

There is a real danger that the 'digital divide' will intensify the gap between those with access to resources and opportunities and those without, internationally as well as within countries. Will ICCE technologies contribute to, or diminish, the problem of technology access and exclusion in the developing world? For developing economies, the challenge of keeping pace in the information revolution goes beyond missing out on the latest technological advances in software or global positioning technologies. There are real dangers that the 'digital divide' will intensify and reinforce the gap between those with access to resources and opportunities and those without, either internationally or within countries.

Although the developing countries connected more than 155 million telephone lines, 105 million mobile-phone subscribers and 4 million leased lines between 1995 and 1998, the wide disparity in access to ICCE technologies in the developed and developing worlds appears to be getting worse, not better. In Africa, with over 800 million people, there are still only 14 million phone lines—fewer than in Manhattan or Tokyo—and 80% of those lines are in only six countries. The average OECD (Organisation for Economic Co-operation and Development) country has roughly 40 times the per capita number of computers of a sub-Saharan African country (South Africa excluded), 110 times as many mobile phones, and 1,600 times as many Internet hosts (Braga *et al.* 2000). ICCE technologies have in many ways brought all the dimensions of human systems—economic, financial, cultural, social, political and ideological—into much deeper and more complex relationships with environmental systems. The overall problem created by these interconnections appears tighter, more turbulent, more global and at the same time more locally immediate, more contested and, in many ways, more irresolvable. To begin to appreciate and understand these issues is a necessary start to their resolution.

The chapters

The scope of the contributions in this book is important. Eighteen chapters offer a range of perspectives—sectoral, national and global—in keeping with the diverse span of the technologies and issues under examination. Nearly 30 university academicians, corporate practitioners, and researchers with independent policy research groups—from Europe, Asia and the US—have contributed to the book. Though there are some overlaps, the chapters are divided into three thematic groups. The first thematic group provides a critical background to the sustainability challenges and implications of an emerging global information economy. As ICCE technologies continue to develop, how will logistic issues affect the environmental management functions of a company? How do supply chain issues and environmental management intersect in an increasingly digital economy? How will the concept of global corporate citizenship be different or changed in the information age?

Chapter 1 ('Sustainable business strategies in the Internet economy') by Klaus Fichter provides an overview of the environmental effects from e-commerce and Internet use. It analyses three different types of linkage: the direct environmental effects of the information technology infrastructure (such as the energy use of networks, servers, receiver systems, PCs, etc.), the secondary effects caused by Internet use, and what he refers to as 'subsequent and rebound effects'. Chapter 2 ('E-logistics and the natural environment') by Joseph Sarkis, Laura Meade and Srinivas Talluri summarises the complex relationship between logistics and the natural environment—at both a practical and a conceptual level. It illustrates how companies and organisations can gain important competitive/ environmental advantage by managing the company's logistics and/or electronic logistics function more effectively.

Chapter 3 ('Greening the digitised supply net') by Michael Totten describes the emergence and convergence of two techno-industrial innovations: 'greening' of the supply chain or network, and the increasing ubiquity of digital technology and Internet-based supply network logistics and procurement operations. This parallel development, he argues, can offer new and unrealised environmental and economic gains if the natural synergy between these innovations is properly harnessed. Chapter 4 ('Dot.com ethics: e-business and sustainability') by James Wilsdon focuses on the 'deafening silence' about the relationship between e-commerce and corporate sustainability. Alongside the economic opportunities being created by e-commerce, he argues that there are some exciting social and environmental opportunities, which must be seized if the new economy is to become more sustainable than the old. With vision, imagination and intelligent policy, there is a better probability that sustainability will be spliced into the DNA of the new economy or the new blend of new and old economies.

Chapter 5 ('Practising corporate citizenship in a global information economy') by Duane Windsor offers some preliminary analysis of the global policy challenges posed by corporate citizenship and the information economy. Specifically, he analyses how the concept and practice of corporate citizenship may evolve in the emerging global information economy using three case studies that deal with energy consumption and urban sprawl, work and workplace practices, and the digital divide. Chapter 6 ('The Internet and sustainability reporting: improving communication with stakeholders') by Bill Weil and Barbara Winter-Watson documents the growing use of corporate sustainability reports by companies with the Internet as the preferred reporting platform. Given the complexity of addressing a diverse, global audience, they argue that the Internet and new communication technologies will play an increasingly important role as environmental reporting develops and matures.

The second thematic group explains how sustainability concerns-related operational, management and business strategy interact with the e-business models and e-commerce initiatives of corporations. The emphasis of this second thematic group is on case-study experiences and evidence from companies that have tried to map out the relationship between sustainability and the use of ICCE technologies. Is the use of e-mail less of an environmental burden than regular mail? Does the digital divide offer new and sustainable business opportunities for corporations in the developing world? Can we even say if or to what extent e-commerce is environmentally and economically sustainable?

Chapter 7 ('Is e-commerce sustainable? Lessons from Webvan') by Chris Galea and Steve Walton challenges the assumption that the wider adoption of e-commerce will lead to greater environmental sustainability. They examine the relationship between e-commerce and sustainability by analysing the triple-bottom-line (economic, environmental and social) impacts of Webvan, an American online grocery delivery service that filed for bankruptcy in July 2001. They conclude that Webvan's business model is less energy-efficient, emits more air pollution, offers no significant improvements in product and delivery packaging compared to conventional grocery shopping, and may lead to unanticipated negative environmental and social outcomes. Chapter 8 ('Information technology, sustainable development and developing nations') by Jim Sheats offers a view of Hewlett-Packard Co.'s World e-Inclusion initiative, which sees ICCE technologies as a way to bring new opportunities for developing countries to access sustainable technologies and business models. Drawing on the ideas from Hart and Prahalad 2000, which identifies the possibility of bringing economic opportunities to the poorest of the poor through new business strategies, Sheats discusses how Internet availability to the rural poor might empower people to make more informed choices about their economy, society and environment.

Chapter 9 ('Environmental impacts of the new economy: Deutsche Telekom, telecommunication services and the sustainable future') by Markus Reichling and Tim Otto provides an analysis of energy and resource consumption as an operational issue in the design and development of telecommunication services and network infrastructure. Although telecommunication services are not inherently more environmentally friendly than the business activities they replace, they do offer new opportunities for energy and resource efficiency under certain circumstances. Chapter 10 ('Environmental impacts of telecommunications services: two life-cycle analysis studies') by Manfred Zurkirch and Inge Reichart continues the discussion of the environmental impacts of telecommunications services based on two life-cycle analyses (LCAs) undertaken by Swisscom. Using a methodology they have developed for the application of their LCA techniques to services, they provide environmental-efficiency examples comparing paper-based versus electronic communication and paper-based versus electronic information retrieval. Their research reveals how complex and context-dependent the environmental burdens of a service can be. Again their conclusion is that, under certain circumstances, e-mail carries a higher environmental burden than hard-copy mail while the reverse is true under other circumstances. One important implication of their research is the need for sophisticated decisions about which systems to use if functional performance and low environmental burdens are the desired goals.

Chapter 11 ('Exploring the global–local axis: telecommunications and environmental sustainability in Japan') by Brendan Barrett and Ichiro Yamada provides a case study of an electronic communications and Internet service supporting local environmental action through the mechanism of a public–private–community–university partnership in Iwate Prefecture, Japan. In a partnership between Nippon Telegraph and Telephone, Iwate Prefecture, the United Nations University in Japan and other community and local education partners, the case study shows how the private sector can work with local community and educational institutions to improve environmental understanding through the Internet and real-time videoconferencing. Chapter 12 ('Product-oriented environmental management: the case of Xerox Europe') by Frank de Bakker and David Foley offers a case study on the experience of Xerox Europe in implementing its product-oriented environmental management (POEM) system. POEM is viewed as an organisational resource that supports the decrease in the environmental burden of a product. Based on a series of interviews with key personnel at the company, the authors explore ways companies can develop the necessary organisational and operational competence to implement and use the POEM system more effectively.

The third thematic group of chapters explores how management concerns of the old economy will be affected, if not transformed, in an increasingly digital business landscape. What is the outlook for energy demand and consumption in the new economy? Can existing regulatory policies meet the environmental challenges posed by the rapidly growing global information economy? In what manner will business travel change with the increased use of information and communications technologies?

Chapter 13 ('Information and communications technologies: boon or bane to sustainable development?') by Josephine Chinying Lang argues that information and communications technologies (ICTs) are likely to result in mixed sustainable development impacts. On the one hand, there may be negative consequences of ICTs from the changing nature of wealth creation, global economic integration and regulatory arbitrage. On the other hand, ICTs may help sustainable development by promoting corporate environmental transparency, facilitating the development of industrial ecology, and promoting online communities. These positive and negative outcomes, she argues, illustrate how the overall impact of ICTs on sustainable development may ultimately depend on how people use ICTs. Chapter 14 ('Information and communications technologies and business travel: environmental possibilities, problems and implications') by Peter Arnfalk discusses and analyses the potential of information and communications technology-based tools such as teleconferencing and webcasting technologies as substitutes for business travel.

Although the environmental impacts, financial costs and time consumption of business travel represent a growing concern for corporations, it is unlikely that there will be a surge in demand for 'virtual meetings' in part due to inadequate infrastructure, training and administrative support.

Chapter 15 ('How fabulous fablessness? environmental challenges of economic restructuring in the semiconductor industry') by Jan Mazurek offers a critical view of the ability of current public environmental policy measures such as the Toxics Release Inventory (TRI) to keep pace with the increasing global dispersal of the US semiconductor industry. She argues that changes in the structure of the industry involve two main trends: first, a move towards offshore production; and, second, a trend away from integrated semiconductor design, production and assembly to an increasingly outsourced model of production and assembly. The implication of her argument is that approaches to environmental monitoring and regulation that track impacts by business entity are becoming less useful. This raises the need for a more global approach to corporate environmental accountability, monitoring and reporting that track the environmental impacts of the global supply chains that link corporate entities. Economic globalisation and business restructuring calls for restructured environmental controls. Chapter 16 ('Micropower: electrifying the digital economy') by Seth Dunn examines developments in micropower technologies to meet the electricity demands of the digital economy. Based on the notion that highly efficient micropower systems are more environmentally benign than centralised generating plants, he argues that micropower systems have the potential to support digital activity in the developing as well as developed world. He also discusses the new conditions in the US that have encouraged developments in micropower, including technical developments in the efficiency of micropower sources and the demand-side pressures arising from the need of commercial Internet users for more continuous, reliable power.

Chapter 17 ('Extended producer responsibility and the european electronics industry') by Lassi Linnanen discusses the policy approaches to managing and reducing waste from the electrical and electronic equipment sector. Based on the recycling and solid waste management systems in Norway, the Netherlands and Sweden, he examines the likely structural and operational changes in the European electronics industry that may result from the adoption of the European Union directive on waste electrical and electronic equipment. Chapter 18 ('Sustainable trade in electronics: the case of the Indian components sector') by Mohammad Saqib, Yashika Singh and Ritu Kumar analyses the sustainability-related issues and questions posed by the complex supply chain and international sourcing that exist in the Indian electronics components sector. They argue that any attempts to green the supply chain of a company have to take into account the dynamic relationships that exist between multinational corporations, contract manufacturers and international sourcing trends. This is particularly the case in an industry such as the consumer electronics sector that is subject to and typically responds to an assortment of changes in the global economy.

Governing the global environment and the new economy

What are the main conclusions to arise from this body of work? First, it is obvious that much more research needs to be done to understand in more detail the environmental and social consequences of ICCE technologies and systems. A critical research issue is the extent to which context and boundary conditions influence the environmental and social impacts of ICCE technologies. Second, this research will be relevant only if it keeps pace with the rapid development of these technologies and systems. Third, ICCE technologies do not bring with them universal benefits for sustainable development. There are benefits to be to be gained, but only under certain circumstances.

This implies that there is an important need for the development and use of sophisticated support tools to aid the decision-making process about when and when not to use ICCE. It also implies, however, that it is dangerous to listen to uncritical advocates or opponents of the ICCE revolution. What we can say conclusively is that both sides are right and wrong, and the answer almost always depends on the context and circumstances surrounding the use of ICCE technologies. ICCE technologies may have a powerful role in promoting global environmental sustainability, especially through their capacity to provide supporting tools in the face of complex choices. But a critical debate has to first take place in order to create the necessary knowledge framework that will guide corporate, public policy and individual choices towards a more efficient use of resources and to meet human needs within the environmental carrying capacity of the planet.

Consequently, one of the most critical issues that differentiate ICCE technologies from previous technological advances is that these technologies are being developed and deployed at a time when the overall level of awareness about the relationship between environmental, economic and social issues has never been higher. We should therefore watch over the development of ICCE technologies with far more wisdom than with previous technological revolutions. Ultimately, achieving these goals will involve tough decisions about what we will permit and the limits and constraints we will accept as individuals and collectively as members of a global society.

Part 1
SUSTAINABILITY CHALLENGES AND IMPLICATIONS OF A GLOBAL INFORMATION ECONOMY

1

SUSTAINABLE BUSINESS STRATEGIES IN THE INTERNET ECONOMY

Klaus Fichter

Borderstep: Institution for Innovation and Sustainability, Germany

1.1 From atoms to bits?

1993 is regarded as the year when the Internet economy was born with the breakthrough of the World Wide Web (WWW). Since then, the Internet has developed into a service-integrated global net with a diversity of multimedia uses. The initial euphoria over the new economy has in the meantime given way to more realistic valuations after the failure of many Internet start-ups and the still low proportion of e-commerce in overall trade turnover. E-business will not be the be-all and end-all in the future, but e-commerce and Internet use will certainly gain in importance.

According to forecasts by the European Commission there will be 500 million Internet users worldwide by 2003 and a rapid increase in e-commerce turnover, especially in the area of business-to-business (B2B). However, when looking at the objectives of sustainable development, the expected effects of the Internet revolution are uncertain. This chapter looks into the environmental effects resulting from e-commerce and Internet use and where the strategic starting points lie for companies who want to use the potential of the Internet revolution for progress towards sustainable development.

What does the future hold in store for the Internet economy? Will *Homo connecticus* lovingly point to the computer touch-screen, be beamed via the World Wide Web around the globe in a matter of seconds and get all jobs done effortlessly, cheaply, in real time and using a minimum of energy resources and without any negative effects? Is this the new economy—clean, pollutant-free and resource-efficient? If you believe the adverts, yes! However, the real world of the digital economy will probably look very different. The proclaimed paradigm shift from atoms to bits (Negroponte 1995: 11ff.) is only half the story.

1.2 Environmental effects of e-commerce and Internet use

The substitution of physical products by electronic alternatives appears at first glance to be a good opportunity for working towards dematerialisation and eco-efficiency. The 'paperless' newspaper on the Internet, for example, could be seen as a contribution to safeguarding natural resources. However, initial estimates show that energy consumption during the entire production process of a screen-readable newspaper is approximately ten times that of a printed newspaper (Plätzer and Göttsching 1998). Digitalisation and virtualisation do not automatically lead to dematerialisation.

For the environmental effects of e-commerce and Internet use, three levels can be distinguished: direct environmental effects of the information technology infrastructure (energy and material use of networks, servers, receiver systems, PCs, etc.); secondary effects caused by the transformation of business processes and markets; and tertiary effects due to subsequent and rebound effects (see Fig. 1.1). This distinction is suitable for classifying environmental effects of information and communications technologies in general.[1]

The core insights of available studies[2] to date may be summarised as follows:

- There is no general answer to the question of whether the use of new media will lead to increased or decreased environmental impacts.

- New and classic media each have their specific environmental advantages: so, for instance, with regard to selective searching for information, electronic media are usually more efficient and more environmentally friendly (time-saving search functions; energy use and environmental exploitation are crucially dependent on use). With regard to entertainment and unspecific background input, conventional media are often more environmentally advantageous.

- Electronic media are often not so much a substitute for but a rather a supplement to printed or other media, thus tending to increase environmental impacts. There is a risk of summation effects and incomplete substitution.

- Digitisation of products and media (music, news, e-mails, etc.) does not automatically lead to dematerialisation but often rather entails subsequent effects. So, for instance, digitised music files downloaded from the Web (e.g. via Napster) are often stored on CDs; received e-mails are printed out on paper, etc. These are rematerialisation effects.

- Side-effects of digitised media, such as packaging of CDs, or printed user manuals, considerably influence the eco-balance.

- The environmental friendliness of Internet use and electronic media depends heavily on electricity production, and the contribution made by the technol-

---

1 A similar classification is presented by Berkhout and Hertin (2001).
2 The number of empirical studies is rapidly increasing; the following are currently available: Kortmann and de Winter 1999; Greusing and Zangl 2000; Reichart and Hischier 2001; Quack and Gensch 2001.

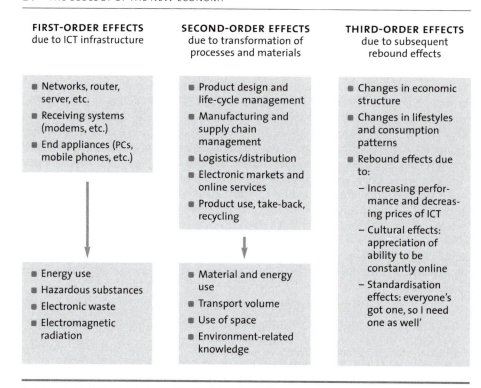

FIRST-ORDER EFFECTS due to ICT infrastructure	SECOND-ORDER EFFECTS due to transformation of processes and materials	THIRD-ORDER EFFECTS due to subsequent rebound effects

■ Networks, router, server, etc.
■ Receiving systems (modems, etc.)
■ End appliances (PCs, mobile phones, etc.)
	■ Product design and life-cycle management
	■ Manufacturing and supply chain management
	■ Logistics/distribution
	■ Electronic markets and online services
	■ Product use, take-back, recycling
		■ Changes in economic structure
		■ Changes in lifestyles and consumption patterns
		■ Rebound effects due to:
		  – Increasing performance and decreasing prices of ICT
		  – Cultural effects: appreciation of ability to be constantly online
		  – Standardisation effects: everyone's got one, so I need one as well'

■ Energy use ■ Hazardous substances ■ Electronic waste ■ Electromagnetic radiation	■ Material and energy use ■ Transport volume ■ Use of space ■ Environment-related knowledge	

Figure 1.1 *Environmental effects of e-business and Internet use*

ogies used for power generation. For printed media, the paper recycling aspect strongly influences environmental effects.

■ The network infrastructure (server, router, etc.), as distinct from terminals, has considerable relevance for energy consumption and environmental effects.

■ Potentials for increasing resource productivity are presumed mainly to lie in the B2B area. US studies (e.g. Romm *et al.* 1999; Cohen 2000) indicate considerable potential in the areas of reducing stocks of flawed products, energy consumption and floor space used for retail and office businesses.

■ Any assessment of the environmental effects of e-commerce on traffic and the environment is linked to multiple assumptions and requires complex modelling. The results of the analyses of environmental effects are thus extremely dependent on the underlying assumptions.

■ Online orders tend to accelerate the delivery of goods and to change the structure of shipped freight towards smaller units; this results in an increase in courier, express and parcel deliveries.

■ On the other hand, Swedish studies show that e-commerce does not necessarily entail more traffic (Jönson and Johnsson 2000). Under certain conditions, online shopping has the potential to reduce the volume of traffic. The realisation of that potential depends crucially on the population density of the home delivery service area, the share of e-commerce users, the delivery distances travelled, and the type of transportation used in the respective region.

■ Only a very few existing studies take rebound effects into account (Romm *et al.* 1999; Laitner and Koomey 2000). Most empirical studies reflect only the effects at a certain point in time.

Examples of the results of existing studies on environmental effects of Internet use and e-commerce are listed in Table 1.1.

Subject of the study	Positive environmental effects	Negative environmental effects
Eco-balance: reading an article in an online newspaper as compared to a conventional newspaper (Plätzer and Göttsching 1998)		An online newspaper uses ten times the energy of a conventional newspaper (with respect to consumption of fossil primary energy) and produces about twice as much waste.
Swedish study: comparing online shopping and traditional shopping for food and goods for daily needs (Jönson and Johnsson 2000)	Dependent on circumstances: the energy consumption for transport of goods is 5%–7% lower with online shopping if the delivery route amounts to a distance of 50–90 km and about 25 families are supplied.	
Eco-balance for desktop personal computers: comparing 'traditional' life-cycle and life-cycle with use of e-commerce (Caudill *et al.* 2000)	If possibilities of e-commerce are used to their full extent in production (B2B, reduction of stocks, etc.), sales (B2C) and in take-back, energy use and environmental impact can be reduced by about 10%.	If possibilities of e-commerce are used in the sales area only (B2C), the energy use surpasses that of traditional distribution channels by about 10%. This is above all due to accelerated shipment by air cargo.
Comparing printed and online catalogues of a mail-order firm (energetic balance of the complete life-cycle) (Greusing and Zangl 2000)		The primary energy consumption of an online catalogue is about 24 times that of a printed catalogue. The main 'energy consumer' is the personal computer needed to read the online catalogue.

B2B = business-to-business; B2C = business-to-consumer

Table 1.1 *Examples of environmental effects of e-business*

To sum up, the overall pattern of environmental effects of Internet use on transport, material and energy use, as well as on environment-related knowledge, is composed of a variety of positive, neutral and negative effects.

1.3 Business strategies: why take environmental aspects into account?

The key question with regard to business strategies is: why should enterprises take aspects of the natural environment into account? Pivotal goals of strategic management are to secure competitiveness and to gain competitive advantage. Besides ethical requirements, there are strong strategic arguments for taking environmental issues into account, since they might directly or indirectly influence shareholder value and competitiveness (Porter and van der Linde 1995b; WBCSD 2001). That is, environmental aspects are worth consideration if:

- Costs can be lowered or avoided.

- A firm can differentiate itself from competitors and thus increase its sales.

- New business areas and markets can be opened up.

- Risks (liability, brand image) can be reduced.

- Markets can be secured through compliance with regulations and resulting acceptance on the part of stakeholders ('licence to operate').

The influence of environmental issues on the competitiveness of an enterprise in the Internet economy depends on the environmental impacts of digital products and online services, the environmental demands by different stakeholders and their influence on profits and shareholder value (Dyllick 1999). The environmental 'exposedness' of an enterprise may greatly vary from sector to sector and from product to product.

Hence sustainable business strategies in the Internet economy will have to deal, apart from other competition-related aspects, with the questions of how far environmental impacts of e-business and e-commerce activities will affect the cost, sales and competition situation of an enterprise, and whether purposive consideration of environmental aspects in e-commerce strategies might allow the firm to win competitive advantages.

The following approaches to sustainable business strategies in the Internet economy are thus to be understood as search paths for finding eco-efficient business solutions. Eco-efficiency is a management philosophy that encourages business to search for environmental improvements that yield parallel economic benefits. It focuses on business opportunities and allows companies to become more environmentally responsible and more profitable (WBCSD 2000: 8).[3] The search for win–win solutions should not be

---

3   The World Business Council for Sustainable Development defines 'eco-efficiency' as follows: 'Eco-efficiency is achieved by the delivery of competitively-priced goods and services that satisfy human needs and bring quality of life, while progressively reducing ecological impacts and resource intensity throughout the life-cycle at least in line with the earth's estimated carrying capacity' (WBCSD 2000: 9).

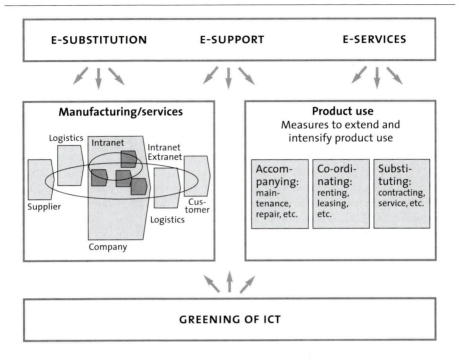

ICT = information and communications technologies

Figure 1.2 **Sustainable e-business strategies**

seen in terms of isolated partial strategies but as an integral part of development, implementation and checking of business strategies.

1.4 Approaches for sustainable business strategies

Whereas the environmental impact of information and communications appliances and technologies has been a topic of discussion in environmental policy (e.g. the EU Directive on Waste from Electrical and Electronic Equipment [WEEE]) for a number of years, the issue of how Internet use and information and communications technologies can actively contribute to sustainable development has not been sufficiently examined. However, the use of information technology in the area of transport is an exception.

To date, positive environmental effects brought about by Internet use and e-business have generally been unintended coincidental side-effects, since telecommunications and the Internet are used primarily to accelerate business processes, to lower costs and to safeguard or open up markets. However, the growth of e-business and the Internet

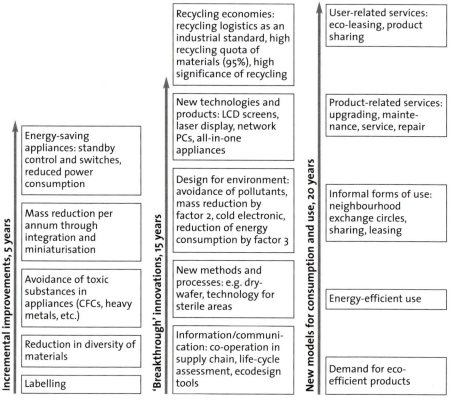

CFCs = chlorofluorocarbons; LCD = liquid-crystal display; PC = personal computer

Figure 1.3 **Sustainable innovation for Internet and communications technologies**

Source: Deutscher Bundestag 1998: 263

means that companies in future will have to take environmental demands into consideration as part of their strategies.

E-business provides four possible environmental strategies for a company's move towards sustainable development:

- **Greening of ICT (information and communications technology):** environmentally friendly production and use of information and communications appliances and technologies

- **E-substitution:** substitution of physical products by electronic and environmentally friendly alternatives for products, mail-order services and uses

- **E-support:** use of the Internet and e-business to safeguard and disseminate environmentally friendly products and services

- **E-services:** use of Internet-based services, business models and networks to safeguard the environment and improve eco-efficiency

These strategies may be applied both to the provision of products or services and their use.

1.4.1 *Greening ICT*

The ecological effects and problem areas of the information infrastructure, especially end appliances, have been the object of scientific examination and the main focus for many manufacturers of information technology equipment (Deutscher Bundestag 1998; Reichl and Griese 2000). The main responsibilities here lie in the development of energy-saving appliances, the avoidance of toxic substances such as PCBs (polychlorinated biphenyls), mercury or cadmium, the reduction of waste through better recycling, and the optimisation of the life and use of appliances: for example, through leasing and sharing. Figure 1.2 shows an overview of innovation paths.

Manufacturers and suppliers of Internet information and communications technology have the task of incorporating environmental considerations in the development and management of information technology.

One example of the many entrepreneurial initiatives in the field of design of sustainable information and communications technology is the 'Eco Vision' programme of the Philips Consumer Electronics Group. This initiative, begun in 1998, is a customer-oriented environmental programme, and focuses on the development and marketing of environmentally friendly products—so-called 'green flagships'. So far, Philips has labelled six products as 'green flagships'. To be selected, a product has to demonstrate outstanding environmental qualities, in particular low energy use, and to rank higher in benchmarking processes than comparable products of competitors.

One example is the 'TV green flagship', a 32-inch television set. While the energy consumption of the most eco-efficient competing product uses 150 W (and 1.5 W in standby mode), the comparable Philips TV set consumes respectively 132 W and 0.3 W. In almost all other environment-related aspects (pollutants, product weight, recyclability), the Philips product ranks as high or better. All Philips business units in the consumer electronics sector are required to develop at least one 'green flagship' (Stevels 2000: 542f.).

Producers and suppliers of information and communications technologies are facing the challenge of integrating protection of the environment in their development, management and product marketing as a way of realising the potential for more environmentally benign information technologies. Apart from the information structure, the way Internet technologies are used is of primary importance for sustainability in the future.

1.4.2 *E-substitution*

The strategic approach of substituting physical products and transport by electronic alternatives is of major importance for companies that sell products and services that can be fully or partly digitalised (answering machines, telephone directories, newspapers, music, online banking, online ticket sales, etc.)—i.e. companies in the telecommunications, media and services sectors. As several studies have indicated, there is no general answer to the question of whether the utilisation of new media and digital products will increase or decrease environmental impacts (Kortmann and Winter 1999; Reichart and Hischier 2001). Frequently, electronic media are not so much a substitute but rather a supplement for printed or other media, thus tending to increase environmental impacts. Digital products and services encompass opportunities and risks for the environment.

The starting point for the strategy of e-substitution is the fact that the use of digital alternatives (online newspapers, music, banking, etc.) is hardly influenced by environmental considerations, but is determined by factors such as convenience, speed, performance, price, etc. Taking this into account, two major aspects have to be the focus of an e-substitution-strategy:

- How to optimise and increase the eco-efficiency of digital products and services?

- How to identify and promote digital products and services that offer a win–win solution and which combine better sales or cost reduction with dematerialisation?

The first step in answering these questions is to estimate the environmental impact of a product or service life-cycle. For this purpose life-cycle assessment (LCA) methodology (ISO 14040ff.) and less complex methods such as cumulated energy use (CEU) have been developed.

One example of an e-substitution strategy can be seen at Deutsche Telekom, Europe's largest telecommunications company. It uses LCA methodology to assess its digital products—for example, the T-Net-Box, a virtual communication and telephone call manager. In 2000, approximately half of all German households were equipped with an answering machine and 24% owned a fax machine, in contrast to the 1.2 million T-Net-Boxes currently active. If the 18 million answering machines in German households were all replaced by the T-Net-Box, it would conserve about 99% of the present energy supply. That would save over 600,000 tonnes of CO_2 emissions and 9,600 TJ of primary energy a year (Quack and Gensch 2001: 147). For customers the costs would remain the same. In both cases the yearly costs are about US$20 (Quack and Gensch 2001: 148). Because of this, Deutsche Telekom is now putting more effort into marketing and selling the T-Net-Box.

1.4.3 E-support

Internet use to support the production and use of products (e-support) may provide great potential for safeguarding the environment. This is shown, for example, in improvements in communications in the field of custom-built products.

The US chemical company ChemStation, which produces commercial detergents, uses the Internet to find out about customer-specific needs and take them into account when determining the composition of cleaners. In this way superfluous additives can be avoided and correct doses of cleaners can be determined more precisely (see Table 1.2).

Other forms of custom-built production, such as printing-on-demand and building-to-order, offer interesting strategies. In this way, for example, Dell Computer succeeded in minimising its stocks of electronic parts for its custom-build order service. Stocks are thus avoided that would quickly lose their value due to accelerating developments in the computer industry. Computers become obsolete so quickly that electronic parts not only lose their value but there is an increase in the amount of waste to be disposed of (Cohen 2000: 3).

Eco-efficiency through e-support	Examples	Environmental effects
Internet support of customer-specific mass production	ChemStation (producer of commercial detergents) (http://chemstation.com)	Reduction of polluting additives, customer-specific dosage
E-commerce and built-to-order strategies	Dell Computers	Reduction of stocks and excess production
Electronic market platforms and auctioneers for used or excess goods	▪ Consumer goods (www.ebay.de) ▪ Capital goods (www.GoIndustry.com)	Extended product use
Internet linkage of consumer goods and mail order articles by means of 'smart tags'	Electrolux: leasing of washing machines, pay-per-use, online accounting via Internet	Incentives for economic use of household appliances

Table 1.2 **Eco-efficiency through e-support**

Another example is electronic market platforms for trade in second-hand and surplus goods. Not only are there Internet auctioneers to be found, such as www.ebay.de, which mainly target private consumers, but also B2B market platforms for the purchase and sale of production facilities and machines. One such example is the Internet platform www. GoIndustry.com, where all services connected to the purchase of used capital goods are offered: technical checks by experts, issues of financing and insurance, and the actual online purchase itself. The managers of this B2B platform emphasise the fact that the efficiency of the service would not be possible without the Internet.

Transponders (smart tags) are an interesting example of how the use of physical products can be augmented via Internet support. These are devices containing a simple microchip and a unit that receives and transmits and thus 'communicates' via the Internet. The wafer-thin transponder can be integrated into products such as household appliances or packaging. The drop in the unit price means that their use has now become economically viable (http://auto-id.mit.edu). With the development of Internet-enabled products, there are now new possibilities for improving product use, product life and recycling. The feedback and complaint process about products and their maintenance is made easier, communication of updates on product safety can be made available more easily, and new incentives to use products economically can be developed. For example, Electrolux, the world's largest producer of household appliances, is testing Internet-enabled household appliances that can be rented to the customer and which will be paid for according to the level of use. This is one way of creating incentives for efficiency of use. In this context, there are questions that need to be clarified, particularly regarding privacy and data protection.

1.4.4 E-services

Internet and electronic networks make it much easier to search for products, compare prices and quality and facilitate trade activities. The potential of e-commerce solutions to cut transaction costs opens up a whole new field of Internet-based services and business models. New business opportunities are the main idea behind the e-services strategy, which focuses on online services that make product use and recycling more eco-efficient.

The Internet makes new business models possible. Entrepreneurs are creating e-markets and offer online services for extending the use of products and for recycling. There are numerous examples of e-markets for surplus materials, waste and recycling.[4] They all reflect the fact that e-commerce offers win–win solutions, combining business opportunities with eco-efficient services.

E-commerce also makes it easier to remarket used products. For example, Hewlett-Packard (HP) has established a remarketing unit that sells 'as new' refurbished products to provide a low-cost solution to customers. HP Remarketing offers a large selection of remanufactured computer products at costs 15%–20% below the price tag of brand new ones.[5]

Further electronic services are provided by Internet portals and online shopping guides for environmentally friendly products and services. One example is www.GreenOrder.com, a web service that helps business and administration to find eco-labelled products on the Internet. There are also Internet portals specific to technology monitoring. They offer information on the latest sector news and technologies, and can be used by development engineers or information managers in the search for eco-efficient technologies and service models.

Various approaches in green e-business strategies, including e-substitution, e-support and e-services, show the variety and potential of sustainable e-business solutions. Examples of individual areas are presented as an overview in Table 1.3. It must be emphasised, however, that these approaches do not guarantee environmental improvements. Whether these strategies actually lead to eco-efficient or environmentally friendly solutions must be examined on an individual basis.

1.5 Conclusions

As a future medium and form of market transaction, Internet and e-commerce are of central importance for sustainable development. At the moment, three clear conclusions can be made:

- There is a scarcity of available data on the environmental impacts brought about by e-commerce and Internet use and there is considerable need for research in this area.

- The use of new information and communications technologies is likely to lead to both positive and negative effects on the environment, but the overall net environmental impact cannot yet be predicted.

4   A good overview is given by the Berlecom B2B marketplace database: www.berlecom.de.
5   www.b2net.co.uk/hp/hp_remarketing.html

Approaches *Functions*	**E-SUBSTITUTION** *Substitution of physical goods by electronic goods*	**E-SUPPORT** *Internet support of production and product use*	**E-SERVICES** *Internet-based services and business models*
Product and service development	▪ Evaluation of environmental impact of electronic products and business models ▪ Digital construction design plans/documents	▪ Use of transponders for linking products and packaging to the Internet ▪ Internet-based benchmarking	▪ Internet-based R&D networks ▪ Career- and task-specific Internet portals for providing information on innovations
Purchase and production	▪ Use of shopping robots for purchase of products that are both eco-friendly and socially acceptable	▪ Build-to-order and print-on-demand strategies ▪ Internet-based co-operation regarding material flow along the value chain	▪ Internet-based markets for surplus materials ▪ B2B platforms for surplus equipment and sites
Marketing	▪ Virtual showrooms and shopping malls: labelling and benchmarking products according to environmental standards	▪ One-to-one marketing strategies on the Internet ▪ Internet-based consumer communication with mass customisation	▪ Internet portals and online shopping guides for eco-friendly products and services
Optimisation of product use and recycling	▪ Software upgrading of household and office appliances	▪ Online support for leasing and sharing models	▪ Internet-based recycling exchanges (e.g. for car parts)
Management of knowledge and information	▪ Manuals on the Intranet ▪ Reporting on environment and sustainability on the Internet	▪ Training support through online learning modules ▪ Internet-based environmental accounting and controlling	▪ Internet communities specific for careers and tasks ▪ Online data banks with product life-cycle data

B2B = business-to-business

Table 1.3 **Approaches for sustainable e-business solutions**

- Despite the dynamism in the development of information and communications technologies and the rapid increase in Internet use, the digital revolution is still evolving and one must not overlook the possibility of guiding and controlling its growth.

The Internet as a medium does not guarantee improvements in the direction of sustainability: this can come about only if it is designed in an environmentally intelligent manner with suitable support from governments, companies and civil society. In addition, its usefulness in this area depends also on to what extent its potential is used to advance eco-efficiency, service design, dematerialisation, recycling and sustainable knowledge management.

2

E-LOGISTICS AND THE NATURAL ENVIRONMENT

Joseph Sarkis   *Laura Meade*   *Srinivas Talluri*

Clark University, USA   University of Dallas, USA   Michigan State University, USA

Many Internet and traditionally based electronic commerce (e-commerce) companies, whether they focus on business-to-business (B2B) or business-to-consumer (B2C) markets, have come to realise that the easy access to information and communication, and the delivery of their products or services are important drivers in developing market competitiveness. Having a supportive electronic logistics (e-logistics) and reverse e-logistics system is necessary to maintain this competitiveness. Billions of dollars will be spent on developing, using and maintaining these systems. According to the US Census Bureau, the B2C market is estimated to be $33 billion in 2001, up from $8 billion in 1998 in the United States. Billions more dollars of services and materials will flow through these systems.

Organisations will feel the economic burden and benefits of such systems when they are integrated into their commerce relationships and delivery mechanisms. Yet the environmental implications of these latest organisational and consumer-driven systems have not been investigated or evaluated. In this chapter we seek to examine the environmental implications of e-commerce from the perspective of the movement of materials and information through the supply chain. In the networked economy, the winners will be those who can take advantage of the benefits of e-commerce while avoiding its liabilities. By assessing the environmental variables at this early phase, we can be better informed about which trends to watch and the policies and practices that need to be put in place to ensure that e-commerce leads to an environmentally sustainable society.

The role of logistics in e-commerce has garnered the lion's share of the focus on the success or failure of Internet-based companies. For a B2C provider such as an online grocery delivery company, having an electronic information portal is not enough. There is a need for appropriate and efficient delivery of goods, which are promised 30 minutes after an order is requested (Hansell 2001). This example shows clearly the economic concerns of the logistics function in the context of e-commerce. In this chapter, we tease out some of the environmental relationships.

We will focus on the two main dimensions of the closed-loop supply chain—forward and reverse e-logistics functions—and begin the discussion by providing an overview of logistics and the various technologies that enable the electronic logistics function. We will also discuss e-logistics elements and their implications for environmental issues, ranging from substitution of delivery mechanisms, variations in packaging, to new methods of managing materials throughout the logistics function. We will then provide a definition of reverse logistics and various practices associated with the implementation and management of the reverse e-logistics function with respect to the natural environment. The final section focuses on the role of industry, government and academia, all of which are heavily involved in the evolution and development of these areas.

2.1 Operational logistics and the supply chain model

Figure 2.1 describes operations within a typical supply chain, with a special focus on the logistics of materials and products. We begin with procurement and inbound logistics activities that bring materials into the system from various vendors. The policies for the selection of vendors represent a central issue for purchasers. These materials are then stored and may be managed under the auspices of the purchasing function. Each of the major functions is profoundly impacted by the design of the product and the process. This impact needs to be managed by including all the functions and vendors in the design of processes and products. This is supported by methodologies and concepts such as life-cycle analysis and design for the environment.

The production function is composed of assembly and fabrication. Within this area, environmental issues such as closed-loop manufacturing, total quality environmental management (TQEM), dematerialisation and source reduction make contributions, even though some of them also influence other functional areas. Outbound logistics includes activities such as transportation determination, packaging, location analysis, warehousing and inventory management (for finished goods and spare parts). Marketing has an important role in these decisions and activities.

External 'use' is the actual consumption of the product, where product stewardship plays an important role. Field servicing may occur at this stage, but, from an environmental perspective, the product or materials may be disposed or returned to the supply chain through a reverse logistics channel. A product and its components can be re-usable or recyclable in this channel. The reverse logistics function may feed directly back to an organisation's internal supply chain or to a vendor, starting the cycle again. Each major supply chain activity consumes energy and generates some level of waste. Reductions in energy use and waste generation need to be addressed throughout the supply chain cycle.

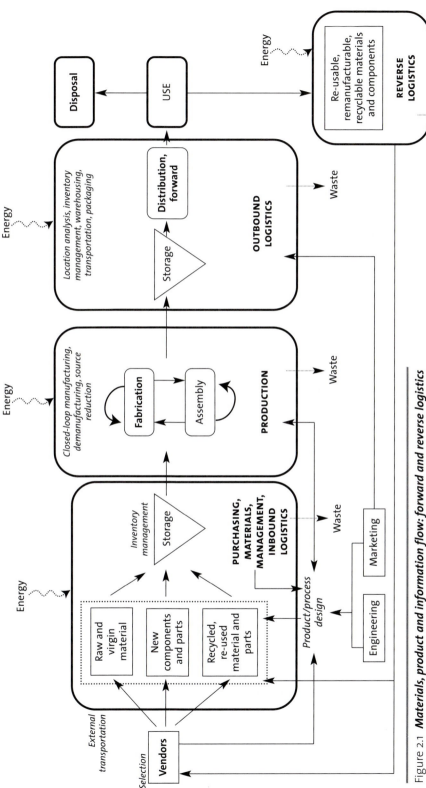

Figure 2.1 **Materials, product and information flow: forward and reverse logistics**

Source: Adapted from Sarkis 2002

2.1.1 Technology

One of the major drivers of the e-commerce and logistics linkage is the technology or the media used to deliver information within and between organisations and to stake-holders. A brief listing of these technologies includes those that have existed for decades and some very recent innovations:

- The personal computer
- Electronic data interchange (EDI) among carriers, shippers and customers
- Barcoding and scanning
- Advance ship notices (ASNs)
- Shipment and package tracking systems
- Satellite global positioning systems (GPSs) and geographic information systems (GISs)
- The World Wide Web
- The Internet, intranets and extranets
- Web-enabled relational databases, data warehouses and data marts
- Decision-support systems
- Electronic signature technology
- Wireless technology
- Enterprise resource planning systems

It is not one technology that has influenced the new environment for logistics, but the electronic, systemic and integrative nature of information and computer technologies. These have radically altered the logistics function of organisations over the past decade. We do not go into these technologies in detail as they are implicitly included in our discussion of the relationships between e-logistics and the environment (see Gulati and Garino 2000 and Simchi-Levi *et al.* 2000 for a more detailed discussion of the role of these technologies in e-commerce).

2.2 Forward e-logistics and the environment

In this section we discuss the impact of e-commerce on the major activities of the forward logistics function, including procurement, inventory management and warehousing, transportation and delivery management, packaging and order management, and present the environmental benefits and costs, or advantages and disadvantages, in each of these areas.

2.2.1 *Procurement*

Software vendors such as Ariba, Commerce One and Clarus have introduced Web-enabled procurement software for effective transactions between buyers and vendors. The primary advantage of these Internet-enabled procurement software packages is that they facilitate electronic transactions over the Internet via e-mail, XML messaging and EDI, which makes it easier for buyers and vendors. In an ideal scenario, these systems would eliminate paper forms for placing orders and bypass paper catalogues. The software provides information on previously ordered items, which makes replenishment decisions easier and allows vendors to route an electronic invoice and receipts back to the customer. The reduction in paper consumption achieved through such systems has a positive impact on the environment since less waste is generated. It is estimated that the net greenhouse gas production could drop as much as 0.25% by 2003 due to the decreased usage of paper (Romm 2000).

On the negative side, technology investments may result in higher energy use and greater reliance on fossil fuels, particularly in the US (Mills 2000, 2001). A rapid increase in new technology investments can also lead to increased levels of electronic waste problems. Electronic hardware is considered to be one of the fastest-growing waste-streams (Europa 2000), and it is estimated that 15 million personal computers are thrown away each year in the US (Witt 2000). Electronic equipment is the source of many toxic substances used in manufacturing and heat treatment, such as lead, mercury, cadmium, chromium and bromine.

Several firms are facing increasing technological problems with existing procurement software systems for managing electronic catalogues for numerous products that make the search process for items easier (Gilbert 2000). Companies are drawn into purchasing additional technology to make these systems work more effectively. This translates into higher energy requirements and potential technology waste. Despite these problems, many companies are buying into the benefits of procurement software, which promises to provide for 'paperless transactions'. While Dell is facing severe cataloguing problems with many of its 1,400 suppliers, the company expects to cut in half the $40 per transaction cost of processing purchase orders after these issues are fixed (Gilbert 2000). The transaction efficiency itself saves significant amounts of the resources required to complete the process.

The supplier relationship is very critical in completing green procurement activities. Information plays a critical role in a firm's e-commerce relationships with suppliers as well as in a number of procurement management issues, including selecting, managing the relationship with and integrating the supplier into the product and process design. Some of the important informational components of green supply chain management include (Bauer 2000):

● Command and control: confirmation of adherence to environmental regulations

● Environmental management systems: ISO 14000-related information

● Information/data transfer:
    – Checkmarked list of banned/discouraged substances
    – Recycled content
    – Recyclability data for benchmarking

- Operational data: bill of materials, process materials, energy use, material emissions

- Data to support OEM (original equipment manufacturer)-level component system design: integrated environmental properties, material emissions, cost, performance of product

- Knowledge to support vertical and horizontal technology transfer

Identifying and locating green suppliers is an area where the Internet has contributed greatly. Green supplier information has been made more available through a number of sites and organisations. Some of these include waste exchanges, which we describe later in the discussion on reverse logistics. Notable green purchasing sites include:

- European Partners for the Environment's Green Purchasing Network (www. epe.be)

- A green purchasing database (www.econexus.net)

- A meta-site that offers information on a number of green purchasing sites, especially in North America (www.nerc.org/gpn)

- Japanese Green Purchasing Network (www.wnn.or.jp/wnn-eco/gpne)

2.2.2 *Inventory management and warehousing*

E-commerce contributes to the better management of inventories through postponement, aggregation and information-sharing. Each of these practices impacts the natural environment. Postponement is the process of delaying the act of product differentiation or customisation as close to the time that a customer order is received as possible. As most e-businesses receive customer orders through the Internet, there is considerable scope for postponement. For example, in the PC industry, Dell maintains inventories of components and postpones the assembly of the PCs until it has received the specific customer order. This allows Dell to hold lower levels of inventories for parts and components compared to its business rivals such as Compaq. Smaller inventories result in lower holding costs from reductions in storage costs (facilities), obsolescence costs (outdated products) and spoilage costs (waste). Smaller storage facilities also result in lower energy requirements, while lower obsolescence and spoilage rates lead to a decline in the toxic waste generated from these components and parts.

Inventory aggregation in e-businesses allows firms to carry lower levels of inventories at fewer numbers of warehouses. The primary reason is that e-businesses do not have to carry inventories at sites close to the customer locations. A decline in the number of warehouses has a positive impact on overall energy consumption. Theoretically, aggregation leads to smaller overall inventory holdings in all organisations with less safety stock required. The reduction in inventory due to improved communication, forecasting and demand management, and aided by an e-commerce system and rapid communication adds efficiencies (and thus, less waste) to the inventory management of organisations. However, it can be assumed that the transportation of products and goods to more distant locations may be less efficient than short-distance transportation.

In e-businesses, the management of information across the entire supply chain allows the 'bullwhip' effect of inventories to be mitigated. This improves overall co-ordination and lowers inventory and warehouse costs. However, the investment necessary to set up an e-business and to streamline a firm's information infrastructure can involve expensive technology investments as well as higher levels of energy consumption. It is not yet clear if the investment and maintenance of these technologies and their potential waste-stream balance the potential eco-benefits in energy and waste generation. Clearly, there is a need for comprehensive environmental and economic cost–benefit analyses of the supply chain decisions.

2.2.3 *Transportation and delivery management*

As technology advances, so does the ability of carriers and shippers to match shipments and capacity. There are now many Web-based transportation exchanges, through which shippers are able to post their loads and carriers post their capacity. When shippers and carriers find a match, they make contact and negotiate price and service. Using these exchanges, shippers and carriers can work together to remove the inefficiencies inherent in the overall transportation network. There are currently exchanges for motor carriers, rail carriers and maritime carriers.

This basic model has developed a number of variations. Most exchanges are based on software that matches the shipments and the carriers, utilising shipment attributes, availability of trailers and so on. Aggregate exchanges have also developed. They are similar to basic exchanges, but they also enable carriers to pool their collective resources to buy tyres, insurance and supplies.

Consortia of carriers combine the aggregate exchange idea with end-to-end logistical services to shippers, whereby they can arrange spot buying or they facilitate entire logistical contract negotiations between shippers and carriers. Efficient partnering of materials through these networks may minimise the amount of energy used to transport aggregated materials. Examples of exchanges such as these include:

- FreightQuote (www.freightquote.com)

- GoCargo (www.navipact.com)

- Logistics.com (www.logistics.com)

- RightFreight (www.relysoftware.com)

- Transplace (www.transplace.com)

Unfortunately, the outbound transportation costs for products may also increase in an e-business setting. For example, the centralisation and aggregation of warehouses may be quite distant from customers when compared to the more traditional retailer stores (in a B2C setting). The increase in transportation costs means higher energy use, which would prove to be harmful for the environment. In situations where the product can be downloaded from the Internet (e.g. music), however, transportation costs are eliminated thereby conserving energy. Information, media and service-based businesses (e.g. engineering, consulting) may see beneficial environmental outcomes from e-commerce whereas the distribution of durable goods and products to distance customers is likely to produce more environmentally damaging results.

2.2.4 Packaging and order management

The marketing of products is also changed through the Internet and e-commerce. Because the online shopping experience is enhanced by the efficiency of the shipping process, e-commerce creates incentives to reduce the size and weight of product packaging. Consequently, refill pouches and super-concentrates—likely to be overlooked on the shelf but easy to ship—could become more appealing to shoppers. Less toxic dyes and inks can be used, as well as more recycled packaging content. Moreover, frequent home deliveries may create the logistical infrastructure for manufacturers to take back their packaging. With delivery costs included in product price, refillable or recyclable packaging material could become increasingly cost-effective (Cohen 1999).

From an environmental perspective, the possibility of unanticipated negative consequences of e-commerce should not be ignored. Electronic texts could *increase* paper use if, for example, consumers print in addition to read e-books or information online. And, unless shipping logistics is carefully planned, increased fuel consumption by vehicles making home deliveries could exceed the reductions in fuel use resulting from fewer trips to the mall. Web-based marketing may in fact encourage more profligate rather than eco-friendly consumption patterns.

2.3 Reverse e-logistics

Reverse logistics is a new frontier in management thinking and practice in the handling and disposal of returned products, and in the use of related materials and information (Meyer 1999). The goal of reverse logistics is to retrieve some value from the returned items as well as achieving environmental gains in the disposal or re-use of returned items. Environmental issues are increasing awareness of the importance of reverse logistics. The Reverse Logistics Executive Council defines reverse logistics as: 'The process of planning, implementing, and controlling the efficient, cost effective flow of raw materials, in-process inventory, finished goods, and related information from the point of consumption to the point of origin for the purpose of recapturing value or of proper disposal' (Tibben-Lembke *et al.* 1998). The economic and environmental implications of reverse logistics are paramount to the greening of industry and environmentally conscious business practices such as re-use, remanufacturing, recycling and reclamation.

From an operational and competitive perspective, industries, especially retailers, have seen the quantity of returned products significantly increase. In 1998, retail returns were around $65 billion per year as compared to over $40 billion per year in 1992. This increase has resulted from a sharper emphasis on customer satisfaction, espoused by such corporate practices as total quality management, and retailers (and other industries) using their liberal return policies as a competitive weapon. Many US firms still believe that a satisfied customer is the most important business strategy for maintaining their competitive advantage. Other countries may not yet have these liberal return policies, but there is a trend towards the spread of these policies as supply chains become more global. With the increasing use of Internet shopping, returns are expected to increase from $1.5 billion in 1997 to a forecasted online return of $11.5 billion in 2004.

2.3.1 *Reverse logistics process operation functions*

A number of possible operational functions and activities can be completed by a reverse logistics service provider or function. Schwartz (2000) and Rogers and Tibben-Lembke (1999) state that every reverse logistics system should include the following steps: **gatekeeping**, **collection**, **sortation** and **disposition**. **Gatekeeping** determines which products are allowed to enter the reverse logistics system; **collection** is the assembly of the products for the reverse logistics system; **sortation** is deciding what to do with each product; while **disposition** is the process of sending the products to their desired destination. Pohlen and Farris (1992) identified the following operational activities in the plastics industry: collection, separation, densification, transitional processing, delivery and integration.

A broad set of activities and duties are associated with the operations of reverse logistics providers. These activities and duties have differing roles and importance depending on the environmental or operational goal of the reverse logistics chain. For example, if the goal of the firm is to use reverse logistics simply for customer service in warranties or in taking returned parts or products, then collection, storage and delivery will play a more significant role. Activities such as the transactional processing for the disassembly of products and components could be integrated back into the forward supply chain while others may not play as large a role. If the goal is more environmentally related, such as reclaiming parts, then the sorting may be more important than the delivery and integration of the parts back into the forward supply chain.

2.3.2 *Electronic commerce reverse logistics challenges*

In the e-commerce arena, reverse logistics is a critical issue, as buyers need to be assured of the validity of the return. The handling of returns is a problem when the following symptoms occur: returns arrive faster than they can be processed or disposed of; large amounts of returns inventory are held in the warehouse; unidentified or unauthorised returns; lengthy cycle processing times; unknown total cost of the returns process; and lost customer confidence in the repair activity (Schwartz 2000).

While devoting time to create a dynamic website, e-tailers often overlook the process of how returns occur. Some of the reasons why e-commerce retailers have not yet fully developed their returns policies and processes include:

- **Relative unimportance.** Why focus on returns when the main priority is to generate sales?

- **Volume unknowns.** Many online retailers do not know everything when they initially start. Volume is a primary unknown.

- **Lack of experience.** Many online merchants have never sold anything before, or they have very little retail experience. They do not know the importance of strong return policies and procedures, and they have not had the years of experience that offline merchandisers have had.

- **Multiple product sources.** In addition, online retailing is often more complex, as many dot.coms sell products from multiple manufacturers who have the packages shipped directly to the customers. Each manufacturer may have its own returns policy and its own procedures, which could create some complex return scenarios (Bayles 2001).

As the market for asset disposition grows, new companies such as The Return Store have begun to appear (Hutchinson 2000). The Return Store, which plans to establish approximately 2,000 locations in the United States, is a place where consumers can bring all their returns, regardless of where they were purchased, and receive credit card processing on the spot. The Return Store then takes the responsibility for the items. This aids e-tailers and reverse e-logistics operations by providing a generic (non-brand name) site for returnables. In a survey of 311 logistics managers, 35% believed company policies would prevent them from installing an effective reverse logistics management system. Another 34% said their companies lacked the proper systems for effectively managing reverse logistics (Meyer 1999). Researchers have advocated the use of third-party logistics as an alternative to developing an efficient in-house system (Brockmann 1999; Gooley 1998; Pogorelec 2000; Rowley 2000).

Third-party reverse logistics providers have an appeal to Internet-based companies who may have a very fragmented distribution chain built around internal warehouses, drop-ship suppliers and, in some instances, third-party providers. Handling returns in-house can be disruptive to the organisation's business operations. I-Vendor, an online fulfilment company that serves Web-based retailers, turned to a third-party reverse logistics source ReTurn Inc. to handle the variety of merchandise that was being returned (Hutchinson 2000). Meanwhile, the large American retailer Kmart is currently reviewing when and for what items to use a third-party reverse logistics provider, and is evaluating how much it can or should take care of this in-house (Heller 2000).

With the advent of e-commerce, third-party shippers have an incentive to devise cost-effective and environmentally sound take-back systems, while expanding their market and increasing the efficiency of their transportation and distribution networks. These strategies have environmental advantages of less fuel consumption and packaging. If efficiently planned, the delivery networks that transport products ordered over the Internet can make pickups simultaneously in the same neighbourhood, delivering goods and returning packaging or discarded products back to the original manufacturer or retailer. Moreover, to reduce the costs of home delivery and make Internet purchases competitive with store-bought products, companies may shift to re-usable shipping containers to reduce the cost of packaging if they are responsible for both deliveries and returns (Cohen 1999). To be feasible, a critical mass of deliveries (a break-even point) and returns must be available. Additional success factors include (Stock 1998):

- A well-defined and charted set of activities, simplified and efficient

- Educational/training programmes, for customers, employees, suppliers, vendors and others in the firm's supply chain, to explain the purpose and relevance of reverse logistics

- Developing long-term partnerships or alliances are necessary to achieve optimal results because multiple organisations must be involved.

- Organisations need to adopt life-cycle analysis/life-cycle costing approaches to reverse logistics activities.

- Measurement systems must be developed and implemented to determine if programme performance is acceptable.

- Sufficient resources must be allocated to reverse logistics and environmental initiatives.

2.3.3 Environmental impacts of reverse e-logistics

A number of environmental issues and impacts arise from the proliferation of information technology and the Internet. Waste disposal of materials and goods can be prevented by increases in the efficiency of secondary markets that facilitate recycling and re-use as well as extend the life of these materials. Efficiencies can be gained from the quick, easy and reliable information that can be provided through Internet channels. For example, a number of websites are currently available for material re-use and exchange, including such products as industrial waste, electronics, wood, glass, textiles, high-tech equipment and even used tights. These materials exchanges are part of the reverse e-logistics arena. The number of these exchanges has proliferated in recent years and includes public, private and not-for-profit organisations. Previous mechanisms for waste-exchange networks were heavily dependent on the published media, which in many cases was outdated by the time the information was received. The Internet provides a number of advantages, including easier and more accurate information dissemination, and more rapid communication among participants.

Used equipment, excess inventory, waste by-products, returned products and remanufacturable goods can all be managed through the Internet. For example, Germany's Henkel company, one of the world's largest producers of washing detergents and other consumer products, has designed an Internet-based market for surplus materials where raw materials that can no longer be used at a specific production site (e.g. old stock), by-products and flawed batches are systematically offered for re-use. This process has provided great savings on raw materials. Internet-based services are also opening up new possibilities for safeguarding the environment by extending the use of products and creating new markets for recycling. However, there is no guarantee that the Internet's net environmental impact will be positive. For decades, technology watchers predicted that the personal computer would result in the 'paperless office', but US shipments of office paper actually jumped 33% between 1986 and 1997 (www.cisp.org/imp/october_99/).

2.3.4 Reverse logistics electronic enablers

Reverse e-logistics services that have environmental implications include for-profit industrial organisations and companies, not-for-profit or non-governmental organisations, as well as governmentally supported organisations that enable the management of materials through a reverse logistics system. Table 2.1 provides a listing of the types of organisation involved in using the Internet to facilitate the reverse logistics of materials and products. It also includes the website address, the type of organisation, a description of the industry and the e-relationship.

The Internet provides an excellent medium for hosting exchange sites. Through an exchange, a single infomediary (an industry consortium or a third party) can bring

Type of organisation	Description	Industry	E-relationship
www.18ocommerce.com			
For-profit	18oCommerce is the leading provider of software that enables companies to focus on their core business by removing the headache of reverse logistics.	Multi	B2B/B2C
www.amazon.com			
For-profit	Individuals may list their used books for sale on the website. The transaction is facilitated between the two parties.	Books	B2C/C2C
www.arcainc.com			
For-profit	Excel in recycling of appliances	Appliances	B2B
https://logistics.bhpconnect.com/default.asp			
For-profit	Provide logistics online software solutions to ensure that unnecessary shipping costs do not occur. Return parts are consolidated for return to a designated facility, returned parts can be tested for no-fault found status and beyond-repair parts can be scrapped locally to save in transit costs.	Multi	B2B
www.ndc-nfi.com			
For-profit	A reverse logistics provider who specialises in the various types of industry and the challenges each industry has in the reverse logistics cycle.	Multi	B2B
www.ciwmb.ca.gov/calmax			
Government	Developed by California integrated waste management board to assist in exchange of discards	Multi	B2B
www.dmcrecycling.com			
For-profit	DMC Electronics Recycling Company offers electronics recycling by developing methods and strategies to minimise electronic waste disposed to landfills.	Electronics	B2B
Epic.er.doe.gov/epic/pages/Matexch.htm			
Government	List of material exchange websites compiled by the US Department of Energy	Multi	B2B/B2C/C2C

B2B = business-to-business; B2C = business-to-consumer; C2C = consumer-to-consumer

Table 2.1 **Example Internet sites and programmes related to reverse e-logistics**
(continued opposite)

Type of organisation	Description	Industry	E-relationship
www.genco.com			
For-profit	GENCO's reverse logistics services include e-returns, return centre management, return centre software, asset recovery services and transportation management.	Multi	B2B/B2C
www.materialsexchange.org			
Not-for-profit	A service that connects businesses with markets and buyers for their re-usable materials	Multi	B2B
www.metrokc.gov/hazwaste/imex			
Not-for-profit	The Industrial Materials Exchange is a free service designed to match King County area business that produce wastes, industrial by-products, or surplus materials with businesses that need them.	Industrial	B2B
www.renet.de			
Government	Car recycling network	Automobiles	B2B
www.rlec.org			
Not-for-profit Education centre	Study the process, technology and disposition options available for products in the reverse logistics cycle.	Multi	B2B/B2C/C2C
www.shiprmx.com			
For-profit	Strategically located processing centres provide the perfect solution to costly cross-country shipments and customer response delays.	Retail	B2C
www.suddathlogistics.com			
For-profit	Return merchandise processing	Retail and manufacturing	B2B/B2C
www.texweb.de			
German government	Internet portals and online shopping guides for environmentally friendly products and services. Internet-based company networks.	Textile	B2B
www.tntlogistics.com			
Profit	Reverse logistics provider of automotive parts	Automotive	B2B

B2B = business-to-business; B2C = business-to-consumer; C2C = consumer-to-consumer

Table 2.1 (from previous page; continued over)

Type of organisation	Description	Industry	E-relationship
www.tsilogistics.com			
Profit	Provider of logistics services and software	Multi	B2B
www.usfreightways.com			
Profit	Reverse logistics for following industries: grocery, pharmaceuticals, health and beauty, automotive parts, food service, convenience stores, music, specialty retail, electronics	Multi	B2B/B2C

B2B = business-to-business; B2C = business-to-consumer

Table 2.1 (continued)

together many buyers and sellers. In the case of recyclable goods, what is one company's waste can be another company's asset. In the e-business world, size does not matter and therefore new entrants facilitating reverse logistics are likely to emerge.

2.4 Industry, government and academia

The environmental impacts of e-logistics and reverse e-logistics have major implications for stakeholders such as business, government and academic institutions. Some of these implications have been previously stated, but we hope to analyse them more fully here.

2.4.1 Industry

2.4.1.1 Adoption
Companies will be adopting these technologies, but the criteria used in their adoption will primarily be driven by economic considerations. The environmental gains and losses may be at best secondary considerations.

2.4.1.2 Technology development
The key role of industry is to lead many of the technological developments required to aid in the integration, dissemination and maintenance of the provision of e-logistics programmes.

2.4.1.3 Investment and integration

Additional investment in e-logistics programmes is needed for their effective dissemination. Difficulties arise in justifying such programmes and technologies when they have to consider the implications not only for their organisations but also for the entire supply chain. This also leads to integration issues, which require knowledge of the requirements and practices of external partners to ensure synergies through e-logistics and reverse e-logistics.

2.4.1.4 Adoption and development of processes

Technological linkage may sometimes be the easiest goal to achieve. Developing supporting business processes and adopting those processes—with associated policies—requires more difficult changes in managerial thinking and practices. It may require acceptance of data standardisation in supply chain management and design decisions. The selection of suppliers and the type of information that they provide represents one example. Another example is to use the industrial ecology concept to advance the ideas and garner organisational support for reverse logistics. Development of virtual eco-industrial parks (EIPs) may be a significant step in advancing e-logistics and reverse e-logistics in a global economy.

2.4.2 Government

2.4.2.1 Awareness development

An important role for government is to promote greater awareness of e-logistics and reverse e-logistics issues among organisations, particularly small and medium-sized ones, and to sponsor programmes, workshops and research related to these two issues.

2.4.2.2 Standards setting

Governments and industry need to develop methods and standards for both technology and practices that apply to the environmental consequences of e-commerce. The trust and reliability associated with standards can aid in the further diffusion of these technologies. However, industrial information standards (which may also fit within the realm of industry standards development) that identify environmental information requirements and methodologies should not be so tight as to constrain innovation.

2.4.2.3 Regulatory oversight

Monitoring of performance and impacts of these practices should not necessarily be relegated to voluntary measures and programmes. The need for regional, national and international regulations needs to be examined periodically, while governments should make sure that environmental regulations and public policy development are not hindering the economic and environmental benefits associated with these practices.

2.4.2.4 Intergovernmental relationships

Am important issue is the scope of intergovernmental co-ordination and management of global regulatory and public policies. Multinational organisations currently have this potential but not necessarily the capability to manage these many complex relationships, whereas the globalisation of the e-supply chain means that smaller organisations need to be aware and compliant with the many international, regional and local standards. International agreements will probably become more necessary though more difficult to negotiate and enforce.

2.4.2.5 Infrastructural support and development

Developing the necessary infrastructure and support mechanisms (e.g. 'Internet2') will further advance the e-logistics frontier. Part of this support includes publicly financing and supporting high-risk–high-payoff research and development within academia and industry. Extending these practices and technologies to developing nations will continue to be a global challenge.

2.4.3 Academia

2.4.3.1 Basic research and development

Many advances in technology and process methodologies will arise from academic research programmes ranging from algorithms and heuristics for effective negotiation and management of logistics relationships to specific hard technologies that increase the speed of transactions and information flow. The practice of reverse e-logistics in business is a critical subject area for organisational researchers.

2.4.3.2 Implications of technology on the environment

Research on the impacts of technologies such as information, manufacturing and biotechnology on the natural environment need to be strengthened. Basic and social sciences including the natural, engineering, economics, policy, sociological and management sciences all have a role to play in this research. The interdisciplinary character of nature and technology requires the integration of academic disciplines.

2.4.3.3 Determining what works and what doesn't

Part of the technology and business process needs to consider *a posteriori* the evidence from industrial practice to determine the efficacy of these advances with respect to the environment. This will require empirical evaluation of economic and environmental results to determine whether a linkage occurs among these outcomes and the various practices. Part of this research is to determine what works and what doesn't work.

2.5 Conclusion

In this chapter, we have highlighted and provided a comprehensive overview of the relationships between electronic communications and information technology, organisational logistics functions, and their impacts on the natural environment. These are three areas of great importance in what has been termed as the 'new economy'. Together these fields and their relationships may have a profound long-term effect and implications for individuals, corporations, governments, society and the environment. Becoming aware of the implications is important for all these groups. The economic implications of these issues are important, but other social and environmental concerns need to be addressed. The implications and relationships still require further study. And, for this reason, there is room for industry, government and academia to be more involved in the development and understanding of the relationship between e-logistics, reverse e-logistics and the natural environment.

GREENING THE DIGITISED SUPPLY NET

Michael Totten

Center for Environmental Leadership in Business,
Conservation International, USA

In many ways, 'greening' the supply network has been an integral part of industrial development throughout history. For centuries many producers of goods and services undertook innovations in their operations and products for productivity gains, capturing value from new technological advances, achieving resource and cost savings, seeking competitive advantages, entering new market niches, complying with regulations, and so on. Pollution and waste reductions and energy and resource savings were realised when innovations resulted in lighter materials, increased re-usability and recyclability of resources, or greater dematerialisation. Prominent examples of such eco-innovations include:

- This past century's shift from the candle to the incandescent bulb and now to the compact fluorescent lamp (CFL) has yielded remarkable efficiency gains. The candle consumes about 80 watts (W) of chemical energy to emit 12 lumens (lm) of light for about seven and a half hours. This was replaced with the carbon-filament incandescent bulb, which used one-quarter less energy (60 W), emitted 15 times as much light (180 lm), and lasted 133 times as long as the candle. When the tungsten filament replaced the carbon one, the efficiency was quadrupled. The tungsten bulb can now match the lifetime output of 8,100 candles, yet the lamp and the electricity cost only about as much as 14 candles. The CFL, however, renders the same lumen output as an incandescent, while consuming 75% less electricity and lasting 13 times longer, displacing the need for 500,000 candles! (Lovins and Sardinsky 1988).

- The locomotive went through a similar dramatic efficiency shift. In 1810 a typical locomotive with a cast-iron boiler had a ratio of weight to power of 1,000 kilograms (kg) per horsepower (hp). The advent of steel boilers enabled a one-third reduction in this value by the mid-1800s. By 1900 the ratio had been reduced tenfold from its 1810 value. By 1950, with wide use of the electric locomotive, the ratio had fallen another fourfold, and by 1980 the ratio had fallen to just 14 kg per hp—a seventyfold reduction over the locomotive's 170-year history (Williams *et al.* 1987).

- Computers offer one of the most extraordinary tales of dematerialisation. ENIAC, the first large-scale general-purpose electronic computer built in the 1940s, was 1,000 times faster than existing mechanical computers or calculators. It used to occupy a large room, filled with 17,400 vacuum tubes and guzzling the output of 180 kW of electricity; its computing power can now fit on a mini-watt microchip. In fact, there is 2,000 times as much computing power in a 5 W Nintendo 64 game player. If car manufacturing kept pace with computer innovations and cost reductions over the past half century, today a person would be able to buy a Rolls Royce for a dollar with a two million miles to the gallon fuel efficiency standard.

As efficiency expert Amory Lovins notes,

> the past quarter-century's efficiency revolution [in the US] is now 'producing' over four times as much energy as the entire domestic oil industry . . . simply by using less energy to do more work in smarter ways. More than half the nation's energy services now come from efficient use (Lovins and Lovins 2001).

This is worth several hundred billion dollars in savings on Americans' annual energy bills.

Despite these myriad productivity-enhancing efficiency innovations, the world is ironically consuming, polluting and wasting more resources than ever in absolute terms. In the past 100 years, the world's industrial production increased more than fiftyfold. Moreover, one-half to three-quarters of annual resource inputs to industrial economies are returned to the environment as wastes within a year (WRI 2000).

What does this have to do with e-commerce and the digitisation of the global economy? A flood of publications written this past decade make varying levels of persuasive cases that the global economy is almost destined in some technologically deterministic sense to become fully digitised. Wireless computers on a chip will become ubiquitous, interwoven into the very fabric of our clothes, appliances, buildings and social ambience (Kurzweil 1999; Martin 2000). Globalisation will be accelerated by the precipitously declining cost of digital communication technologies (Gilder 2000; Schwartz *et al.* 1999), business productivity will soar to new heights as a result of digital information and communications technologies (Slywotzky and Morrison 2000; Tapscott *et al.* 2000). And, as one recent report effusively noted,

> We may be living through the business equivalent of the Cambrian explosion when after 3.5 billion years of sluggish evolution, a vast array of life forms suddenly appeared in only 10 million years. New business models and ways of organising and operating businesses are appearing in comparably rapid profusion, driven by stunning advances in the information technologies (Geoffrion and Krishnan 2001).

This quote unwittingly captures the great potential of these new technologies as well as their potential for great harm. If digital information and communications technologies enable the traditional business goal of minimising the cost per unit of product or service, while externalising waste, pollution and environmental damage onto society and nature, then the 21st century will confront humanity with an ecological crisis of global and historical magnitude.

If businesses pour their ingenuity into streamlining their logistics so that anyone can click on a computer and have products shipped anywhere on the planet, the efficiencies and environmental gains that may be captured by these extraordinary productivity-enhancing tools will be overwhelmed by the accelerated pace of human consumption.

Swiftening the pace of ceaseless, careless human production and consumption would clearly worsen the two most notable perils confronting humankind: a species extinction spasm that scientists say could result in the irreversible loss of upwards of two-thirds of all the planet's species by the second half of this century, constituting one of the six largest extinctions in the history of the planet (IBC 1999); and climate change that threatens to cause severe health problems and massive economic and environmental damage for several centuries to come.

On the other hand, if businesses seek to minimise the cost per unit of service as well as maximise the social value gained per unit of environmental impact, and employ these powerful digital technologies to help achieve this goal, then humanity and nature may reap the fruits of this sustainable development (Chambers and Lewis 2001; Hawken et al. 1999; Lovins 2001). Industrial ecology experts such as INSEAD (European Institute of Business Administration) Professor Robert Ayres spell out a robust vision of a zero-emissions economy by shifting from the consumption model to a closed-loop service model, and making extensive use of advanced information and telecommunication technologies (Ayres 1998).

These are two among a number of possible scenarios by which the future is likely to unfold. Given the complex, non-linear nature of the world's diverse sociopolitical–economic activities, I will argue in this chapter that nobody really knows what surprises will arise or if the environment will in the end emerge as a winner or a loser in an increasingly digital economy. As information and communications technologies do not have any intrinsic qualities directing them towards environmentally benign directions, human decision-making remains the decisive factor in how productivity- and efficiency-enhancing technologies will be applied.

3.1 Changing corporate and commercial decision-making

Corporations have become in recent years the focal point if not targets of accountability for the environmental damage caused by human consumption. Corporations are pushed and pulled in new directions by internal and external drivers. Historically, compliance with regulatory regimes has been the overwhelming driver of corporate environmentalism (Tankha 1999).

But an additional driver is emerging resulting from the changing cultural attitudes about the environment. One major study of environmental attitudes concludes that the concern for the environment has become integrated within core American values such as parental responsibility (Kempton 1995) and that this sentiment is even more deeply held by Europeans. The Internet has infused this with an extraordinary momentum which promises to get stronger over time (SustainAbility 1999).

The information technology revolution has become a power-enabling mechanism behind the transformation in consumer/stakeholder and corporate relationships, greatly enhancing consumer education and sophistication. A report on corporate sustainability notes:

> The ease and economy of the Internet provides a vehicle for even the smallest stakeholder groups to potentially reach a global audience. Large corporations are therefore under greater public scrutiny than ever before. At the same time, the ease of electronic mail promotes communication between and among stakeholders and corporations. These mushrooming communications technologies have thus conceived a new concept—stakeholder capitalism (Tankha 1999).

A second driving force in consumer/stakeholder and corporate relationships—stakeholder activism against large-scale industrial and infrastructure projects, or product and process scares—is also intimately linked to the growth in digital technologies. This has been facilitated by the declining cost of computing and high-speed communication links formerly limited to multi-million-dollar supercomputers. The capacity to do sophisticated graphics and mapping with multiple databases, compile sophisticated economic and financial analyses with spreadsheet software, and then distribute the information with a click of the button to Internet users around the world truly represents a revolutionary tool (Totten 1993, 1998, 1999).

These structural changes in cultural beliefs and technological capacity for engagement appear to be influencing and changing an increasing number of corporate internal drivers. Leadership on sustainable practices is emerging, driven by a hope for competitive advantage, reduced risks and costs of doing business, new market opportunities, enhanced corporate reputation, and associated business reasons (Rowledge *et al.* 1999).

Among a growing number of examples, Volvo stands out as an intriguing case of taking sustainable business change to heart. The company adopted a sustainability strategy in the 1990s that views

> environment as a validated 'property', like reliability or strength, with a set of defined aspects, such as fuel-efficiency or material intensity, to be carefully targeted, monitored and improved at each stage of the product development process. Its aim is to have environmental considerations as ingrained in people's thinking as cost—in the sense that no new idea is considered without determining how much it will cost (Rowledge 1999).

This has involved approaching strategy and decisions from a 'high-integrity, holistic, integrated life-cycle perspective'. A dramatic change stemming from this approach was Volvo's view of product development, which traditionally was limited to assembly and use (warranty). Now it looks upstream to the extraction of raw materials, materials production and component manufacturing, as well as downstream to dismantling and sorting, re-use and recycling, and final disposal.

A key component of the company's green management strategy is managing its relations with the suppliers. Suppliers are viewed as development partners and are involved early in the product development process. Volvo's 'Environmental Requirements for All Major Suppliers and Contracts' require each supplier to have a certified environmental management system in place, including goals and action plans for the continuous decrease of their environmental impacts. Open data-sharing and dialogue are fundamental parts of the process.

Another important internal driver for Volvo is the digitisation of its environmental and business strategy. Every aspect of Volvo's management strategy is data-intensive, information-rich and knowledge-driven. The company recognises that digital tools enable the continuous gathering, rapid analysis and widespread, instantaneous distribution of information to its employees and extended supply network partners. Digital tools represent the vehicle for interactive design, communication, feedback and adaptive management that enable the company to monitor, evaluate and verify progress on its sustainability goals.

3.2 The digital supply network

As Adrian Slywotzky and David Morrison once observed:

> The Internet is ultimately about innovation and integration. Innovation is what your objective is—in cost structures, selling, marketing, sales, supply chain. But you don't get the innovation unless you integrate Web technology into the processes by which you run your businesses (Slywotzky and Morrison 2000).

This analysis begins with a simple assumption that it is cheaper, faster and cleaner to manage digital bits than physical atoms. By managing bits through manipulation of information (i.e. gathering, analysing, modelling, sorting, sharing and replicating data), a firm can eliminate or reduce its management of atoms (e.g. manipulation of physical assets such as stockpiling inventory, shipping products, buying equipment, installing machinery, building factories).

Digital business designs are not limited to large corporations but are, in fact, proving indispensable for start-up entrepreneurial firms attempting to market 'disruptive technologies' (Christensen 1997). The 100+ mpg, ultra-lightweight, high-performance concept car being pioneered by efficiency expert Amory Lovins and his colleagues at Hypercar Inc. is a case in point. It is not just the intensive computer modelling that goes into the design process of the hypercar, as this is true also of steel-stamped vehicle designs by all auto companies.

Metaphorically, the successful, well-managed mainframe computer industry was disrupted by the mini-computer technology, which in turn was disrupted by the PC revolution. The hypercar is following the PC model of radical redesign instead of incremental changes. Unlike the century-old auto industry which is locked into the steel-stamped car and can only deliver around 15%–20% of the energy of the car's fuel to the wheels, the 'hypercar designer starts with platform physics because each unit of saved road load can save in turn ~5–7 units of fuel that need no longer be burned in order to deliver that energy to the wheels' (Lovins 1997).

A critical component in transforming the hypercar to commercial reality has been the microchip revolution. This breakthrough design relies heavily on crash-impact-resistant polycomposite carbon fibres and computer-aided manufacturing techniques for creating shape-to-mould body parts and aerodynamically slippery surfaces. This in turn relies on resin transfer moulding processes that combine computer-controlled resin injection, online process monitoring, statistical process control, optimised low-pressure mould design, electron-beam moulding and adhesive bonding (Hawken *et al.* 1999).

3.3 Greening the digitised supply network

Business-to-business (B2B) supply network operations have emerged in recent years as critically important global e-business platforms. Projections of worldwide B2B e-commerce is estimated to be anywhere from $1.4 trillion to more than $7 trillion by 2004 (eMarketer 2001).

To date, the primary motivator for this shift to digital procurement has been to cut costs and save time. For example, IBM's internal e-procurement team has saved the company hundreds of millions of dollars in the purchasing of non-manufacturing supplies (paper, pens, corporate services, etc.). More than 6,700 suppliers are plugged into IBM's e-procurement system (Slywotsky and Morrison 2000).

Xerox Europe, a $6 billion 'document' company with half a million customers and 50 million documents to process annually, is aggressively pursuing e-procurement as a market opportunity that derives both productivity and some environmental gains. Xerox Europe plans a paperless future for its 50 million documents. The project is set to save $300 million a year and transform Xerox into a showcase e-business (Xerox 2000).

While environmentally preferable attributes are not a top priority in these cost-reducing efforts, there are indicators they could be brought into the digital procurement process. The issue of 'greening' the supply chain is gaining a lot of attention from companies, governments and academics (BSR 2000; CSP 2001; GEMI 2001; Baumgarten and Arnold 2000). Some of the important green supply chain issues include extended supplier networks, Global Reporting Initiative efforts, ISO 14001 management standard and choiceboards.

3.3.1 Extended enterprise supplier networks

First, companies such as Toyota and DaimlerChrysler are using extended enterprise supplier networks to create partnerships, and to promote knowledge-sharing and trust-building. Advances in information and communications technologies have led to impressive environmental gains in the company supply chain. Working with a supply network offers new opportunities to reduce environmental burdens over the entire network and limits the possibility of shifting environmental burdens from one link in the supply network to another (Dyer 2000).

3.3.2 *Global Reporting Initiative (GRI) efforts*

Second, a growing number of national and multinational companies are voluntarily participating in tracking their social, environmental and economic performance, and transparently reporting progress through adoption of guidelines developed by efforts such as the Global Reporting Initiative (www.globalreporting.org). Web supply networks and B2B e-commerce sites could facilitate the tracking of purchases to indicate a company's environmental gains and identify lost opportunities as a result of less energy- and resource-efficient product purchases.

3.3.3 *ISO 14001 management standard*

Third, the connection between good environmental practices, operational excellence and improved financial performance (World Bank 2000) is leading more corporations to certify their business operations and those of their suppliers to the ISO 14001 environmental management system.

The ABB Group uses the ISO 14001 standard as a starting point for measuring its progress and continuous improvement on social and environmental indicators. In 2000 ABB used a set of 39 operational performance indicators (OPIs) to monitor environmental performance, six more than the previous year.

The quantity of emissions and use of chemicals are calculated with the mass balance method, and then go through a two-tier internal verification and audit to check for accuracy and consistency, as well as external review by Det Norske Veritas (DNV), an internationally accredited classification society, as part of the annual verification process.

To communicate the company's environmental performance to the company's stakeholders, ABB issues and posts the company's environmental product declarations (EPDs) and environmental declarations (EDs) on its website. Based on a formal life-cycle analysis, an EPD describes the environmental performance of a product, a system or a service over its entire life-cycle, while an ED describes the environmental performance of the engineering, construction, service and other activities of an entire business area or other organisational unit. ABB intends to make even greater use of information and communications technologies to facilitate interaction with its suppliers and improve the company's life-cycle environmental performance (ABB 2000).

3.3.4 *Choiceboards*

Fourth, the rapid development of powerful software algorithms such as 'choiceboards' is leading to enhanced product or service information. As described by business management expert Adrian Slywotzky, 'In a wide variety of markets, customers will soon be able to describe exactly what they want, and suppliers will be able to deliver it to them without compromise or delay' (Slywotzky 2000). E-business tools such as choiceboards build on existing Internet capabilities of companies such as Dell or Sony Corporation, which let their customers design their own products and services by choosing from a menu of attributes, components, prices and delivery options.

E-business functions such as choiceboards open new market opportunities for environmentally preferable products and to assist buyers in selecting products that help shrink their ecological footprints. A growing number of Internet sites already use a wide range of environmental attributes to identify products with recycled content, EnergyStar-compliant labels and other green qualities.

Web-based selection algorithms (including screeners, comparators, locators, configurators) offer opportunities to electronically integrate procurement decisions with continuous learning mechanisms (Slywotzky and Morrison 2000). For example, some products may offer preferable attributes for achieving green-building certification, or ensuring success in voluntary programmes for pollution prevention, water efficiency, hazardous waste reduction, energy efficiency, zero emissions, zero-waste pollution, climate- (carbon-) neutral operations, and so on.

Web-based operations can also open up new possibilities in sharing and validating information on consumer products. Using a peer-to-peer forum such as 'e-pinions' (www.epinions.com), an individual can share his or her experiences and discuss the environmental attributes of products or services.

3.4 Greening public policy for the digital economy

Virtually all technologies are double-edged swords with gains and losses, an upside as well as a downside. In the nexus of the environment and the digital economy, there has been extensive discussion on the environmental impacts from the logistics and shipping industry as the supply chain logistics move increasingly from ground to air transportation (Hendrickson *et al.* 2001; Matthews *et al.* 2000).

As former US EPA Strategic Futures Director David Rejeski points out, 'When we opt for trucks instead of boats or rail, energy use goes up by a factor of four to five (from 400 or 500 BTUs per ton-mile to over 2,000). Moving the same package by air freight again increases the energy use dramatically (to over 14,000 BTUs per ton-mile)' (Rejeski 1999).

Some companies such as Sweden's SJ Rail are responding to this environmental concern by marketing their environmentally superior transport services ('Green Cargo'). They also offer corporate customers online software that allows for a comparative analysis of environmental costs of different transport modes and logistical arrangement (Rowledge *et al.* 1999). However, additional, innovative public policy efforts are likely to be necessary in dealing with some of the environmental downsides associated with an increasingly digitised economy.

The example of increased pollution problems from the air freight industry is one of the many vexing uncertainties in a more digitised economy. Another troublesome trend is the outfitting of cars with advanced digital communication, information and entertainment systems, as well as the growing pervasiveness of web phones. This ability to access information anytime, anywhere is, in effect, transforming cars into roving offices, or detachable, mobile-home office and entertainment rooms. Society could make great gains in greening our buildings, products and factory processes, only to see these environmental benefits swamped by people driving polluting vehicles more frequently.

Just as some European countries have been at the forefront in crafting a range of innovative public policies to spur commerce in a more ecologically sustainable direction, many of these same policies—if widely diffused—will be a critical asset in ensuring digital commerce moves in a similar direction. Europe's leadership in addressing extended and shared producer responsibility of products also holds out some hope of realising closed-loop industrial ecology opportunities (OECD 1998).

3.5 Digitisation unbound

Internet growth trends remain wildly speculative, but a number of projected trends suggest that e-commerce activity may very well be global in the next five years. It is well worth noting that 80% of installed appliances, consumer electronics, office equipment and other energy-consuming products in the developing world will be purchased over the next several decades. Whether these new products are environmentally sound or energy-efficient will have a large impact on the environmental and natural resources of our planet.

E-procurement is not likely to make much of a difference among consumers in developing countries (or in wealthier countries for that matter). However, e-procurement choiceboards may serve a valuable role in helping corporate or institutional purchasers identify and order low energy-intensive and environmentally friendly, high-quality products.

In the end, the digitisation of commerce and society is so fraught with uncertainties that no one can presume to know how it will unfold. Hence, it behoves us to vigorously participate in its unfolding, whether as willing participants, sharp-eyed critics, or just plain disbelievers.

DOT.COM ETHICS
E-business and sustainability

James Wilsdon
Demos, UK

In the digital age, entrepreneurs are the new rock and roll. Teenagers who previously fantasised about becoming pop stars have swapped guitars for laptops in a bid to become the next Jeff Bezos, CEO of Amazon.com, or Martha Lane Fox, chief operating officer of Lastminute.com. But what motivates this new breed of entrepreneurs? How do they see the role of business in society? Will they automatically head down the old-economy route of putting profit before people, or can they lead the way towards more sustainable, accountable models of capitalism?

In exploring these questions, a good place to start is Louise Proddow's *Heroes.com*, a recent tribute to 50 prominent members of the English digerati. Proddow suggests that e-entrepreneurs have a number of defining characteristics, including (Proddow 2000: xii-xv):

- Passionately embracing the dot.com era

- Recognising that the Internet changes everything and opens up new opportunities

- Rethinking how they do things; making dot.com central to their strategy and life

- Playing by new rules, being more open, more flexible, more dynamic

- Acting in Internet time and making things happen fast

- Recognising the value of partnerships and outsourcing

- Living for today and enjoying the momentum and buzz of the Internet

From a sustainability perspective, this is a bit of mixed bag. Thumbs up for flexibility, dynamism and recognising the value of partnerships. But the emphasis on speed and 'living for today' may give some cause for concern. Despite their much-vaunted creativity, what actually comes across from reading *Heroes.com* is a striking narrowness of vision. Few of the entrepreneurs profiled seem willing to raise their sights above the economic bottom line to say anything about the wider responsibilities of business. There is a lack of what we might call 'three-dimensional entrepreneurship'—using technology to create environmental and social, as well as economic, benefits.

4.1 Dot.com ethics survey

To explore the relationship between e-commerce and corporate sustainability, Forum for the Future commissioned a survey of the attitudes of information technology and dot.com business executives towards social and environmental issues between July and November 2000. From the original sample of 150 companies, they received responses from 103. Just under half of these were completed by the CEO and the rest by senior managers.

Companies were selected to represent a cross-section of the e-commerce marketplace, ranging from large multinationals to small start-ups, and including a wide mixture of business-to-consumer (B2C), business-to-business (B2B), Internet service providers, software and hardware companies. The main criterion for inclusion was a business model based on the Internet. For this reason, we did not include traditional companies that are now involved in e-commerce.

Contrary to some of the negative stereotypes about dot.com entrepreneurs, the results of the Forum for the Future survey were overwhelmingly positive:

- 65% said that social and environmental issues are important or very important to their companies (28% said they were slightly important; 7% unimportant).

- 92% said that environmental and social issues are important or very important to them personally.

- 53% thought these issues would be more important three years from now.

- 79% agreed that the positive effects of e-commerce on society would outweigh the negative (21% neither agreed nor disagreed).

- 58% agreed that e-commerce would have a positive effect on the environment (29% neither agreed nor disagreed; 13% disagreed).

- 62% agreed that e-commerce would enable companies to be more responsive to consumers' ethical and environmental concerns (17% neither agreed nor disagreed; 21% disagreed).

- 57% agreed that companies with a good environmental and social reputation would be likely to benefit from improved financial performance (30% neither agreed nor disagreed; 13% disagreed).

According to the survey, e-business leaders were broadly supportive of the sustainability agenda even if they do not articulate their concerns in precisely these terms. In some ways this is unsurprising considering that the majority of the companies surveyed are run by highly educated, creative people aged 35 or under, who are likely to have a reasonable level of environmental and social literacy. The e-generation has, in the words of Don Tapscott, 'grown up digital' (Tapscott 1998), but it has also 'grown up green', with a high level of awareness of global issues, and an unconventional if not radical approach to doing business. This new wave of 'knowledge workers' is 'mobile, skilled, affluent, hard-working, ambitious, environmentally conscious, and a group who can trade on their skill, expertise and intellectual capital'. They also believe strongly in freedom, collaboration and choice—values that are likely to be reflected in the way they run their companies (Leadbeater 1999: 178).

Unfortunately, our survey also reveals a sharp gulf between theory and practice. On the question of whether their companies have any systems or policies to address environmental and social issues, the survey found that:

- 79% of companies do nothing to measure or manage their environmental impacts.

- 66% do nothing to measure or manage their social impacts.

- 82% do nothing to measure or manage their transport impacts.

- 83% offer no staff training on environmental or social issues.

This suggests that information technology and e-commerce companies still have a lot to learn about the basic principles of environmental and social management. Recent surveys by Business in the Environment and the Pensions Investment Research Consultants support this view. The research carried out by these two groups concludes that the information technology sector is one of the worst-performing industries in terms of environmental policies and reporting (PIRC 2000).

When we asked why these high-tech companies had no policies and systems in place regarding environmental and social issues, three reasons stood out:

- **Lack of perceived impacts.** The myth of virtuality is very powerful, and the survey shows that many companies do not recognise that they have any significant impacts.

- **Lack of time.** The e-world operates at breakneck speed, leaving little time to reflect or act on these issues.

- **Lack of expertise and resources.** Many e-businesses operate under considerable financial pressure, and cannot devote resources to these issues. Often there is insufficient staff expertise to develop policies and put systems in place.

These obstacles should not be underestimated, but they can be overcome with commitment from senior managers. Closing the gap between ideals and action is a priority for any e-business—or for any company for that matter—seeking to establish a reputation for good corporate citizenship.

Fortunately, there are encouraging signs of a growing interest in corporate environmental and social responsibility. In the US, groups such as the Seattle-based Digital Partners and the Silicon Valley Community Foundation have sprung up to channel newly acquired wealth towards social and community-based initiatives.[1] Several high-tech and e-commerce companies have set up charitable trusts. For example, the online auction company eBay allocated 1% of its shares to the eBay Foundation at the time of stock flotation. Meanwhile, individuals such as Microsoft co-founder Bill Gates and former chairman of Netscape Jim Clark have donated millions to health and education initiatives, with a particular focus on the developing world.

In Europe, fewer people had a chance to make their millions before the downturn in the market. However, a handful have started to invest in social projects. In March 2000, Tim Jackson, the founder of QXL, established a £70 million charitable trust and said 'it is important that entrepreneurs who have made a lot of money very quickly put some of that money back into the community'. Kate Oakley, a leading writer on the new economy, suggests that e-entrepreneurs will eventually make a contribution to the social fabric of our towns and cities equivalent to that of the great 19th-century industrialists. Just as the Victorians built museums, libraries and universities, so these 'new Victorians' will seek to 'channel their wealth into good works of all sorts, from soup kitchens to school programmes, AIDS hospices to playgrounds' (Oakley 2000).

Nonetheless, the bulk of this activity still takes place in the realm of philanthropy, and it is less common to find e-businesses that deliver social and environmental benefits through their core activities. There are exceptions—mostly small start-ups; some pioneering examples are noted in Box 4.1. A handful of larger companies are now tackling the digital divide as a strategic business issue: for example, AOL, which has an active social inclusion programme, and Hewlett-Packard, which recently announced a $1 billion initiative designed to market tele-medicine, e-learning, e-commerce and microcredit schemes to 1,000 villages in the developing world.[2]

The examples in Box 4.1 illustrate some of the diverse ways in which e-commerce can blend economic, social and environmental innovation. A lot more, though, could be done to foster social and environmental entrepreneurship:

- There is a need for support networks for entrepreneurs—perhaps as offshoots of existing Internet business networks such as First Tuesday—to assist with finance, advice and business development, and ensure that innovative ideas succeed.

- Government and NGOs (non-governmental organisations) should join forces with progressive IT, telecom and e-commerce companies to establish a 'sustainability incubator', able to provide advice and start-up capital to social and environmental entrepreneurs.

- New companies aiming for a stock market flotation should follow the example of eBay in allocating at least 1% of their shares to a charitable trust.

- Government and NGOs need to engage the venture capital industry in a more active dialogue on social and environmental issues, and encourage it to support community-based business ventures.

---

1   www.digitalpartners.org; www.siliconvalleygives.org
2   www.aol.co.uk/info/corporate/community_programme.html; www.hp.com/e-inclusion

www.greenstar.org—supports communities in the developing world through a network of Internet-enabled community centres, which offer a combination of Web access, education, tele-medicine, renewable energy and microfinance.

www.ethical-junction.org—a B2C portal for organic and fair-trade products, with its own virtual 'ethical high street'.

www.greenorder.com—a B2B site enabling public- and private-sector organisations to purchase environmentally friendly products, ranging from building materials to office supplies.

www.flametree.co.uk—supports companies and employees seeking a better 'work-life balance', with Web-based advice and consultancy on sustainable work patterns.

www.drparsley.com—an ethical incubator working to bring sustainable dot.com businesses to market. Currently working on projects with *The Big Issue* and a network of organic food producers.

www.publicsector.org—a news and consumer site for UK public-sector workers which promotes green lifestyles, products and services.

www.goodcorporation.com—encourages companies to meet a set of social and ethical standards set out in the online *GoodCorporation Charter*.

www.ushopugive.com—enables consumers to donate a small portion of the profits from online purchases to a charity of their choice.

B2B = business-to-business; B2C = business-to-consumer

Box 4.1 *Some ethical dot.coms*

4.2 Stakeholders.com

> In the dot-com era, trust—the direct result of integrity and reputation—remains critical . . . The only difference now is that reputations, which still take time to build, can be tarnished more quickly (McNealy [CEO, Sun Microsystems] 2000).

How will e-commerce affect the relationship between a company and its stakeholders? Could it usher in a new era of transparency and accountability? One of the best descriptions of the changing nature of corporate power in the new economy can be found in the book *The Cluetrain Manifesto*. Written by four Web aficionados, this consists of a set of 95 theses, designed to show how the Internet has radically altered the rules of business. The first of these run as follows (Levine *et al.* 2000: xiv-xx):

- Markets are conversations.

- Markets consist of human beings, not demographic sectors.

- Conversations among human beings sound human. They are conducted in a human voice.

- Whether delivering information, opinions, perspectives, dissenting arguments or humorous asides, the human voice is typically open, natural and uncontrived.

- People recognise each other as such from the sound of this voice.

■ The Internet is enabling conversations among human beings that were simply not possible in the era of mass media.

■ Hyperlinks subvert hierarchy.

The Internet enables these conversations to take place more easily. It is a perfect medium for promoting inclusivity: '[It] invites participation. It is genuinely empowering' (Levine *et al.* 2000: 17). Through e-commerce, traditional boundaries can be dissolved, and companies can become more responsive to stakeholder needs.

But are all stakeholders getting a piece of the online action? A lot is said and written about the changing relationship between companies and consumers, but there is very little about other groups. The Forum for the Future survey asked e-businesses to rank their stakeholders according to importance. The results are revealing (see Fig. 4.1). Customers, employees and investors are regarded as critical; the media, on-line communities and suppliers as important; government, geographical communities and NGOs as fairly unimportant; and trade unions as totally irrelevant.

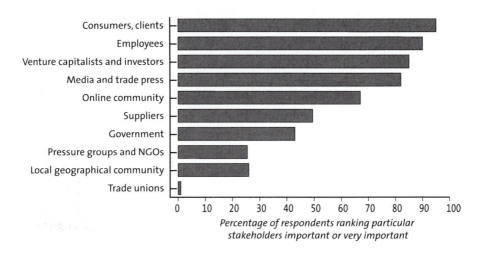

Figure 4.1 **How important are the following stakeholder groups to your company?**

4.2.1 *Consumers*

As the book *The Cluetrain Manifesto* suggests, the Internet changes the balance of power between companies and consumers. The most obvious benefit of this is cheaper products and services as consumers learn to compare prices at the click of a mouse. However, this new wave of empowerment also offers the tantalising prospect of an upsurge in ethical consumerism.

In the B2C market, companies will need to find new ways to add value and differentiate themselves from their competitors as prices are driven ever lower. Focusing on ethical and environmental performance is one route to a rapidly expanding market. A recent survey by The Co-operative Bank found that 30% of us take some account of ethical issues when shopping for products and services (Cowe and Williams 2000). Fast-growing sectors include ethical investment, which is now worth £3.3 billion in the UK, and organic food, which is predicted to be worth £1.5 billion in the UK by 2003.

Traditionally, the barriers to ethical consumerism have been the difficulty of accessing products and the limited availability of reliable information. E-commerce is ideally suited to overcoming these obstacles, and it can only be a matter of time before a large retailer launches a green or ethical shopping site. At the moment, this market has been left to a handful of small players such as ethical-junction.org that lack the scale to reach a wide consumer audience.

For e-tailers, there is a strong business rationale for investing time and money in improving ethical performance. As well as opening up new markets, it can help to build more meaningful bonds of trust and loyalty with consumers. Currently, debates about trust on the Internet are focused on privacy and the security of transactions. As e-commerce becomes more sophisticated, consumers are likely to want assurance on a wide range of issues—including the social and environmental credentials of products and services—and companies will have to capitalise on their reputation to offer that assurance.

4.2.2 *Employees and trade unions*

In the knowledge economy, human capital is a company's greatest asset. The importance of recruiting and retaining high-quality staff underpins many of the benefits—particularly stock options—that information technology and dot.com companies offer their employees. Across the sector as a whole, employment practices and management structures are broadly progressive.

But in the e-commerce gold rush, some companies have taken advantage of their employees' dreams of getting rich, and failed to apply the same kind of innovation and creativity to ownership structures and career development that they apply to other parts of their business. Andy Law, the founder of the advertising agency St Luke's, has drawn attention to this problem: 'Dot-coms are terribly traditional. They're owned and managed absolutely conventionally and rather than redefine business, they exist to enrich a tiny few . . . You see the fallout every day. Employees are burned out, alienated and disillusioned' (Law 2000).

In many e-businesses, for every well-paid knowledge worker reaping the benefits of his or her intellectual capital, there is likely to be someone else working long hours for modest pay in a technical support centre or fulfilment depot. When dot.com stocks were riding high, employees accepted poor conditions and a lack of job security in return for stock options. Now that share prices have slumped, workers are turning to traditional forms of collective bargaining to prevent redundancies, and companies such as Amazon and eTown are facing calls for union recognition. The fact that only 1% of our survey respondents consider unions to be an important stakeholder shows that there is still a long way to go before good employment practices are established across the sector.

It does not have to be this way. As Bill Thompson points out in a recent pamphlet on 'e-Mutualism', the Internet is the ideal environment for new forms of co-operative ownership and management (Thompson 2000). It is not an organisation that anyone can join, it is a set of relationships, and should therefore lend itself to more inclusive employee- and stakeholder-driven models of capitalism.

4.2.3 Community

In its 95 theses, *The Cluetrain Manifesto* goes on to discuss the importance of community: 'To speak with a human voice, companies must share the concerns of their communities. But first, they must belong to a community' (Levine *et al.* 2000: xvi). As our survey shows, community is understood first and foremost in a virtual sense for many e-businesses. This shift in perception requires us to revisit traditional stakeholder models and update them so that they remain relevant to the e-business environment. Tools and concepts such as corporate community investment will need to be adapted to cope with these new forms of virtual community.[3]

This emphasis on the virtual can be a positive thing. As recent research by the think-tank Demos shows, despite the fears that the Internet will erode social relationships, the trend is in the opposite direction towards the creation of online communities as an addition to, not a substitute for, existing social networks (Jupp and Bentley 2001). More often than not, electronic communication is supplementing relationships and allowing people to find out more about the organisations and individuals they are dealing with. There are also exciting opportunities to use the Internet to create new forms of community participation and civic institution. In his magisterial study of community life in modern America, the sociologist Robert Putnam concludes that 'the internet will not automatically offset the decline in more conventional forms of social capital, but it has that potential. In fact, it is hard to imagine solving our contemporary civic dilemmas without computer-mediated communication' (Putnam 2000: 180).

Yet it is still important to reflect on the lack of connection that many dot.coms feel with their local geography. Writers such as Richard Sennett have drawn attention to the corrosive effects of a wired workforce that fails to engage with its community. Sennett describes how his home area of Clerkenwell, once home to printers and small manufacturers 'is now becoming a neighbourhood of lofts, sold to the young financiers working nearby in the City, or to the officer class in the army of graphic design, fashion and advertising which has occupied London' (Sennett 2000). These people use the city as a backdrop to their lives, rather than actively involving themselves in the community. They have few links to local people, local politics, and no understanding of the social capital that was ploughed into the parks, the cinema, the bookshop.

A few e-businesses are now working to reverse this trend—for example, Amazon.co.uk has an active community programme in the urban area where its head office is located. However, more could be done across the e-business sector to learn from existing best practice in the bricks-and-mortar world. There are economic as well as ethical reasons why this makes sense. As the 1998 Competitiveness White Paper of the UK Department of Trade and Industry puts it, 'commitment to the local community and its economic, social and environmental concerns, builds reputation'. And reputation in turn underpins company value (DTI 1998).

---

3   CCI (corporate community investment) has been pioneered and promoted by organisations such as Business in the Community (www.bitc.org.uk).

4.2.4 *Suppliers*

Most analysts agree that B2B e-commerce is where the real growth will happen over the next five years. The Internet research company Forrester predicts that consumer spending on the Internet will increase from $7.8 billion in 1998 to $108 billion in 2003, while B2B transactions will rocket from $43 billion to at least $1 trillion. The basic selling point of B2B e-commerce is that it cuts costs. Estimates vary, but the scope for savings in some sectors is thought to be anywhere from 20% to 30%.[4]

Online trading exchanges are seen as a way of achieving these efficiency gains. In every sector, companies are joining forces with competitors to build huge trading hubs, where all procurement can take place under one virtual roof. The volume of transactions that will pass through these exchanges is mind-boggling. For example, the auto-industry exchange Covisint, born from an alliance between Ford, General Motors and Daimler-Chrysler, is set to bring together 35,000 component makers with an annual trading volume of $250 billion (Henig 2000).

In sustainability terms, it is not yet clear whether B2B e-commerce will have positive or negative effects. Taking the supply chain as a whole, B2B undoubtedly has the potential to deliver gains in environmental productivity alongside economic efficiency. But the narrow focus on price in the purchasing protocols that govern many transactions, particularly through automatic exchanges, creates the real possibility that environmental and ethical considerations will be downgraded or ignored altogether. The speed and volume of transactions through such exchanges may make it difficult to know who you are dealing with, and this creates reputational risks that might have been avoided in traditional supply-chain relationships. There is a danger that so-called 'stealth corporations' start using the anonymity of B2B exchanges to sell low-cost, environmentally or socially destructive products (SustainAbility 1999).

Currently, many e-businesses are flying blind, with few of the safety-checks and systems that are required. How long can it be before a prominent e-tailer gets hit by a sweatshop scandal, similar to those faced by Nike and Gap in recent years? Dot.coms should be conscious that companies that live by the Web can also die by the Web. In recent years, NGOs have become extremely adept at using the Internet to orchestrate campaigns against companies with poor track records (examples include shameonnike.com and mcspotlight.com). Dot.coms are more vulnerable than most to new forms of online campaigning.

To cope with these challenges, ethical audit and compliance systems need to enter the digital age. There are already systems, such as those offered by Clicksure.com, which provide online assurance on issues of quality. These should be extended to cover environmental and social issues. B2B exchanges will also need to develop protocols to ensure that trading partners meet environmental and social standards. It will take time for these systems to develop, but it should one day be possible to click on a website and review the quality of the environmental or social standards of a particular supplier or a contractor. Another click should take you to the website of the auditing agency, and even allow you to exchange e-mails with the individual auditor (Babcock 2000).

4   www.forrester.com

4.3   An agenda for a sustainable digital economy

> We've been called everything—Amazon.con, Amazon.toast, Amazon.bomb—
> and my favourite, Amazon.org, because clearly we are a not-for-profit corpo-
> ration (Bezos 2000).

After the rollercoaster ride of the past year, it is time to take stock. There is no inevita-
bility that the new economy will see the emergence of more ethical models of business.
But we could use the opportunities we have in front of us—opportunities to combine
technological innovation with social and environmental innovation—to take a major leap
forward in the pursuit of sustainability.

Forum for the Future's survey shows that e-entrepreneurs have a clear sense of their
responsibility to society and to the environment. The challenge is to act on this, so
e-commerce is about more than just 'the soundless scrape of coins over the wire' in the
future (Levine *et al.* 2000: 165). New-economy business leaders need to take stock of their
impacts and of their potential to make a difference.

Internet technology provides us with ample opportunity for e-materialisation: replacing the real with the virtual, reducing energy use and increasing the efficiency of supply
chains. This potential needs to be realised through new business models, through chan-
nelling innovation towards environmental goals, and through rethinking whole systems
of production and consumption.

The Internet also changes the way we relate to each other, and creates new forms of
accountability. The responsible company can use the Internet to let everyone know how
well it is doing; the irresponsible company can be easily named and shamed. The Web
makes it easier to reach out to your stakeholders, and to source products and services that
meet ethical standards. It also makes it easier to trace where companies have gone
wrong.

How will all these opportunities be realised? In part through policies and systems
(through measuring, managing and reporting on environmental and social impacts); in
part through learning from others in networks that allow ideas and experience to change
hands; and in part through leadership of the most committed and the most influential,
who set a standard for others to follow. E-business leaders need to translate their progressive values into a template for inclusive and responsible business.

In addition to policies, systems and declarations, there are two further principles we
can draw on in developing sustainable e-business: 'joining the dots' and 'taking time'.

4.3.1   *Joining the dots*

Dot.coms are no strangers to partnership. Web success depends on forging alliances:
with suppliers, technology firms and content providers. But as e-business begins to
tackle sustainability, these networks must expand to include meaningful partnerships
with government and NGOs. We need, literally, to join the dots. Dot.coms, dot.orgs and
dot.govs need to share ideas and work together to embed sustainability in every area of
the new economy.

The barriers to these alliances are not as great as one might imagine. Dot.coms and
dot.orgs have a surprising amount in common. Both seek to challenge the established
conventions of the old economy and are prepared to take risks and push for change.

E-commerce blurs the old boundaries: it brings the high street into our homes, and brings government out of its Whitehall and Washington corridors. The Web is a neutral meeting point for new partnerships and new alliances.

It is not just a matter of asking business to adapt. Non-governmental groups are good at pressuring companies, but they also need to build trust, identify common ground and support companies to get things right at the design stage. And government needs to work hard to counter its image as a barrier to be leapt over, an obstacle to innovation. It needs to seek out good practice and use its influence to encourage it elsewhere. It should not shy away from intervention, but should intervene creatively, to foster innovation, not stifle it.

4.3.2 *Taking time*

In the new economy, speed is critical to success. Technology moves fast and, because first-mover advantage is so powerful, Internet companies have to move even faster. There are said to be three or four Internet years to one calendar year.

But slowness can also be a virtue. The e-business community does sometimes need to think in longer time-horizons, which encompass not just the next investment decision but also the social and environmental changes that those decisions will bring about. In thinking about e-business and sustainability, we need to cope with several different time-cycles: cycles of investment and innovation on the Internet, which are measured in weeks and months; cycles of investment in the physical infrastructure of energy systems, roads and towns, which are measured in decades; meanwhile, cycles of change in the natural environment are typically measured in centuries or millennia.

The way we view time is the key to creating a sustainable digital economy. It does not mean abandoning the hectic pace of e-life, but it does require us to switch lanes occasionally. Things look different from the slow lane. There is time to pause, reflect and consider the long-term issues that really matter.

Now and then we need a bolt of inspiration to stop us in our tracks. The Long Now Foundation (www.longnow.org) is one such attempt. Initiated by a group of technology entrepreneurs, including Kevin Kelly, co-founder of *Wired* magazine, and the musician Brian Eno, the Foundation is building a clock that will keep time for 10,000 years. It will tick once a year, bong once a century, and, once every millennium, the equivalent of a cuckoo will come out. Such attention-grabbing reminders of the long-term implications of our actions are essential.

Taking up the sustainability challenge requires creativity, innovation and alliance-building. It requires a different way of thinking. But this is what the dot.coms are so good at. We need to channel their dynamism and creativity for the benefit of all: to turn the new economy into a force not just for economic good, but for social and environmental good as well.

PRACTISING CORPORATE CITIZENSHIP IN A GLOBAL INFORMATION ECONOMY

Duane Windsor
Rice University, USA

The 21st century will probably see the emergence of an integrated global economy built around communication, investment and trade linkages. The fundamentals of corporate citizenship and social responsibility will remain constant, but practices and motives will continue to change with circumstances. Globalisation is likely to provide a very complicated set of forces and changes, many inconsistent, such that specific predictions may prove unreliable (Held *et al.* 1999). Indeed, there are significant counter-forces operating against the trends discussed here (Harvey 1995). Speaking broadly, however, the world's societies are becoming increasingly interlinked and interdependent with respect to business and capital market activities, communications, and environmental and technological impacts. The coming global economy will probably feature two relevant developments. First, on Peter Drucker's authority, organising information will be the key resource of both firms and individuals (1999: 110). Second, global corporate citizenship—that is, social responsibility behaviour by firms (see the linkage suggested in McIntosh *et al.* 1998)—will probably spread (Conference Board 1999b). The relationship between these two developments is the concern of this chapter.

The term 'social responsibility behaviour' is used deliberately. While *behaviour* may reflect purely economic motives, to which social responsibility is instrumental and subordinate, *conduct* should reflect some moral sentiment to which increase in economic wealth is irrelevant, or at least subordinate. Corporate citizenship can be simply an appearance of social responsibility. The fundamental distinction is between goals and means. Frederick (1994) distinguishes between corporate social responsibility (CSR1) and corporate social responsiveness (CSR2): the former is goal-oriented and normative; the latter is purely instrumental, an unavoidable precursor to wealth acquisition. In a tradition stretching back to Adam Smith in *The Wealth of Nations* (1776), wealth is penultimate only: its social worth turns on whether it is the key, in democratic capitalism, to alleviation of poverty and ecological sustainability of the planet (Chilton 1999).

Kinsley (1987) makes the point that, if corporate charity is 'actually a hard-nosed business decision, why give the corporation credit for generosity?' The point traces back to Adam Smith's view in *The Wealth of Nations* (Modern Library edn, 1973: 423) castigating 'affect[ing] to trade for the public good' as tending to under-perform with respect to the public good plain economic self-interest maximisation. Smith assumed conditions of security, justice and social harmony. The issue is whether corporate citizenship implies corporate assumption, in whole or in part, for assuring these conditions—and now doing so globally during the change to an information economy. Social responsibility (CSR1) was intended as a normative conception of the social role of the firm: the conception argued that the goals of the firm were more complex than strict profit maximisation. Corporate citizenship is a refurbishing of social responsiveness (CSR2): it is a strategic and instrumental use of corporate resources to build long-term markets and corporate reputation (for a revealing exposition, see McWilliams and Siegel 2001) that appears to be CSR1 responsibility. The goal is strict profit maximisation, achieved by behaviour recognising that the firm's environment is not simply a marketplace (see Szwajkowski 2000 for a revealing exposition). The situation need not be viewed as cynical: profit and market deepening (as Smith explained in 1776) comprise the natural bent of the business executive; and the business and society literature is arguably confused concerning CSR1, CSR2 and citizenship, so that it is easy for the business executive to mistake natural behaviour for good conduct.

Key elements in the coming global economy will be multinational enterprises (MNEs) and international policy regimes. MNEs are concrete organisational entities operating in multiple domestic marketplaces. Little conceptual refinement is therefore needed here for present purposes. However, two points to appreciate are that: (1) important MNEs are largely domiciled in the mostly advanced and democratic countries holding membership in the Organisation for Economic Co-operation and Development (OECD); and (2) the fundamental driver of MNE behaviour in the 21st century, appropriately or not, is likely to be share-owners' wealth maximisation. Indeed, Drucker (1999: 59-60) expects this driver to increase in intensity, on the argument that institutional ownership of such firms will largely represent future pensioners and their wealth expectations for retirement in an economically uncertain world. It is the global corporate citizenship, or responsibility and responsiveness, of these MNEs that will be central to this chapter.

International policy regimes are arguably more awkward to define and describe, but even so they are becoming increasingly important with growing interlinkage and interdependence (Preston and Windsor 1997 provides various examples of such regimes). Krasner (1983: 2) proposed the following definition: 'A regime is composed of sets of explicit or implicit principles, norms, rules and decision-making procedures around which actor expectations converge in a given area of international relations.' A regime is problem-specific (e.g. environmental, financial, investment, technological, trade, etc.). Regimes are now commonly embedded in multilateral institutional arrangements and agreements (such as the World Trade Organisation), but neither formal consent nor institutional structure is strictly speaking necessary. It is rather functional and behavioural relationships and expectations that are the core element of regimes. The spreading social demand for and corporate supply of global corporate citizenship behaviour is becoming a behavioural regime without a formal institutional framework. (The British Foreign Office established a global citizenship unit in 1998 intended to encourage UK firms and charities to act responsibly abroad.) International policy regimes can embed and reflect 'norms' for behaviour (Windsor and Getz 1999 gives a detailed exposition). From this viewpoint, 'Markets are probably the social institution most dependent on normative underpinnings' (Kratochwil 1989: 47). Friedman (1970) accepted the need of business for external setting of moral and legal 'rules of the game'.

The important dimension of globalisation addressed in this chapter is the increasing role of information and the supporting technology and infrastructure. In part, this role is captured in the popular terms 'digital economy', 'e(lectronic)-economy', 'information economy' and 'new economy'. Information is something told or facts learned, news, knowledge, or data stored in or retrieved from a computer. This broad definition thus encompasses communication, intellectual property rights, and computer and transmission technologies as well as certain aspects of organisational capabilities involving those dimensions. The global information economy suggests a fundamental transformation of society and culture, as well as markets and businesses. This transformation includes the expected replacement of traditional 'command-and-control' management by new organisational models emphasising the implications of knowledge workers for work practices (Conference Board 1999c).

This chapter examines the concept and practice of corporate citizenship, essentially a recent refurbishing of the notion of corporate social responsibility (CSR1), in the emerging global information economy. The topic is inherently broad, so emphasis will be placed here on certain specific aspects of corporate citizenship in a global information economy. The purpose is to obtain some insight into corporate citizenship issue framing and practice. There are a number of difficulties to be addressed in the examination. First, corporate citizenship and social responsibility are not yet adequately defined. Second, we are at the very beginning of the global information economy. Hence we have to predict future phenomena (and their implications), such as virtual work, organisational networks, global communication village, global digital divide, and so on. Third, advanced- and developing-country conditions may generate different corporate citizenship and social responsibility issues (and the conditions may be in conflict). Advanced technology both (1) separates advanced from developing countries even more, and (2) separates technology-enabled 'cosmopolitans' even more from 'locals' (Windsor 2000b)—although nanotechnology holds enormous promise for distributing access to resources much more widely (Cromie 2000).

The remainder of this chapter after this introduction is developed in the following manner. Section 5.1 discusses the theory of corporate citizenship and corporate social responsibility, with particular attention to difficulties of concrete definition and issues of interpretation. Section 5.2 examines three particular aspects of corporate citizenship and responsibility in the global information economy: energy consumption and sprawl development (as related to aspects of sustainability) (Section 5.2.1); work and workplace practices (Section 5.2.2); and the digital divide (Section 5.2.3). A brief concluding section (Section 5.3) summarises the chapter's findings and implications. Attention is directed to what I term 'progressive corporate citizenship': if the concept of citizenship is to have moral substance, then responsibility rises with wealth and power.

5.1 Conceptions of corporate citizenship and responsibility

The concepts 'corporate citizenship' and 'corporate social responsibility' are not adequately defined in the business and society literature. A brief, and suggestive rather than systematic, historical overview is useful in this connection. Schlesinger (1986) suggests for US political history a cyclical theory of alternating periods of private and public interest. While probably too mechanical and simplistic, the perspective may provide some useful insight here in understanding fundamentals and practices. The prevailing business philosophy of the Gilded Age following the American Civil War (1861–65) was one of Social Darwinism castigated in Jack London's *The Sea-Wolf* (1906) and summarised in William (son of 'Commodore' Cornelius) Vanderbilt's notorious comment 'The public be damned!' (William Vanderbilt, a key railroad magnate, was strongly opposed to regulation of the industry.) In the early 20th century the prevailing view was that corporate donations were illegal gifts of shareholders' assets made without their consent (Conference Board 1999a), and that consumer and employee rights were strictly limited and secondary.

That view of charity echoed in Friedman's (1970) characterisation of discretionary CSR1 as 'theft' by management from the other primary stakeholders. Yet even in the Gilded Age there was a developing sense of post-game philanthropy (Carnegie 1900). Carnegie, Rockefeller and Cornelius Vanderbilt all engaged in important charitable activities. Chernow (1999) characterises philanthropy as a 'redeeming aspect' of the 'so-called robber barons of the Gilded Age'. The Reverend Russell Conwell (founder of Temple University in Philadelphia) in his Chautauqua circuit lecture 'Acres of Diamonds' (delivered 6,000 times) preached the acquisition of wealth for the ultimate purpose of doing good for others. The Progressive era followed with emphasis on public regulation of business excesses and economic cycles (Hofstadter 1963; Jenks 1917; Wood 1986). Drucker (1999: 59) suggests that by the late 1920s business balancing of multiple stakeholder interests had in fact become established practice.

Even so, the Michigan Supreme Court in *Dodge v. Ford Motor Co.* (170 N.W. 668, 1919) adopted a corporate governance standard of primacy of stockholder wealth maximisation and the business judgement rule constraining judicial intervention. As Nunan (1988) explains, Henry Ford had wanted to suspend the special (i.e. double) dividend paid for years in order to fund (by cutting the effective dividend in half) price reductions to consumers and compensation increases to employees. Ford's purpose was to share the fruits of industrial civilisation with other stakeholders, and not to expand the business (although that effect might have followed). Ford's philosophy echoes in Bartlett and Sumantra's (1994) argument that purpose is superior to strategy, and that purpose is stakeholder welfare. The Dodge brothers, shareholders in the firm, sued for continuation of the special (i.e. second) dividend and won. Berle (1931) expounded the purely fiduciary responsibility of managers as agents of owners, to which Dodd (1932) responded with a multiple-constituency theory of managerial responsibilities. Heald (1970) published a history of business–community relations during the period 1900–60. The global information economy updates this long debate over corporate purpose and stakeholders' rights to unfolding 21st-century conditions.

The 1950s began an intellectual systematisation of the corporate social responsibility (CSR1) notion. Bowen (1953) published the seminal modern work *Social Responsibilities of the Businessman*, although one can trace back to Clark (1916). Counter-arguments against social responsibility followed from Levitt (1958) and Friedman (1962, 1970). Friedman (1970) argued that CSR1 was ambiguous and that discretionary CSR1 by management constituted 'theft' (i.e. unprofitable allocation of corporate resources) from other participants (explicitly customers, employees and owners). He admitted, however, to a prudential altruism in which immediately unprofitable allocation might be practised with an eye to future conditions; and he specified a role for government in setting legal and moral 'rules of the game' that could not be established by competing businesses themselves. Davis (1960) responded that business could ill afford over the long run not to be socially responsible. A business-and-society field subsequently developed built around notions of business ethics, corporate social responsibility (CSR1), corporate social responsiveness (CSR2), social auditing, corporate social performance (CSP) and stakeholder management. Carroll (1991) depicted CSR1 as a four-step pyramid of responsibilities ordered as: economic (required), legal (required), ethical (expected) and discretionary (desired philanthropy). Wood (1991) systematised the CSP approach as an integration of society-dictated responsibility (CSR1) principles, organisational responsiveness (CSR2) processes and performance outcomes (corporate social policies and programmes and corporate social impacts).

The 1980s witnessed a resurgence of what Schlesinger (1986) might characterise as private interest. Corporate management shifted towards shareholder wealth maximisation in a movement pioneered by, among others, Jack Welch ('Neutron Jack') at General Electric (GE). Workforce downsizing, corporate portfolio restructuring, profit orientation, organisational change management and market value enhancement became hallmarks of the new era in business philosophy. President Reagan espoused dramatic tax cuts, reduced growth of civilian spending, and volunteerism by business, non-profits and individuals in place of government action. An aspect of the 1980s and 1990s has been the rise of the global corporate citizenship movement (Handy 1997). The term 'corporate citizenship' is evidently not of much later origin than CSR1 (Gossett 1957).

In contrast to CSR1, corporate citizenship has been more of a managerial movement subsequently incorporated into the academic literature partly as a means of refurbishing CSR1 and CSP in an era of unabashed shareholder wealth maximisation. The Conference Board has been an important promoter of corporate citizenship broadly defined. Corporate citizenship is, however, both an old and a newly refurbished notion. The historical roots of the idea of citizenship of corporations reach back before the mid-19th century. In 1839, Chief Justice Taney of the US Supreme Court declined to accept a 'citizenship' fiction for corporations (Miller 1968: 8). In 1886, in the pro-property era of the Gilded Age, a subsequent US Supreme Court accepted a 'person' fiction for corporations that wrapped 14th Amendment substantive due process protection around virtually anything businessmen wanted to do to stakeholders (Miller 1968: 54). Miller (1968: 60) comments that 'calling a corporation a person is a convenience, not a fact, and to equate the power of the natural person with the artificial person is utterly fallacious'. Similarly, corporate citizenship may be mostly rhetoric, and one should carefully examine substance. Many American states adopted so-called corporate constituency statutes; but Orts points out that these statutes (typically adopted as anti-takeover measures) simply increase managerial discretion by reducing fiduciary responsibility without increasing any other constituency's legal rights (1992: 72-73, n. 381).

Awards have been established to signal the desirability of corporate citizenship. The Ron Brown Award for Corporate Leadership, announced in 1996 by President Clinton, and managed by The Conference Board's Global Corporate Citizenship Program, covers employee relations (workforce diversity, work–life balance, development–education–training, health–safety–workplace security) and community relations (education, economic development, environmental management, community outreach). The initial 1997 winners were IBM (diversity programmes) and Levi Strauss ('Project Change' anti-racism initiative). IBM was in 1999 the initial recipient of The Herbert W. Hines Award for Corporate Citizenship from SeniorNet for its Global Workforce Diversity Program for volunteerism. The Council on Economic Priorities gives Corporate Conscience Awards (Carroll 1998: 6). Many firms now issue corporate citizenship reports in some form.

The positive view of corporate citizenship is that it reflects a firm's voluntary and socially desirable commitment to improve the quality of community life through 'active, participatory, and organised corporate involvement' (Conference Board 1999a: report abstract). Key dimensions of corporate citizenship are community affairs, corporate contributions, corporate ethics (Conference Board 2000c) and environmental management (Conference Board 2000a), this latter linked to global ISO 14001 environmental processes and system performance certification. In one sense, the corporate citizenship idea rejects the pure trickle-down theory that a sole focus on economic growth will solve poverty (Conference Board 2000b). The World Resources Institute and Aspen Institute joint report *Beyond Grey Pinstripes* (1999: 2) asserts 'a new model for corporate citizenship' going beyond the philanthropy and compliance of the past 'to seek business opportunities in solving significant social and environmental problems'.

The shift from intellectual movement to corporate movement, signalled by the change in language from CSR1 to corporate citizenship, arguably has a darker side. While identifying a 'triple bottom line' of social, environmental and financial goals, Elkington (1998) characterises corporate citizens as cannibals who have learned to dine with forks. A key element in corporate citizenship strategy is corporate image or reputation building (Conference Board 1996). A company spokesman stated of Allied Domecq's sponsorship of the Royal Shakespeare Company (£5.5 million over the previous five years) that 'the principal aim of the sponsorship is to enhance the corporate image of Allied Domecq among its predominately City-based audience of investors, analysts, business media and politicians' through a mutually beneficial marketing partnership (Jones 1999).

The story behind corporate citizenship is partly one of managerial recognition of the power of positive reputation. Reputation may be little more than a polite term for modern-age propaganda (i.e. 'spin'). Aggressive media influence may be the object and reputation the means, rather than vice versa. 'The real story about Big Oil in many countries is less and less about misbehavior, more and more about the expanding frontiers of corporate citizenship . . . These companies must aggressively tell their stories to the news media . . .' (Wasserstrom and Reider 1999). By the end of the 20th century, corporate philanthropy had become a strategic tool (Altman 1998) contributing, through building of corporate reputation, to the firm's business strategy (Conference Board 1995, 1999a). Doubt has been cast on the very notion of *global* corporate citizenship: 'We are not "citizens of the world". We cannot be: the very concept is a contradiction in terms' (Selbourne 1999). The notion of global corporate citizenship, like corporate constituency enactments, may simply increase managerial discretion and encourage 'footloose' global corporations that bear no enforceable social responsibilities anywhere (Windsor 1992).

In fairness to corporate managers attempting to balance competing demands, there is a readily apparent and not-easy-to-resolve difficulty baked into the corporate citizenship and responsibility ideas. Allen (1992) distinguished between a 'property conception of the corporation' and a 'social entity conception' (Blair 1995: 208-15). A property conception or finance model is based on an inherent view assigning a residual profit right to capital owners. A social entity conception accepts that there is a public concession to operate. But Allen argued that the two approaches make for a schizophrenic conception of the business corporation (unless the social entity approach is always the most profitable strategy). Carroll (1998: 1-2) linked the four CSR1 dimensions to corporate citizenship as the latter's 'four faces' of being profitable, obeying the law, engaging in ethical behaviour, and giving back through philanthropy. 'Profit-making is not antithetical to good corporate citizenship. Indeed, it is *required* of good citizenship' (Carroll 1998: 2; cf. Conference Board 1999d).

In the same general sense, Fombrun (1997) identifies ethics, social benefit and profits as the 'three pillars' of corporate citizenship: the model or theory must be that ethical behaviour yields both social benefit and firm profitability. There need be no fundamental conflict between profit and responsibility, as long as profit is not taken to mean strict short-term wealth maximisation: but, while '[m]ost of us don't try to squeeze every penny out of life', the corporate system may tend toward such value-maximising behaviour (Kinsley 1987). Kinsley criticises both 'corporate charity and cultural benefaction, which amount to executives playing Medici with other people's money' (cf. Friedman 1970) and strict share-owner value maximisation. And that theme of criticism is to be found in the legal literature as well (see Knauer 1994). Keim (1978: 67) argued that the evidence from corporate philanthropy indicated that businesses were simply responding to changing social expectations (i.e. rules of the game), and that responsiveness to such constraints did 'not support the contention that businesses are pursuing social goals'. And estimated corporate giving, measured as proportion of pre-tax income, fell from 2% in 1986 to 1% in 1996 (*Business Week* 2000: 14). The estimate may not provide a truly accurate picture, as employee volunteerism and other forms of philanthropic activity may have been substituted for traditional cash giving. Much therefore turns on moral sentiment.

Corporate citizenship is today judged managerially as an investment in the social environment of the firm. If the firm can help that environment prosper, the firm itself may benefit from a rising tide and, furthermore, the environment may view the firm's reputation more positively as a separate matter. This strategic approach is, of course, Friedman's notion of prudential (i.e. strategic) altruism (see McWilliams and Siegel 2001 for a formal exposition). McWilliams and Siegel (2000) concluded that the empirical relationship between CSR1 and corporate financial performance is neutral: there is no fixed empirical relationship. Even so, the situation need not be viewed cynically. First, it is better that even amoral managers exhibit, if only as a surface attribute, socially responsive behaviour rather than socially irresponsible behaviour. Responsive practice is still some distance, however thinly in motive, from William Vanderbilt's notorious statement 'The public be damned!' Now tobacco executives allegedly lie under oath and engage in influence purchasing rather than openly defying public sentiment. The path to true corporate citizenship and responsibility may simply have to begin with amoral responsiveness.

5.2 Practising corporate citizenship in an information world

The implication of the argument just made concerning the possibly schizophrenic nature of corporate citizenship makes systematic appraisal of corporate conduct issue by issue fundamental to evaluating the practice of citizenship and responsibility. One may arguably still define appropriate rules of engagement at the potentially conflicting interface of wealth and social purposes. For example, as noted earlier, it has become commonplace for large businesses to issue corporate citizenship (or social responsibility) reports in some form (see Council on Foundations 1996). Naturally, such reports will tend to highlight what a firm has done right. A standard for evaluation is that such reports be candid concerning bad as well as good social performance. The firm will inevitably attempt to 'spin' a positive balance, but the vital principle is full disclosure of information to stakeholders and the public at large.

This chapter examines three important dimensions of corporate citizenship in the emerging global information economy: (1) energy consumption and sprawl development (as related aspects of ecological sustainability); (2) work and workplace practices; and (3) digital divide. These issues occur in both advanced and developing countries. Due to limited space, the appraisals must be brief, but a single issue would not be sufficient to convey the highly diverse aspects of practising corporate citizenship in an information world.

5.2.1 *Energy consumption and sprawl development*

The greener-business theme is an important dimension of the emerging global information economy (Lovins *et al.* 1999; Shrivastava 1995). How can corporations contribute to global ecological sustainability by more efficient (and preferably reduced) energy consumption and also by a reduction of historical pressures towards inefficient sprawl development patterns of land use? The linkage between the two phenomena is that low energy costs and rising wealth have promoted decentralisation of land-use patterns, particularly in North America and also around the large cities of many developing countries. Is there sustainable technology development (Weaver *et al.* 2000) meeting Elkington's (1998) triple bottom line of financial, environmental and social performance? As noted at the outset of this chapter, specific predictions may prove difficult, because globalisation is a complex and multidimensional process. Technology may both drive and conserve energy consumption and sprawl development.

The California electricity and heating crisis of winter 2000–2001 highlighted the problem of energy consumption in the 21st century for many Americans. And that problem is intimately tied to the development of the global information economy. A significant proportion of electricity in the US is probably consumed (directly or indirectly) by computers, and computer technology production (much of which is in California's Silicon Valley) uses both electricity and chemicals (for which greener substitutes are being developed). Yet California is also highly environmentally sensitive. As a result, in that state, demand for electricity greatly outpaced production capacity. The 1996 California deregulation scheme reduced and essentially fixed retail energy prices while floating wholesale energy prices (presumably on a prediction of long-term decline) and preventing utilities from taking long-term wholesale contracts. (The major utilities in the state acted differently under deregulation, so that, while some utilities got into grave difficulties, others did not.)

Sourcing shifted nationally towards cheaper and cleaner natural gas, so that supply did not meet up with demand. A hot summer followed by a cold winter, combined with drought in the Pacific region reducing hydroelectric supply and a large proportion of California's generating capacity offline at the time for various reasons precipitated requirements for spot-market purchases when spot-market prices jumped markedly. Major Silicon Valley manufacturers had evidently anticipated some problem and diversified energy sourcing so that production could continue (but was hardly necessary given the sudden increase in inventories as the US economy teetered on the edge of recession after years of sustained, non-inflationary growth).

It is difficult to isolate communication technology from mobility technology (in the advanced societies) and the culture of poverty (in the developing societies and less developed regions within advanced societies) associated with the global digital divide (to be discussed below). Sprawl development is a controversial topic (Windsor 1979). There are both critics (Duany *et al.* 2000) and defenders (Gordon and Richardson 2000). The latest metropolitan sprawl analysis (Galster *et al.* 2000 for the Fannie Mae Foundation) argues that sprawl is a pressing problem involving traffic congestion, environmental degradation, and central city decline which can be corrected by smart growth, to which is unavoidably attached social equity issues (e.g. access to housing, jobs, transport). The Clinton–Gore administration (Report 2000) addressed the building of liveable communities: can a sense of community be created within sustainable prosperity? Global corporations themselves are a form of 'sprawl' in the sense of requiring multiple locations for operation (Celarier 1999 discusses the situation of Citibank in this regard).

Technology—in the forms of lower-pollution autos and improved mass transit—may both address the problem and create in the global information economy a social choice between virtual work (i.e. telecommuting) and greater individual mobility (Conference Board 1998). Nanomachines, now being developed, may combine high computing power and information memory with extremely low electricity requirements, and may ultimately be wearable or even implantable (Cromie 2000). Assuming price drops dramatically along with electricity consumption, then usage should spread, as has cellular technology. Huber (2000) argues that rising wealth will tend to reduce sprawl through the effects of technology and increased ability to reconcentrate activities.

5.2.2 *Work and workplace practices*

The global information economy implies virtual knowledge management teams functioning across organisational networks and national boundaries (Windsor 2000a). Blair (1995) argues that the shift to knowledge work implies fundamental changes in corporate governance to the degree that knowledge employees are entitled (both instrumentally and normatively) to ownership shares. Changes in work and workplace practices are under way. But in light of energy consumption and sprawl development patterns, should firms promote telecommuting or mass transit mobility for employees? The proposed Corporate Code of Conduct Act (HR 4596), introduced in summer 2000 by Congresswoman Cynthia McKinney (Democrat–Georgia), would require corporate codes of conduct for any US-based firm with more than 20 employees abroad (Kelly 2000c: 9). Under the act, a code (applying to all subsidiaries, joint ventures or licensees) would have to include paying living wages, respecting international labour standards, and providing public documentation concerning where business is conducted. Enforcement would be by US government preference to complying firms in contracts and export assistance, and private suit in US courts by affected victims (including non-US citizens). The National Labor Relations Board (NLRB)'s Division of Advice issued a memorandum that employees have a right to organise through company-owned e-mail (Kelly 2000b: 9).

It has been alleged in a proposed class action lawsuit, filed in June 2000 in federal district court (Philadelphia), that New York Life Insurance during the early 1990s financed its new line of 'MainStay' institutional mutual funds from its employees' pension plans and 401(k) assets (Kelly 2000c: 9). The suit was brought by a fired vice president under the Racketeer Influenced and Corrupt Organisations (RICO) Act and the Employee Retirement Income Security Act.

Business Ethics in its March/April 2000 issue listed IBM as No. 1 of 100 Best Corporate Citizens. Receiving complaints from more than three dozen IBM employees, Kelly and Klusmann (2000) readdressed the matter. The controversy was provoked by IBM's announcement on 3 May 1999 that it would shift defined-benefit pensions to cash-balance plans; in the case of older employees, the result might be a pension cut of as much as 50%. (The plan was allegedly overfunded at the 1998 year end by $450 million and the cash-balance shift would allegedly save an additional $200 million.) At that time, the online benefit estimator allegedly disappeared from the firm's intranet site (on 1 May). The Equal Employment Opportunity Commission (EEOC) opened an investigation into possible age discrimination. In May 1999, IBM also announced a lifetime post-retirement cap of $25,000 per family for health insurance premiums (historically promised as lifetime benefit). In September 1999, allegedly under pressure, IBM allowed an additional 35,000 employees to choose either plan. Upon further inquiry, the authors alleged significant losses for 15,000 employees. Kelly and Klusmann comment (2000: 5) that the goal of the 100 Best Corporate Citizens list was

> to point to companies serving *all four* key stakeholder groups: employees, customers, the community, and shareholders . . . We'll come right out and say it: serving shareholders at the expense of other stakeholders is not right. It's not what we expect from our best corporate citizens—least of all from citizen No. 1.

IBM employment fell from 405,000 in 1985 to 220,000 in 1993. In 1995, IBM doubled the 401(k) match; stock options are now offered to 30,000 of 305,000 employees.

Hicks (1996) commented somewhat similarly on 'Caterpillar Flunks Corporate Citizenship Test'. At its York, PA, plant, Cat initially refused entry to National Institute of Occupational Safety and Health (NIOSH) investigators inspecting for chemical hazards with a warrant. The United Auto Workers (UAW) had claimed that cadmium exposure in the oil cooler department greatly exceeded OSHA (Occupational Safety and Health Administration) standards. NIOSH obtained an emergency court order for access.

5.2.3 The digital divide

As with many types of economic and social change, the emerging global information economy involves both promise (for winners) and peril (for losers) (Luttwak 1999; Tapscott 1995). A recent source of strong feelings has been the complaint that, in various guises, the information economy has created a 'digital divide' in society. It would be most proper to say that the information economy has left large segments of the world population behind. The term 'digital divide' connotes a lack of access to the information economy by various information and technology have-nots defined in terms of region, rural location, income class, ethnicity and so on (Dunham 1999). This digital divide occurs both within and across societies (see Jarrett 2000 on Asia; and Lerner 2000 on Latin America). It may be that, as some authors have discussed, digital divide is a mostly political issue raised for purposes of increasing funding to public education and so on (Bolt and Crawford 2000; Fattah 2000; Levine 2000). But the broad context of the digital divide is that the new economy might arguably worsen the gap between haves and have-nots in society by devaluing relatively unskilled labour (Conference Board 2000b) and increasing the disadvantages faced by those who lack ready access to information and technology.

One aspect of this divide is the prevailing global regime for international property rights (see Windsor forthcoming). Intellectual property rights are becoming more valuable in a knowledge-oriented world. Napster has been prohibited by the courts from its previous conduct of allegedly facilitating distribution of copyrighted music without the users having to pay royalties. Pharmaceutical firms argue that high prices are necessary to fund sophisticated research and development. The argument is somewhat confused or mis-stated. It may well be that high prices are due to high costs, but this situation does not automatically imply high profits. Generally major pharmaceutical firms enjoy quite high returns to owners. The true argument, never stated as such, is that high profits are required to stimulate pharmaceutical research and development. The argument in this form may or may not be valid. Outside the US, where much of the research and development is conducted, various countries engage in price control of pharmaceutical products. Developing countries often contend that they should not have to pay prevailing market prices for the fruits of intellectual property rights. In effect, they argue that prices should be reduced to reflect their special needs and limited resources (see Jensen 2000).

Cellular technology reduced the capital costs of connecting users outside the US with ready access to telephonic communication. Along the same lines, nanotechnology may in the future greatly reduce costs of access to the global information economy. The citizenship and responsibility issues turn on what to do in the interim. It is valuable to the reputation of technology firms to contribute computer equipment to educational institutions, and such contributions may generate additional customers in the future. In the recent inventory pile-up in the winter of 2000–2001, firms could respond by giving equipment to employees both as benefit and as a means of reducing inventories more rapidly. But should firms donate or reduce prices on equipment to conquer the digital divide more rapidly? Firms are more likely to view the digital divide as a matter of public policy allocating costs to taxpayers.

5.3 Towards a theory of progressive corporate responsibility

This chapter has addressed the practice of corporate citizenship, and its implied corollary corporate social responsibility, in the emerging global information economy of the 21st century. The emphasis has been on the application of the corporate citizenship theme to certain specific dimensions of the global information economy: (1) energy consumption and sprawl development; (2) work and workplace practices; and (3) the digital divide. In each instance, a similar finding is that the global information economy appears to involve contradictory effects difficult for firms to address. Perhaps this similarity of findings reflects that the global information economy involves both promise (for winners) and peril (for losers). Detailed predictions are unreliable here.

Information generation and use, and the supporting technology and infrastructure, have been energy-consuming, as illustrated in my interpretation of the winter 2000–2001 energy crisis in California (including Silicon Valley), and supportive of sprawl development, as implied in virtual networking. By the same token, however, scientific and technological advances may move in the direction of nanotechnology that is at once more portable and cheaper, and more energy-efficient. And wealth and technology in combination may ultimately facilitate urban reconcentration. Such changes suggest that what defines corporate citizenship and responsibility issues are the transition costs.

The information economy is steadily transforming work and workplace practices in various ways. Knowledge work is becoming more valuable and employment is moving towards greater mobility in terms of physical location and also movement of individuals among firms over time. The divide in the world economy between knowledge work and manual labour (however assisted by technology) is becoming more pronounced. The transition from the latter to the former must, on the whole, be socially beneficial. It is the transition costs that define corporate citizenship and responsibility issues. The digital divide similarly defines who has access and who does not to the global information economy. Improved technology and reduced technology costs may reduce this divide with time. Again, it is the transition costs that define corporate citizenship and responsibility issues. In each dimension, there may be short-term spikes in economic costs and undesirable impacts, followed by longer-term cost reductions and socially desirable benefits. But the changes leave stranded individuals as well as formerly valuable locations and investments; it is the transition costs of the changes that may importantly shape how corporate citizenship and responsibility should be practised. It is not simply a matter of how the future benefits outweigh present costs, but of how the changes are managed.

More broadly, corporate citizenship and responsibility have been and remain ill defined in the literature as a guide to concrete management action. A dramatic range of views varies from (1) discretionary corporate altruism of any type is misallocation of resources, through (2) corporate responsibility should focus on profitable opportunities, to (3) corporate responsibility must be moral choices imposing economic costs on the firm (a view that McWilliams and Siegel [2001] make matters of public policy). The evidence cited here suggests that corporate citizenship has emerged mostly as a managerial movement aimed at strategic use of external pressures calling for responsibility that transforms those pressures to the benefit of the firm, in terms of both return on investment and reputation-building. Perhaps no other behaviour is to be expected of MNE executives, and true citizenship and responsibility may of necessity have to proceed from such a beginning point. McWilliams and Siegel (2000) find a neutral relationship between corporate responsibility and corporate financial performance.

The implication, in my view, is that the conception of corporate citizenship and social responsibility must become progressive if it is to be morally convincing. A widespread approach in business management is benchmarking against the best practices of other firms. Benchmarking suggests that, if the most successful firms increase citizenship and responsibility activities, other firms will tend to follow. By the same token, the bench-marking process works in reverse. So, for example, if charitable giving on average declines from the present 1% (down from 2% historically) to 0.5% (data discussed earlier), then a firm will tend to adjust its own philanthropy downwards as not competi-tively necessary or economically remunerative. Progressive citizenship and responsibility implies that corporate duty rises with wealth and power. And such conduct becomes an acid test for citizenship and responsibility.

Progressivism is a difficult and awkward notion. In effect, the proposal constitutes a tax on capital; and both capital taxation (Atkinson *et al.* 1999) and the very notion of pro-gressive taxation (see Blum and Kalven 1953) are under assault, and some of the reasons for such assault have merit. But, as Blum and Kalven point out, however uneasy the case for progressive taxation (and the case has always been uneasy, although introduced by Adam Smith in *The Wealth of Nations*, 1776), the very notion of citizenship suggests that greater civic duties fall on the rich, powerful and successful than on those less fortunate. How to work this general notion into concrete practice is the very substance of corporate citizenship and responsibility. Selekman (1958) long ago pointed out that the funda-mental problem with management was that it tended to treat conditions, including labour, as abstractions in profit-oriented decision-making. 'Few corporations would risk damaging the natural environment nowadays, for fear of harsh penalties. But many damage the human environment, suffering no penalties at all' (Luttwak 1999: xi).

THE INTERNET AND SUSTAINABILITY REPORTING
Improving communication with stakeholders

William B. Weil and Barbara Winter-Watson
Environmental Resources Management, USA

6.1 Introduction

What seemed daring a decade ago is becoming commonplace as more corporations issue public reports on their economic, social and environmental performance. These reports serve as important tools for promoting and preserving a company's reputation among local communities, regulators, customers, employees, non-governmental organisations and investors. This chapter highlights and analyses the emergence of corporate sustainability reports (CSRs) with a growing trend of using the Internet as a reporting platform.

As transparency gains ground as a management strategy and reporting standards (e.g. the Global Reporting Initiative) increase their reach, CSRs look to become a standard business practice. The global boom in reporting indicates that the commonly cited benefits, including improved public relations and internal communication, outweigh any concerns from the voluntary disclosure of environmental information.

CSRs must speak to a diverse global audience of internal and external stakeholders, who all have a distinct set of communication needs and perceptions. Given the complexity of the target audience and the content, new communications technologies will play an important role as environmental reporting advances.

The Internet offers several capabilities and characteristics that lend it advantages over the traditional paper report: ease of updates; decreased distribution/production costs; and interactivity, allowing content customised to the user and instant feedback. While the current lack of standardisation limits usefulness by making comparisons difficult, and the ever-present digital divide makes distribution through one medium impossible, the Internet is bound to play an increasing role as this communication channel develops and matures.

6.1.1 Social pressures on corporations

Throughout history, social pressures on corporations have ebbed and flowed, including: the Jewish law of biblical times directing investment according to ethical values, anti-Apartheid boycotts, Greenpeace and other activist groups today (Socialfunds.com 2001). Today the differences are in the relative strength, reach and the impact of social pressure groups and movements, most notably increased and unregulated communication, connectivity and collaboration. It is time for proactive corporations to embrace the concept of 'radical transparency' and voluntarily disclose their performance data, to open lines of communication or run the risk of violating their implicit social contract, threatening their right to operate (Lash 2000).

Given the increasing global nature of business and shifts in the way businesses engage clients, suppliers and communities, corporate reporting needs to be seen in the larger context of engaging stakeholders for growth enhancement. In the 20th century, there were several major pushes in corporate responsibility. In the 1930s, after the Great Depression in the United States, social pressure demanded the disclosure of financial information by companies. The US Congress established the Securities and Exchange Commission in 1934 to enforce the newly passed securities laws, to promote stability in the markets and, most importantly, to protect investors. In the 1970s, the increasing calls for corporate responsibility were again encouraging reporting.

Corporate environmental reporting is relatively new, spurred by accidents such as the disastrous release at Bhopal, India, and the *Exxon Valdez* spill, as well as regulatory drivers such as the development of the Toxics Release Inventory (TRI) in the United States. The former US Environmental Protection Agency Administrator Carol Browner acknowledged that, 'putting high-quality environmental information into the hands of citizens is one of the most powerful tools for protecting public health and the environment' (SustainAbility 1999). Since the development of the TRI in 1987, national pollutant release and transfer registries have been developed in many European and OECD (Organisation for Economic Co-operation and Development) countries with varying coverage and levels of public reporting.

Recent efforts to make environmental information available to the public via the Internet have yielded impressive results. When Environmental Defense's scorecard.org website was launched in 1998, the site received 1.3 million 'hits' in the first 24 hours (Barnum 2002). In our experience, clients have seen notable increases in the number of visits to the sustainability sections of their corporate websites.

Further study is needed to determine exact trends; however, anecdotal evidence shows that there is a relatively small but rapidly growing interest among stakeholders for information on corporate sustainability reporting.

6.2 The state of corporate sustainability reporting

While exact figures are difficult to obtain (and in the world of the Internet are rendered instantly obsolete), there has been a clear qualitative trend in management towards an increasingly open style in connecting with stakeholders both inside and outside the company. With increased outsourcing blurring the lines of corporations, issues such as external engagement and reputation management have gained greater importance.

As of November 2000, 46% of the British FTSE (*Financial Times* Stock Exchange) 100 companies and 40% of *Fortune* 100 firms feature environmental content on their websites, though these numbers are growing rapidly (Winter-Watson and Weil 2001). Industries that are resource-intensive and/or have had historically significant environmental or social impacts are more likely to report. Reporting levels are much greater in the utilities, automotive, pulp and paper, and chemical industries than 'new-economy' firms in service industries (including financial and high-technology), which are not highly visible (Winter-Watson and Weil 2001; SustainAbility 1999).

Geographically, there are significant trends in corporate reporting, with the bulk coming from firms based in the EU, US or Japan. Latin American and African firms are just beginning to feel the public pressure and performance demands from multinational clients (Jones *et al.* 1999). While Asian companies have been quick to incorporate ISO 14000 and green accounting, they have been slow to warm to the notion of expanded transparency, often reporting anecdotal evidence of performance than a full-scale standardised performance report.

The majority of the reports to date have been published by large companies. The one issue yet to surface is how reporting applies to small and medium-sized enterprises (SMEs). The 2000 Dun & Bradstreet Small Business Survey found that nearly 40% of small businesses have their own websites, up from just over a quarter last year, and that 70% now have Internet access, up from 57% last year (Dun & Bradstreet 2001). PSI Global's Small Business Survey corroborated the Dun & Bradstreet findings that small businesses have quickly embraced the Internet as a new information channel, but found that most have no plans for truly interactive communications or commerce (PSI Global 1999). Whether this important sector of the economy has the necessary resource or drive to report on their performance continues to be an unknown quantity.

Initially, reports tended to be at either end of the spectrum in terms of inclusion of detail: either a 'bare-boned "just the facts" presentation, or a superficial sugar coated approach . . . more public relation than performance information' (Axelrod 1998). There has been a push in recent years to combat this and move towards standardisation and co-ordination of corporate reporting.

Currently, a number of global reporting frameworks—including the Global Reporting Initiative (GRI), United Nations Environment Programme (UNEP), the Public Environmental Reporting Initiative (PERI), European Eco-management and Audit Scheme (EMAS)—introduced over the last ten years muddle the landscape and inhibit some of the more progressive analysis of performance (see FEE 2000 for additional guidelines) (McLean 2000).

Combine these with industry-specific reporting and certification schemes (e.g. Forest Stewardship Council, CEFIC/Responsible Care, Green Seal, Energy Star, Blue Angel, EU Eco-label) and issue-specific indicators (e.g. GHG Protocol for greenhouse gas emissions, Institute of Social and Ethical Accountability's AA 1000 for ethical issues, the World Business Council for Sustainable Development's eco-indicators) and the picture becomes even less clear. This natural progression is appropriate and impressive when compared to the state of financial reporting, which still is not standardised internationally after more than 500 years since the development of the first double ledger.

6.3 Why companies report

Before we analyse the most effective platform for reporting to enhance reputation and achieve competitive advantage, we need to first clearly establish the risks and the benefits. Why should companies report at all?

One of the primary issues firms raise against the voluntary disclosure of environmental performance and impacts is the spectre of increased liability risk. 'The failure to carefully consider legal issues and concerns before voluntarily disclosing environmental data in a formal corporate environmental report has the potential for causing serious adverse consequences to the company' (Case 2000). These reports can include voluntarily disclosed information, which regulators can use to discover non-compliance or conclude that the submitted report is not in full agreement with required disclosure regulation.

David Case of the Environmental Law Institute describes several additional examples of 'inappropriate' statements, including information that could offer ammunition for a pending suit, accepting responsibility for costly environmental clean-up, or violating a confidentiality provision of a settlement. Finally, there is the issue of whether firms should 'report' environmental performance of particular products (e.g. as it is currently done by electronics manufacturer Philips) or document the substantiation of marketing claims of certain products (Case 2000).

Moreover, reporting has the potential to allow competitors access to proprietary information. A 1998 study by the Reason Public Policy Institute describes how it was able to derive a profile of a chemical company using publicly available information including

> descriptions and estimates of main production lines, consumption and operating rates, main products manufactured, chemistries used, throughput rates, operating temperatures and yields. These estimates were found to be within ten percent of the plant's actual numbers (Case 2000).

Finally, the potential loss of competitive advantage has been cited by firms who feel that sharing the details of their programmes entails exposing their systems to the spying eyes of the competition and potentially losing the industry expertise.

Despite these risks, there are several benefits from reporting, including: meeting regulatory requirements; enhancing corporate trust and reputation; maximising stakeholder value; and communicating internally.

6.3.1 Meeting regulatory requirements

There has been an international debate over whether environmental or sustainability reporting should be made mandatory. Denmark, New Zealand and the Netherlands have already introduced legislation requiring some form of environmental reporting. Both ISO 14001 and EMAS also require that environmental statements be produced, though only EMAS specifies that they be made publicly available (Jones et al. 1998).

In the United States, various regulatory acts have mandated reporting of certain environmental data and information to the general public. The Emergency Planning and Community Right to Know Act (EPCRA) §313 requires covered companies to submit annual data to the US Environmental Protection Agency (EPA) on amounts of specific toxic chemicals released to the air, water and land or transferred off-site. Additional disclosure is required in financial reports filed with the US Securities and Exchange Commission (SEC) (regarding regulatory compliance, judicial proceeding and liabilities) (Case 2000). The group of required reporters has been expanded recently in the US, as new companies and facilities must submit mandatory risk management plans under the Clean Air Act and on releases of toxic chemicals in an expansion of the TRI reporters in 1999 (Axelrod 1998).

6.3.2 Enhancing corporate trust and reputation

The most significant driver for public reporting is 'reputation, reputation, reputation'. The Harris Interactive poll of reputation lists social responsibility—defined as 'perceptions of the company as having high standards in its dealings with people, good causes, and the environment'—to be one of six key attributes of reputation (Harris Interactive 2001). As discussed above, the importance of reputation is bound to increase in the future given the growing communication capabilities.

Although few consumers (25% according to a Philips study) are willing to spend additional money for 'environmentally friendly' products, over half of those surveyed in North America and Oceania had 'punished a company seen as not socially responsible' in the last year, while an additional one in six had considered doing so. Globally, two out of three people surveyed want companies to go beyond their historical role of making profit, to contribute to broader societal goals as well (Ottman 2001; Environics International 1999). Given the importance of reputation, this is obviously a key potential benefit of communicating sustainability performance.

Once the reputation is established, interactive reporting can help identify stakeholders and create new opportunities to learn from and collaborate with them as partners. Companies inevitably encounter environment-related management issues in their products or business processes from time to time. The central premise is that it is too late to communicate once the problem has already developed. By building a reputation for environmental or social concern, a company will over time reduce the risk of criticism and enhance its image with customers, shareholders and regulators.

While the current readers of these reports are often limited to the academic and environmental NGO (non-governmental organisation) community, one only needs to look at the Shell/Brent Spar incident or Nike's experience with sweatshops to recognise the importance of establishing communication and trust. (Contrast the response of the activist group community to the Shell incident and the Ford/Firestone tyre scandal in light of Ford's historic retreat with leading critical NGOs only months before, and the importance of outreach becomes clear.)

While the Web has allowed well-informed protest groups to become a global force, only 14% of companies utilise any tools to formally track environmental information about themselves that may be on the Web (GEMI 2000). If the discussion can be brought to the corporate site (see Royal Dutch/Shell 2001), it may be easier to provide background information to relevant issues and concerns.

Companies making the first moves into reporting tend to be at either end of the sustainability performance spectrum. The best-performing firms clearly see the positive impacts of publicising the good news. Some of the worst-polluting industries have also been early adopters of reporting, seeking to frame the issues and put performance results in their own context.

6.3.3 *Maximising stakeholder value*

As value chains become longer via shifts to outsourcing, stakeholders (including sup-pliers and corporate clients) increasingly demand proof of the social responsibility of companies with which they do business. Only by means of balanced reporting of the value that a company creates for its stakeholder—whether shareholder, employee, cus-tomer, partner or society at large—will the stakeholder be able properly to value the company.

A case in point is the rise of socially responsible investments. Although a relatively small portion of total investments, socially responsible investing continues to grow and become more mainstream and influential. According to a 1999 report by the Social Investment Forum, total investments using at least one social investment strategy have grown from $40 billion in 1984, to $639 billion in 1995, to over $2 trillion today. More-over, social investments now account for about 13% of the estimated $16.3 trillion under professional management in the US (Socialfunds.com 2001).

With expectations moving beyond compliance, concerns about lack of disclosure of significant environmental risks will play a role for evaluation of exposure by stakeholders inside and outside the supply chain (Repetto and Austin 2000a). Intermediaries between investors and corporate information such as the Investor Responsibility Research Center, Innovest, Council on Economic Priorities and others compile this information for digestion on a global scale. One very real use of the reporting standards is to provide information to these interests in one package, to eliminate the burden on corporate EHS (environment, health and safety) officers of customising the response for each.

Annual reports provide an excellent forum for businesses to commit publicly to continuous improvement in their sustainability efforts. This commitment allows a busi-ness to build and protect its reputation, opening possibilities with this burgeoning branch of socially responsible investing.

While companies may have 'shied away from connecting economics and the environ-ment . . . to avoid criticism that companies might only be meeting responsibilities that were economically prudent', improved management and accounting systems and the opportunities to demonstrate environment as value-added rather than a cost centre have begun to outweigh these concerns in recent years (Axelrod 1998). In ComEd's 1998 report, the CEO writes that, 'the meshing of economic and environmental performance is among the most promising and beneficial trends in industry today' (ComEd 2001).

6.3.4 *Communicating internally*

The tremendous internal impacts of the reporting process (including data-gathering and internal discussions of integrating environmental and business strategies) are difficult to calculate and generally overlooked. Experts acknowledge, however, that 'the real benefit of environmental reports is not merely to disclose information, but to help your company measure and analyse its own performance' (*Green Business Letter* 2001). A published report can complement a management system by making performance transparent and by providing a concise reference document for an organisation's environmental issues. It is quite remarkable how many targets managers agree to in the period shortly before pro-duction of the environmental report. The report, therefore, acts as a catalyst for improv-ing the environmental programme.

Reporting can also take the format of an intranet site. Many companies find these to be extremely valuable, allowing exchange of best management practices and performance among global facilities. Lack of internal communication is often one of the largest stumbling blocks for successful environmental projects to become replicated internally.

6.3.5 Building competitive advantage

As greater numbers of companies publicly disclose information, pressure for non-reporting companies to increase transparency will create a positive feedback loop. When reporting is the norm, non-disclosure will become a disadvantage. Early adoption can allow firms to influence the direction of reporting standards. Additionally, current response to reporting is generally heralded as a positive step, regardless of which direction performance numbers are headed. This advantage will not last, and laggards will not be afforded the luxury of such a grace period.

In today's increasingly competitive markets, whether the impetus comes from the push of the regulators or the pull of the eco-consumer market, reporting can offer a distinct competitive advantage in terms of existing clients, as well as opening new markets. Firms seek to enhance their brand image by portraying their environmental or sustainability achievements in a positive light, while maintaining some sense of humility in acknowledging larger issues surrounding the firm's operations. Further, the establishment of new award schemes for reporting can provide incentives in themselves.

6.4 Targeting the CSR report

As is evident in discussing the potential benefits of reporting, the report must address a heterogeneous audience with varying interests and goals. To effectively assess the impact of the reporting effort, we must first discuss the key internal and external target audiences and what they seek to learn from or contribute to the discussion (*Green Business Letter* 2001).

As summarised in Table 6.1, the target audience for corporate sustainability communications is quite broad and includes distinctly varied objectives (*Green Business Letter* 2001). Some firms, such as Sainsbury's, Anheuser-Busch, Kodak and others, produce reports with varying levels of detail in an attempt to target specific audiences (Environment97. org 2001). This effort will probably become more common as communication through the supply chain becomes more important and part of accepted business practice. Before we address how the Internet is specifically capable of managing this issue, let us quickly investigate some other likely developments.

6.5 Why report online (versus paper)

In the short term, debating whether to issue a paper report or convert to a fully Web-based report ignores the reality of the widely varied target audience. The focus has shifted from

Target audience	Focus
Internal	
Facility managers, employees	Want to know about job safety, job security, and to have pride in their environmental efforts. Employees can also be an excellent source of money-saving ideas. As the eyes and ears of the corporation, establishing goals and starting a dialogue can lead to impressive environmental improvements.
Management, boards of directors	Mainly concerned with reputation (e.g. any potential major boycotts or protests), compliance and financial aspects (i.e. how investments in sustainability initiatives will affect your financial performance, both in the short and long term, environmental liabilities, potential regulatory changes with financial effects).
Public relations, sales teams	Can be alerted to new initiatives and provided information to be used as a sales tool to differentiate the firm. These stakeholders can also provide invaluable real-world experience in how to target the market and should be actively involved in the design of the communication media.
External	
Shareholders, investors, analysts, bankers, insurers	Fully focused on the financial information discussed above for management.
Potential employees	Progressively more concerned with reputation of potential employers; corporate websites are often the first stop for investigations about a company.
Communities	Primarily concerned with health effects of operations to neighbours, including toxic chemical use and release and risk management plans, local economic (employment) impacts of corporate strategies, and local community involvement in the form of philanthropy and volunteerism.
Non-governmental organisations, activist groups	Interested in specific, quantitative performance data, acknowledgement of environmental or sustainability issues yet to be addressed.
Regulators, international standards bodies	Investigate compliance with standards, agreement of reported performance results with required disclosures.
Suppliers, business clients (directly, and via sales force), end-consumers	Review overall sustainability commitment and performance, and how this may affect product quality, cost and safety. These stakeholders can contribute greatly to overall performance through discussions of co-ordinated process changes and holistic focused partnerships (e.g. 'servicising' rather than product delivery, unique contracting methods).
Competitors	Seek to gauge effectiveness of efforts, benchmark opportunities within own operations.

Table 6.1 **Target audience for corporate sustainability reports and their focus**

'how to translate the hard-copy report for the Internet, but how to translate information on the Internet to hard copy for those to whom access to the Internet is denied' (Jones *et al.* 1998). The importance of selection of the appropriate medium should not be underestimated: 'handing an interested stakeholder a printed report as they attend a community meeting sends a very different message than providing them with a Web address' (Axelrod 1998).

The most often-cited benefit of Web-based production is a decrease in distribution, production and inventory costs with a much-trumpeted saving in paper. Without spending too much effort towards a life-cycle analysis of paper-based versus Internet-based reporting, it would help to discuss the clear benefits of this alternative communication medium.

As is the case with many new Internet-based projects, corporate reporting should not be funded and measured as with other investments (Cook 2001). While traditional business measures are still applicable, they should be supplemented with non-quantitative measures of impact and effectiveness.

The same problems are faced in the shift from a hard-copy report to the Web as in many of the ventures into the e-economy: lack of knowledge/familiarity, lack of recognition of the new medium needing a specific strategy ('Just put our brochure on the Web'), and concluding that the effort is not internally justified.

Unfortunately, these factors build on each other in a self-fulfilling prophecy. If a company posts a single large PDF (portable document format) file of their report (the cheapest way to build a sustainability 'website'), it is not likely to generate much interest in the target community (Scott 2001).

Furthermore, even if the site is more substantive than a PDF file, the likelihood of the intended audience finding their own way to the site is low without proper publicity to generate traffic. Publicity should be directed both internally and externally, consistent with the stakeholders described above. Once they have been lured in, several aspects of site design must be considered for effective communication: **usability**, **features**, **content** and **connectivity**.

6.5.1 Usability

File size is a key factor in the usability of a site. One should not expect Internet users to have a great deal of patience. The PDF is a useful tool for reproducing documents for the Internet; however, companies should be wary of the large file sizes, leading to long download times for those with slower connections.

Presenting the option of downloading specific chapters or sections and including file size and probable download time is recommended to enhance usability. These same warnings hold true for large image files and the trappings of modern websites with extraneous audio and video or animation. Large files and long downloads will probably be an even more significant barrier to stakeholders in the developing world.

Given the notion of global responsibility and global distribution of the report, the inclusion of local data is very helpful for those seeking information about the plant in their neighbourhood, state or country. This again goes back to the notion of radical transparency as mentioned earlier. To some it seems an insurmountable challenge or foolish venture, but progressive companies such as Bristol-Myers Squibb have included data and contact information for local facilities with positive results and numerous accolades from its stakeholders.

Recent software developments allow impressive monitoring of Web usage, including statistics on demographics of visitors (geographic location and sector), which areas of the website they viewed, and so on. A Global Environmental Management Initiative (GEMI) study found that 71% of the firms performed at least basic monitoring of activity on their website. The capabilities in this area are increasing rapidly and will probably become a significant opportunity to enhance the content and design of websites (GEMI 2000).

6.5.2 Features

With some reports growing to overwhelming tomes (averaging between 25 and 40 pages, though some are significantly longer, with Ford's latest reaching 98 pages), the use of search, site map and hyperlink features makes this depth of information more palatable and more useful (Jones *et al.* 1998).

This will only become more important as content contained on EHS or sustainability websites becomes more complex, incorporating press releases, articles (as does the AT&T site), training manuals, environmental education and other outreach materials (AT&T 2001). However, the inclusion of a site map and search capability will never substitute for an intuitive and simple site design.

Interactivity of the medium is another key benefit (e.g. an early warning of trends of what 'people are saying about your company') as well as a potential risk (e.g. traceable evidence of awareness of liability can have legal ramifications). Overall, these threats appear minor, and the feedback mechanisms should become an integral feature of a comprehensive sustainability website.

E-mail addresses should be provided, preferably an individual's name rather than info@ . . . or environment@ . . . to lend a sense of personal contact. Reflecting back to the issue of the digital divide, physical mailing addresses should always be provided for those without an e-mail account (Jones *et al.* 1998). Companies should be prepared, however, to respond promptly to comments and suggestions. In a recent study of response time to e-mail enquiries sent to addresses posted on firms' sites, 41% responded within two business days and 5% within a week. Disappointingly, however, the majority (55%) never responded (Winter-Watson and Weil 2001). Clearly there is room for improvement.

Tenet 6 of the book *The Cluetrain Manifesto*, which discusses the impact of the Internet on business, states that 'the Internet is enabling conversations among human beings that were simply not possible in the era of mass media' (Levine *et al.* 2000). Even companies that are already attempting to interact with their critical audience (see Royal Dutch/Shell 2001) should be encouraged to perform outside searches to scan the Internet for emerging issues.

6.5.3 Content

The report itself should be as detailed as far as the firm can support with regard to performance results (while maintaining discretion with propriety information), goals and verification specifics. The site should at a minimum address a full range of EHS and sustainability issues as prescribed by the current reporting standard.

Depending on the nature of the report, sites should also include education outreach to explain the performance metrics and put the results in context. As Kevin Butt, head of environmental affairs for Toyota Manufacturing of America, observed, 'if people don't understand what they're reading, [the Internet] can also be a dangerous tool. Ultimately, it is critical for us to be sure that the public understands' (KPMG 2001).

Electrolux has an extensive section dedicated to 'Eco Know How' and 'Eco Savings' (describing how minimising resource use can save you money over the life of a product), and International Paper's 'Sustainable Forestry Challenge' serves to frame the debate. However, both of these represent only the beginning (Kolk 1999; Electrolux 2001; International Paper 2001). To reach effectively the bulk of consumers, these educational sites need to have prominent links from the main corporate and product page, and not just subsections of the environment area of the website.

Larger business trends such as globalisation and outsourcing the supply chain are having significant economic (e.g. distribution of wealth created, local sourcing, transfer pricing policy, profit repatriation), trade (e.g. fair trade, compensation of indigenous peoples for use of resources and knowledge), product stewardship, human rights and health impacts, particularly in less-developed countries (SustainAbility 2000). Combine these impacts with the estimate that over half of the online population accessed the Internet in a language other than English in 2000, a figure expected to grow to 75% by 2005, and we quickly see the importance for companies to ensure that they design the sites appropriately to present the broad range of issues to an international audience (Global Reach 2001).

Another benefit of the electronic medium is the capability of visitors to tailor it to their language and content-area focus or interest level and visitor demographic (student, investor, etc.). These improvements in connectivity allow expansion of both richness (depth of details provided) and reach (access to the target audience) (Evans and Wurster 1999).

Finally, Internet users expect that the information on sites be updated on a regular basis. Though this ability leads to some concern that history may be quietly changed, it has not dramatically impacted the perceived value of the information presented (Scott 2001). Currently less than half of *Fortune* 100 firms' reporting pages post information on when the data was last updated, which negates one of the key potential benefits of real-time reporting using the Web as a communication medium (Winter-Watson and Weil 2001).

6.5.4 Connectivity

Increased internal hyperlinks (to and from main corporate and product pages) should be encouraged to reflect the larger integration of sustainability concerns into the overall vision of the firm. On average, access to the primary environmental homepage from the main corporate page requires more than two links (Winter-Watson and Weil 2001). This may arguably be one too many for a company purporting to have a corporate environmental vision.

One goal of many corporations, especially in Europe where the impact of protest sites is most forceful, is to counteract the increasingly sophisticated, Web-savvy and well-connected protest websites. In the spirit of radical transparency, firms should be encouraged to include external links, particularly to associated NGOs. Currently, such links to external sites varied significantly, from 34% as reported in the 1997 UNEP/SustainAbility study, 22% in an ERM (Environmental Resources Management) survey of US *Fortune* 100 firms and 9% of FTSE 100 (British) companies (SustainAbility 1997; Winter-Watson and Weil 2001). With groups such as Corpwatch.org and Ethicalconsumer.org monitoring what was once the secret inner workings of corporations, radical transparency is upon us, whether acknowledged on the corporate website or not.

6.6 Future reporting trends

With the state of corporate sustainability reporting currently in flux, there is a window for progressive companies to capture a significant first-mover advantage. In the next five to ten years, reporting schemes are likely to be increasingly regulated, standardised and become an expected aspect of the implicit social contract. As communication technologies improve and connectivity continues to increase, corporations need to guard their reputations by utilising the communication media to establish channels of dialogue, acknowledge imperfections, fulfil their implicit social contract, and achieve competitive advantage.

With recent developments in the UK pension plan disclosure requirements and increasing awareness in the financial sector, the importance of environmental and social performance data to the financial markets will only multiply in years to come. As the standardisation of sustainability communications increases, financial markets are starting to recognise that improved environmental performance is linked to enhanced financial performance (though causality is an ongoing debate).

Increasing number of studies (e.g. Repetto and Austin 2000a, 2000b) indicate that current environmental reporting understates many financially significant environmental risks. A company such as Baxter, which maintains environmental expenditures and savings in a financial framework, is able to provide a more targeted set of data and information to the investor community (Baxter Healthcare Corporation 1999). Green accounting (as standardisation and compatibility improve) will be a critical component in more effectively communicating sustainability issues to the financial sector.

The Global Reporting Initiative, an important corporate reporting platform, has expanded its 2000 guidelines to include social sustainability indicators and increased the relevance of quantitative and qualitative reporting of social impacts (see ITT Flygt 2001; Novo Nordisk 2001; Bristol-Myers Squibb 2001; British Airways 2001). There is now a movement to develop pilot versions of sector-specific supplements to the core guidelines over the 2000–2002 period.

Partnerships with former critics (e.g. numerous NGO–private-sector initiatives: Nature Conservancy–International Paper; NRDC–Dow Chemical; Environmental Defense–UPS; Conservation International–Starbucks Coffee) have proved to be tremendous opportunities to open new lines of communication. Increasingly, stakeholders (particularly critical audiences) expect firms to disclose negative environmental performance and to address the 'elephants in the bedroom'—that is, large-scale sustainability issues (SustainAbility 2000).

Tackling these issues improves the credibility of the report, but they should be undertaken cautiously and with the input of legal experts to mitigate any potential liability risks. Report verification, including third-party certification of data validity, the data-gathering mechanisms or the report itself, lend credibility to the reporting process. Currently, 65% of the FTSE 100 firms surveyed have some third-party verification, while the comparable figure was only 12% for the *Fortune* 100 companies (Winter-Watson and Weil 2001).

Part 2
E-BUSINESS STRATEGIES FOR A SUSTAINABLE WORLD

IS E-COMMERCE SUSTAINABLE?
Lessons from Webvan

Chris Galea
St Francis Xavier University, Canada

Steve Walton
Emory University, USA

At the end of the week of 6 March 2000, the Nasdaq stock exchange hit a record high of 5048.62. In the months leading up to that event, e-commerce was being touted as changing every rule and assumption of business. At the peak of the Nasdaq run-up, many people suggested that e-commerce would be a significant driver of sustainability and business performance on social and environmental dimensions. For example, in a presentation to the Sustainable Enterprise Academy,[1] Jonathan Lash, president of the World Resources Institute, described how the Internet economy would change the way things were acquired, with one efficient truck trip replacing multiple car trips by individuals. By 6 March 2001, the Nasdaq was halved to a value of 2052.78 and e-commerce and the Internet were viewed differently. Although many e-commerce firms, including the online grocery retailer Webvan, have ended up in bankruptcy, e-commerce continues to be a major part of the global business and economic landscape. Therefore, there is still a critical need to systematically evaluate the relationship between e-commerce and sustainability. Using Webvan as a case study, the goal of this chapter is to explore this relationship between sustainability and e-commerce in the context of the online food-retailing sector. Some of the results we describe will not apply to other forms of e-commerce, but many will.

7.1 E-commerce and sustainability

Acceptance of the Internet has given rise to claims that the 'old' ways of doing business are dead, and that the 'new economy' reigns supreme and will revolutionise many aspects

---

1   16 October 2001, CIBC Leadership Center, Toronto, Canada.

of business. Unsurprisingly, one of the claims is that e-commerce is critical to achieving more sustainable forms of business. This claim arises from the assumption that sustainability and e-commerce are complementary initiatives (e.g. even using common language such as 'dematerialising products' and 'substituting information for products'). However, major divergences do exist since sustainability and e-commerce use different strategic benchmarks.

A 'sustainable' business strategy requires a company to adopt a more holistic measurement system than companies typically use (i.e. a triple-bottom-line measurement system that includes social, environmental and economic performance), while rethinking the boundaries of their decisions and including issues that have traditionally been viewed as external. E-commerce, on the other hand, requires first and foremost that companies embrace speed and innovation as core strategies. Beyond the conflict in the strategic mission, there are also important operational similarities and differences between sustainability and e-commerce. A fundamental similarity is that each draws on resource productivity perspectives to argue for places on corporate agendas (e.g. Porter and van der Linde 1995a). In this model, e-commerce is viewed as a tool to achieve sustainability. A key difference is that e-commerce argues for global reach whereas sustainability argues for local actions.

The synergies from the similarities and the tensions from the differences are magnified by the operational gaps in theory versus practice. For example, many proponents of business-to-business (B2B) e-commerce transactions argue that the information shared between trading partners is a powerful tool for reducing inventories. However, Solectron, a US-based electronics contract manufacturer, was left with $4.7 billion in inventory when Ericsson, Cisco, Lucent and other major customers supplied the company with end-item demand figures that were at best optimistic (*Business Week* 2001). As a result, Solectron had to lower its financial targets for the next two quarters, announce a workforce reduction of 10%, and watch almost 10% of its share price erode (*Wall Street Journal* 2001).

These synergies and tensions have led to two competing perspectives on the relationship between e-commerce and sustainability. The first perspective is described succinctly by *The Economist* (2000b) when it suggests that the Internet will influence sustainability only to the degree that using the Web 'genuinely displaces real-world activities'. For example, e-commerce will deliver environmental gains only to the extent that it causes people to reduce auto trips or read newspapers online and companies to reduce packaging. The second perspective is captured in Nevin Cohen's work published in iMP (Cohen 1999) and other journals. This perspective tends to be more forward-thinking about potential long-term impacts of e-commerce on the environment, including changed supply chain structures from e-commerce. As Cohen points out, however, the early stage of the life-cycle of e-commerce makes long-term prediction risky. Table 7.1 presents several critical issues concerning e-commerce and sustainability and their relationship.

One way to illuminate the relationship between e-commerce and sustainability is by example. This approach, however, is limited, as the issues that are relevant for a B2B company are different from those for a B2C (business-to-consumer) company. We examine Webvan in this chapter because it illustrates characteristics that make the relationship between e-commerce and sustainability hard to understand, such as 'last mile' delivery timing, significant product inventory, trade-offs in transportation modes, delivery patterns and differential access to service based on race and income. We will briefly describe

Issue	E-commerce	Sustainability	Relationship
Speed	Critical—faster is better	Optional—better is better	Potentially conflicting
Reach	Global—'distance is dead'	Local—'proximity matters'	Conflicting
Customisation	Critical—recognise individual differences	Critical—enhances local solutions	Complementary
Information substituting for product	Yes	Yes	Complementary. Dematerialising product.
Information substituting for productive assets	Yes	Yes	Complementary. Supply chain information, for example.
Access	Limited to those with Web access	Unlimited	Conflicting. Hardware access limits relationship.
Consumerism	Enhances—easier access to more products	Discourages— unbridled consumerism increases waste and energy use	Conflicting

Table 7.1 *Critical issues in the relationship between e-commerce and sustainability*

Webvan's operating business model, including pertinent financial information, and use this to synthesise a model of the relationship between e-commerce and sustainability.

7.2 Webvan and the online grocery market

Before filing for bankruptcy in July 2001, Webvan, an online grocer based in Foster City, California, once operated in ten cities in the United States. Following their acquisition of HomeGrocer in 2000, Webvan was acknowledged as the leading online grocery retailer in the US, and as recently as October 2000 the company had approximately 524,000 customers with an average of $103 per order. Furthermore, Webvan had been one of the top five funded e-commerce start-up companies ever, and received $1.2 billion in venture funds from such notable sources as Goldman Sachs, Sequoia Capital, CBS and Knight-Ridder. Like many e-commerce start-ups, Webvan had only limited success in converting its venture funding into a profitable business. At their IPO (Initial Public Offering) in November 1999, Webvan traded for $25 per share. By 23 March 2001, Webvan was trading for 12.5 *cents* per share, giving it a total market capitalisation of $89.5 million, less than the $117 million in cash Webvan reported in their 30 September 2000 10-Q SEC (Securities and Exchange Commission) filing. Comparing Webvan's share price to two competitors is revealing. Although each company's shares fell in 2000, Albertson's and Winn-Dixie (two conventional American grocers) more than recouped their losses by March 2001 (see Fig. 7.1).

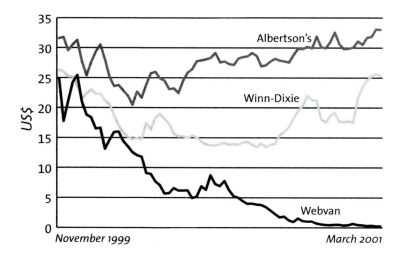

Figure 7.1 ***Historical share prices for Webvan and two competitors***

What accounts for Webvan's failure? Many of its economic problems can be traced to the design of its operating business model. Webvan delivers groceries within one hour of a target time set by the customer from a choice of available times. Often this requires planning for a grocery delivery two or three days in advance. One change in shopping habits is that customers must become accomplished inventory planners if they wish to avoid the frustration of following the Webvan truck out of the neighbourhood to make their own trip to the grocery shop for the last few critical items that ran out between the order and the delivery. One of the authors has used Webvan's service at least six times and can attest to the frustration that this 'out of stock at replenishment' engenders. To some degree, the difficulty of making this change in behaviour explains why customers who love the Webvan service order only seven times a year, when, according to the Food Marketing Institute, consumers visit the grocery store an average of 2.3 times per week.

Moreover, the company chose to build highly automated distribution centres outside of the urban centres it serves. Each of these distribution centres, built at a cost of $35 million, is 330,000 square feet and is capable of handling the volume of 20 supermarkets. Based on assumptions about order size and profit margin per order, Webvan calculated that it must process 3,000 orders per day to break even on its distribution centre. At the end of 2000, however, it was processing only 2,150 orders per day at its San Francisco distribution centre (Hansell 2001). Given an average order size of $103, this distribution centre suffered a daily revenue shortfall of $87,550, which amounted to an annual revenue shortfall for the distribution centres combined of $283.7 million.

Adding in other operations management and marketing costs, the reasons for Webvan's loss of over $450 million in 2000 are clear. In order to break even on distribution centre operations, the average daily order volume needed to increase by 40%. Although the investment in distribution centre technology led to impressive automation, it did not always allow for the efficient processing of orders and inventory management of the more than 50,000 consumer items that Webvan handles. Within each distribution centre, pick and pack is first divided into temperature (ambient, refrigerated and frozen). Managers bragged about 'pick and pack' workers having to move less than 19 feet to pick any item for an order in the ambient temperature zone.[2] However, the conveyor in the frozen section did not work as expected. At a temperature of −20° Fahrenheit, the conveyors moved so slowly that it became more efficient for the workers to use shopping carts rather than the conveyor belt to pick up groceries (Hansell 2001).

Webvan's operating model required shipments from the large distribution centre to serve selected substations around the city. Atlanta, for example, was served by nine such substations. Totes were packed at the distribution centre, loaded onto large trucks and routed to the appropriate substation where the totes were then loaded onto one of several smaller trucks that deliver to customers. The additional capital required to operate these substations was not included in the cost of building and operating the distribution centres, and they became yet another drain on available cash. Hansell (2001) had suggested that a less capital-intensive distribution centre structure, such as that of HomeGrocer prior to their acquisition by Webvan, would have been more appropriate. Perhaps, but it may have been insufficient to offset the behavioural and social changes required to use online grocers. Although this may change in the future, the online grocery business is currently not lucrative in size or profitability (see Table 7.2).

Applying lessons learned from Webvan to other online retail services suggests that many may not be sustainable economically. According to *The Industry Standard* (Couzin 2000), few online retailers are profitable regardless of their industry (see Table 7.3). For example, as of October 2000 only three North American online retailers showed profits. Even Amazon's promise of profitability by the end of 2001 is suspect, as they are promising only an operating profit (i.e. they will soon be able to sell things for more than it will cost to acquire and deliver them). Less clear is whether these issues signal a core difficulty with making money through e-commerce or a fundamental difficulty with the business models used to date. We hold to the latter.

7.3 Social impacts of Webvan

Webvan's business model extends beyond personal habits and has a lot of potential to influence larger social institutions and habits. Marketplaces are not just shopping outlets; they are also meeting places that represent a significant social/recreational compo-

2   *The Economist*, 24 February 2000.

Issue	Amount	Source
Number of Internet users	104 million	Pew Internet Project
Of those, number buying online	56% or 58.24 million	Pew Internet and American Life Project (Rainie and Packel 2001)
Of those, number buying food or clothing	11.2% or 6.52 million	Toop 2000
Of those, number buying groceries	9.6% or 626,196	Toop 2000
Average annual revenue per Webvan customer	$700	October 2000 10-Q and Hansell 2001
Profit margin of a traditional grocery store	2%	Food Marketing Institute
Number of pure-play online grocers	7	Food Marketing Institute
Number of clicks-and-mortar online grocers	19	Food Marketing Institute
Total market profit available	$8,766,744	Calculated
Average profit per competitor	$337,182.46	Calculated

Food Marketing Institute Website addresses:
www.fmi.org/facts_figs/keyfacts/chains.html
www.fmi.org/e_business/e_retailing/on_line_shop.htm
www.fmi.org/e_business/e_retailing/supermarket.htm

Table 7.2 **Estimate of the profitability of the online grocery business**

Company	Revenues ($ million)	Profit (loss) ($ million)	Current projection
Amazon	638	(240)	Operating profit in 4Q 2001
eToys	25	(60)	Out of business
FragranceNet	1.7	0.10	October 2000*
FTD.com	18.2	0.25	October 2000*
Homestore	62	0.55	October 2000*
Webvan	87	(120)	Out of cash by June 2001[†]

* From Couzin 2000
† From Webvan's October 2000 10-Q

Table 7.3 **Third-quarter-2000 profit of selected online retailers**

nent to shopping. Frequent shopping at specialised retail outlets (e.g. butchers and greengrocers) contributes to regular, friendly social interactions and creates important connection stations where one can interact with other members of one's community.

Typically weaker in large urban centres, marketplaces remain a mainstay of many towns and villages in North America where going grocery shopping continues to give people a chance to meet up with friends and acquaintances. The resurgence of speciality retail food outlets (e.g. boutique grocers such as Pusiteri's in Toronto or Harry's Farmers' Market in Atlanta) increases the likelihood that urbanites will identify with shops and shopkeepers. Grocery shopping on the Internet eliminates these social features and substitutes impersonal technological 'interactions'. Human contact may occur only when the groceries are delivered. Webvan excelled in this sense by hiring associates who provided knowledgeable and professional faces for the service, but the chance of getting to know a Webvan driver was low and, at best, minimally gratifying.

This limited source of social interaction may be threatened as well. Secure, refrigerated boxes can be installed at a customer's residence so that deliveries can be made at any time, thus eliminating the only point of human contact, as the customer need not be home for delivery. In the final analysis, this loss of contact with one's community threatens the development of a sustainability consciousness. The social side of sustainability implies a local human scale of operations, which affirms the core of our identity rather than depersonalises our interactions. Three important social impacts and implications of Webvan's business model should be noted: digital divide; social capital and community-building; and personal lifestyle.

7.3.1 Digital divide

Clearly, Webvan's business model worsens the digital divide—the disparity of Internet access according to income, education and social status. Webvan's services target businesses and higher-income stay-at-home parents (mostly mothers). To use Webvan one must have access to a personal computer with Internet access. According to *Business 2.0* (2001), almost 90% of all Internet users have incomes of $25,000 or greater per year. Thus, Webvan's services are more available to those with more money, which deepens perceived inequities between the rich and the poor.

7.3.2 Social capital and community-building

Economic effects of shifting to online grocery shopping often have direct social implications, such as the effect on local job markets and the local tax base. Centralised distribution centres shift jobs away from neighbourhoods and into industrial parks. This shift could potentially diminish the local property tax base as the property taxes paid by grocery shops often represent a substantial portion of the local tax intake. In turn, this reduces the ability of the community to deliver local services. These trends can be seen as socially regressive because they tend to erode self-sufficient, sustainable communities.

Webvan also undermines community-building by reducing the social capital available in a community. Putnam (2000) describes social capital as the value of social networks and suggests that reducing social capital will reduce community cohesion, leading to the phenomenon known as 'bowling alone'. Reduction in cohesion emerges from eliminating the sense of general and specific reciprocity individuals feel when engaged in social interaction. In this sense, Webvan substitutes physical capital (the infrastructure associated with its business model) for the social capital that is generated naturally when people interact with each other.

7.3.3 Personal lifestyle

Online grocery shopping is faster and more efficient than conventional shopping; thus it should free up personal time and improve one's quality of life. This argument assumes that all shopping is essentially a chore. Perhaps, but not necessarily. Shopping can be enjoyable: witness the enjoyment that most people display shopping at local farmers' markets or at speciality food boutiques. Unfortunately, some modern grocery stores seem designed to remove the sensory pleasure from food shopping, although there has been a recent resurgence in designing the layout of stores to make the shopping experience more satisfying. In contrast, shopping on the Internet exemplifies non-sensory experiencing. The objective is to order what one needs as quickly as possible and then to move on to other activities. There is little, if any, sensory interaction with the goods being purchased and almost no chance of a serendipitous shopping event that injects pleasure into what the Italians call *il terribile quotidiano*, the daily grind of life.

Another impact on personal lifestyle is the time saved. Undoubtedly, time is saved if one avoids an excursion solely to shop for food. Yet people typically combine various shopping trips, or shop while they are near to the shopping outlet, as, for example, when one shops after work before driving home. To evaluate the impact of online grocery shopping on personal time one must evaluate how the time saved is used. Time saved from shopping online that is used for socially constructive activities (e.g. tutoring at a school or volunteering in a soup kitchen) represents a gain for society. Yet a paradox exists: the more 'free' time people gain, the busier they seem to be. Accordingly, more time does not lead necessarily to a higher quality of life, especially if the extra time is used for stressful activities, such as working longer hours (often on the computer!).

7.4 Environmental dimensions of Webvan

Online grocery shopping can have a major impact on the environment. Differences in degree of environmental change arise from distribution-centre operations, distribution/ transportation patterns and alterations in land use. Shopping online changes the stocking and distribution patterns in several ways. One major change is the use of large centralised distribution centres outside of the city core from which orders are shipped to regional substations and then to customers. Contrast this to stocking groceries in individual stores. The main environmental impacts of this model are in fuel use and emissions due to changes in transportation methods and in the operation of distribution centres.

Changes in transportation are from suppliers and to customers. From suppliers, Webvan's model of stocking substitutes truck deliveries to grocery stores in congested urban centres with deliveries to centralised distribution centres in a suburb. Theoretically, this should result in benefits to the environment with regard to air pollution and congestion. Practically, however, the frequency of deliveries is significantly higher: Webvan aims for an inventory turnover that is 50% higher than the bricks-and-mortar equivalent.

The other main change in transportation patterns is how groceries are brought to the consumer. Individual trips to the grocery store in a personal vehicle are replaced by deliveries with a refrigerated truck or cube van. A high-level analysis of the impacts of these changes is revealing. Table 7.4 shows that switching to home delivery will significantly increase both the volumes of emissions generated (by at least a factor of 25) and of fuel consumed (by over 50%) to serve the same number of households.

Packaging is another environmental issue that is influenced by Webvan. By delivering in plastic totes, Webvan initially avoided the difficult 'paper versus plastic' bag problem and removed a huge source of packaging waste. Recently, though, they began to package orders in paper bags and then place the bags in the plastic totes. This made unloading more efficient and increased the number of deliveries in each driver's route, but it added superfluous packaging. Furthermore, there was minimal opportunity to reduce the packaging that manufacturers use for items due to the storage, freshness and handling requirements that arose from the pick-and-pack operations at the distribution centre.

Issue	Supermarket	Webvan	Difference
Number of households	10,000	10,000	0
Average round trip of complete route (miles)	5	62*	+57
Number of trips per month	8	4**	–4 trips
Per cent of route dedicated to groceries	25%[†]	100%	+75%
Grocery miles driven per month	100,000	97,600	–2,400
Fuel consumed (gallons)[††]	3,994	6,177	+2,183
Carbon monoxide emissions (grams)[‡]	340,000	10,022,300	+9,682,300
NO_x emissions (grams)[‡]	40,000	3,879,600	+3,839,600
Particulate matter emissions (grams)[‡]	8,000	387,960	+379,960

* Webvan's systems are designed to serve substations within a 50-mile radius from the distribution centre (DC). Deliveries to the consumer are made from the substations. The 62 miles include a 40-mile round trip from the DC to the substation and a 22-mile delivery route.

** Assumes that people are sufficiently good planners to reduce by half the number of grocery trips required. Relaxing this assumption only makes Webvan less environmentally attractive.

† Assumes that some portion of the trips are used for other purposes, such as other errands or going to work. Moving towards a higher proportion makes Webvan more environmentally attractive, but the fuel and emissions offset is so large that even at 100% dedicated grocery trips, Webvan is not environmentally preferred.

†† 25.04 mpg for cars (*EPA Fuel Guide*, 2001, available at www.epa.gov/otaq/fedata.htm) and 15.78 mpg for trucks (*Transport Canada Fuel Consumption Guide*, 2001, http://autosmart.nrcan.gc.ca/online_e.htm)

‡ Auto emissions from the US Federal Regulations for Auto Emissions. Truck emissions are derived from the EPA's Emission Standards Reference Guide for Heavy-duty and Non-road Engines.

Table 7.4 *Model of environmental impacts of Webvan's delivery model*

Finally, Webvan's operating model affects land use. Moving warehouse operations away from the city core may accelerate urban and suburban sprawl. This could lead to further urban deterioration in the city centre. The net environmental effect will probably be negative as sprawling cities are less efficient than compact ones, given that the same level of service (e.g. for roads, sewers) must be provided, despite the population dispersion. The result is that more of these services must be provided to obtain the same level of benefit.

7.5 Conclusion

Much rhetoric has been spouted about the effects of online economic activity such as retailing and grocery shopping. However, little rigorous work has been attempted so far to assess the impact of online retailing on sustainability. Our analysis suggests that the model of e-commerce chosen by Webvan is not sustainable economically, socially or environmentally, a result that does not apply solely to Webvan. Any business model that tackles the 'last mile' delivery challenge must find a way to overcome the emissions and fuel-usage problems associated with setting delivery schedules according to consumer desires.

Many e-commerce models specifically aim to remove personal interaction from business and personal transactions. For example, companies that offer online purchasing have found that public exchanges do not provide the opportunity to develop long-term relationships with suppliers. Regardless of the e-commerce context, removing social interactions from conducting transactions will decrease the community's social cohesion.

Our analysis raises a number of important issues and questions for academics, researchers, entrepreneurs and members of society to ponder. One compelling question might be, 'how do we use the vast resources of the Internet to deliver goods and services in a way that is economically profitable for business, socially beneficial for people in their communities and environmentally safe for the planet?'

INFORMATION TECHNOLOGY, SUSTAINABLE DEVELOPMENT AND DEVELOPING NATIONS*

James R. Sheats†

Hewlett-Packard Co., USA

The discussion and practice of sustainability has become a prominent feature of many industrial as well as government and international development forums since the Brundtland Commission published its 1987 report, *Our Common Future* (WCED 1987). The Rio 'Earth Summit' of 1992 and the Kyoto meeting in 1997 on global warming placed a further, very public, spotlight on the issues of physical resource usage, development, industrial practice and government policies. The extent to which these themes have gained credibility and serious attention is illustrated by the fact that the World Business Council for Sustainable Development has now over 140 members, most of which are multi-billion-dollar transnational corporations. Business for Social Responsibility has more than 1,400 members or affiliates, who collectively represent revenues of over US$1.5 trillion. Professor Stuart Hart's 1997 article in the *Harvard Business Review* won the McKinsey award for best paper of the year (Hart 1997). This paper outlined with uncommon clarity the positive role that developing nations could play in the pursuit of sustainability.

The concept that developing nations could be an important locus for sustainability action is not controversial. There was significant tension during the Rio Summit, for example, between countries from the developing world and those such as the US. With the diplomatic overburden stripped away, the debate reported in the press went like this. The richer nations wanted the poorer ones to agree to participate in global greenhouse gas reduction targets since, as their development plans unfold, they will become major

---

*   HP's World e-Inclusion would not exist without the dedicated work of many people, including everyone currently employed on the project. Here I would like to acknowledge the contribution *sine qua non* of Joel Birnbaum, Lyle Hurst, Carly Fiorina and Barbara Waugh, and apologise that all the other deserving individuals cannot be listed in this space.

†   The opinions expressed here are those of the author.

contributors to global warming. On the other hand, the developing nations insisted that the US and Europe, as the major contributors to greenhouse gas emissions (and reaping the majority of economic and social benefit therefrom), clean up their acts before the developing nations are expected to make any sacrifices.

This vignette is typical of a divide in opinion that is still quite widespread, despite lip service to the 'triple bottom line' concept (the simultaneous necessity of ecological, social and economic sustainability). A casual survey of people and organisations devoted to the elimination of poverty and those devoted to ecological sustainability does not reveal a strong synergy. Yet a closer look at the issues involved suggests that the two issues are inseparable (Sheats 2001).

It is clear that the elimination of poverty, a goal set by Dr Muhammed Yunus of the Grameen Bank to be reached within the next half-century at most, cannot be contemplated without incorporating the principles of sustainability from the outset. Should one make the attempt without doing so, one might temporarily alleviate poverty, only to create impoverishment for *all* the planet's inhabitants a short time into the future. Certainly, the practices of the roughly one billion richest inhabitants of the Earth are unsustainable. About this there is little serious disagreement. The dismal outcome of these activities can only be accelerated by having the rest of the world adopt them.

At the same time, however, sustainability assuredly cannot be achieved without the elimination of poverty and the gross inequity in income distribution that exists today. The fundamental reason for this was articulated in Hart's 1997 *Harvard Business Review* article, which emphasised the interaction of poverty and population growth. Without enquiring into the sociology of why population growth is correlated with poverty, the strength of this correlation tells us that we will not see population stabilised—an essential element of sustainability—without dramatic increases in living standards for 80% of the world's population.

We are thus confronted with a pair of issues of fundamental importance to society. Each of these is being driven by large constituencies of activists in industry, civil society, and government and quasi-governmental bodies, which should really have strongly overlapping, if not identical, agendas; yet the protagonists in many cases barely communicate.

Several events have occurred recently that underpin hope for a major change in attitudes toward these issues. One of these is the conference sponsored by the World Resources Institute (WRI) entitled 'Creating Digital Dividends' (16–18 October 2000, Seattle, Washington; www.digitaldividends.org). This meeting brought together over 300 leaders from industry, NGOs and government. They worked for two and a half days in an action-oriented format designed to develop a business agenda for achieving sustainable solutions to the so-called 'digital divide' which is a prominent part of the increasing gap between rich and poor nations today.

During the planning phase of this conference, the draft of a seminal paper (entitled 'Strategies for the Bottom of the Pyramid: Creating a Sustainable World') by Stuart Hart and C.K. Prahalad was circulated. This paper sets out its themes with a clarity and comprehensiveness that led the CEOs of Hewlett-Packard, DuPont, Ford, Citibank and Unilever, as well as WRI, to write supporting commentaries.

A few days before the conference, Hewlett-Packard Co. (HP) announced a major initiative called 'World e-Inclusion', whose goal is to bring sustainable e-solutions to the world's rural poor. The initial programme goals, described in a speech by CEO Carly Fiorina at the Digital Dividends conferences, have been followed up by several initiatives, including a major programme in Senegal in collaboration with the Joko Foundation and Sonatel, investments in and alliances with a number of companies and foundations, and establishment of a research lab in India whose purpose is to engage developing-country scientists and engineers in the innovation process for their own environment.

8.1 The fundamental problem of sustainability

While it is often asserted that the meaning of sustainability is unclear, this probably arises from confusing the question of what sustainability is with what it takes to achieve it. Sustainability is at heart a simple concept: people have to live within the framework of the Earth's dynamic systems. Change is a normal, indeed ubiquitous characteristic of nature. However, it occurs on definite time-scales dependent on a variety of complex underlying dynamics, and, if large perturbations are introduced on a much shorter time-scale, the other entities in the system will not be able to adjust, with results for many ecosystem members that can be catastrophic. The goal that we are all moving towards, therefore, is a social system in which we satisfy our basic needs, and as many of our desires as possible, without introducing perturbations into nature that rapidly shift eco-systems irreversibly away from the steady-state conditions in which we found them. The time-scale of any changes that we cause should be comparable to the time-scale with which the system can adjust continuously. In current practice, however, the extraction of materials from the Earth, their processing and their return in the guise of waste constitute just such large-scale perturbations, leading to the ecosystem crises we face today.

Stated in this way (which is not conceptually different from the definition of sustainable development stated by the Brundtland Commission), the inseparability of social and ecological sustainability is evident. If people's needs are being satisfied, they will not be poor, since 'poor' implies a wide separation between classes, with some people not getting what others consider basic services. At the same time, economic sustainability is similarly built in, if by economics we understand the process by which people attach value to what they do. Society will not meet its needs if its members do not attach value to the processes that are proposed to achieve this goal. This thematic unity can scarcely be overstressed, and should be kept in mind when one thinks of the 'triple bottom line' (a concept perhaps more appropriate to pragmatic focus on specific tactics).

The human effects that we call 'environmental impact' can be usefully summarised by the simple formula first used by Ehrlich and Holdren in 1971: $I = P \cdot A \cdot T$ where I represents impact, P population, A affluence or standard of living and T technology, or the efficiency by which the affluence is achieved. The product AT is consumption, which can be measured, for example, as a mass of material processed per person per unit time. Thus A may be thought of as a type of **state function** representing our needs and desires: where we are now and where we want to be at some future moment. For example, we need to get to our workplaces, and we want to be able to go to recreational facilities (e.g. the beach, mountains or the golf course). There are many ways to provide this mobility, ranging from walking to private helicopter, with different amounts of resource usage per unit of distance travelled.

The method that reduces I the most, of course, is not to go at all. While it is hard to go surfing without actually being at the ocean, telecommuting provides a means of going to work with no travel, costing only the electricity of the communication system, and the very small fraction of the hardware materials claimed by the activity. These examples illustrate the type and range of possibilities and how our technological choices affect the results. Thus T is the **path function** describing how we get from one state to the other, and the science of kinetics teaches us that such paths can vary tremendously in the energy (work) required, even though the initial and final states are the same.

Sustainability is viewed here from the perspective of what the business community can plausibly hope to affect. One may well suggest that perhaps one should simply not go to the beach or the golf course; one may suggest that the people of developed nations should reduce consumption to the levels of the typical Bangladeshi before worrying about the developing world. One may even wish to suggest that the developed world adopt policies that discourage the spread of consumer goods into the developing world since the production of these contributes in many ways to global unsustainability. This is precisely the argument that the developing nations rejected rather vigorously in the 1992 Rio Summit and its aftermath. These are social choices that should be discussed in a variety of venues. But to ask business to rein in consumption, in the context of the economic system we have today, is quite impractical and without chance of success. The purpose of business, as seen here, is to supply, as cost-effectively as possible, services people ask for. The components of these services must be decided in other arenas, which involve government, schools and many types of social organisation as well as private conversations. What we must ask here is how, if at all, the familiar processes of business can generate positive change in the existing social context.

8.2 The implications of current ecosystem stress

Returning to the $I = P·A·T$ formula, it is known that world population, now at about 6 billion, will rise to somewhere around 8–12 billion before stabilising (WRI 1999). The uncertainty includes many political factors that affect the use of birth control and family-planning procedures, but this demographic juggernaut is impossible to eliminate.

A second factor is affluence. Today, 20% of the world's population uses 86% of its resources. Yet that 20% has an essentially stable population, while the poorest half of humanity generates 90% of the population growth. The correlation between poverty and population growth has been recognised for some time, and is why global living standards must rise dramatically in order for population to be capped at a tolerable (sustainable) value. There are without doubt many factors that enter into this correlation, including: education (especially for women); the social and economic status of women; the degree of expectation of rising standard of living and potential for achieving personal fulfilment; expectations for financial support in old age; infant mortality; children's health quality; and so on. Without attempting to delve deeply into any of these details, it is a reasonable first approximation to assume that our current standard of living in the developed world is what is required to achieve population stability. This assumption is consistent with the observation that our own population was increasing until relatively recently.

Taking these two factors together we find that, in the absence of changes in technology, environmental impact is due to rise by about a factor of ten during the next 25–50 years. This prediction rests in part on a demographic basis, and has an inherent momentum that is unlikely to be altered. Failure to achieve the economic gains that reduce and eliminate poverty leads to population growth that overwhelms any advantage of low resource usage per person. Even if population growth is limited by regulatory force, material growth is left unchecked. Thus we see that not only should we not discourage economic growth in the developing world, it is an obligation to foster it.

Since the global environment is already under substantial stress, however, this factor-of-ten increase in environmental burden represents the makings of a major catastrophe; its consequences will prevent the very industrial progress that gives rise to it (a simple example of negative feedback). Bangladesh, for example, will not be able to realise improved living standards if major parts of the country are under water and others are frequently flooded, yet just such effects are predicted by the most recent report issued by the Intergovernmental Panel on Climate Change. Nor should we assume that the developed world would be immune to these effects. Apart from obvious issues of international interdependence and the sourcing of most material resources from the developing world (especially oil), a warming climate has worldwide health ramifications that are poorly understood but generally ominous.

These considerations further reinforce the interrelationship of the sustainability themes. The viability of the fundamental ecosystem services that make life possible is now seriously threatened because of human impacts, yet we are not addressing the basic needs of a large fraction of the existing human population. From a global perspective, poverty and environmental degradation are virtually one and the same problem. Without eliminating poverty, the world cannot hope to achieve a stable, appropriate population size; without truly sustainable industrial practices, current gains in living standards will lead to even greater impoverishment for generations to come.

Fortunately, technological and economic capability for addressing these needs has never been greater. Technologies exist today that, when coupled with innovation in business models to deliver them in people-centric form, can reduce environmental impacts by a hundredfold while actually increasing the quality of the services provided. Most importantly, this can be done in a way that generates profitable returns for all participants. HP's World e-Inclusion Initiative seeks to implement these themes within the context of the company's competence and strategic thrust. One essential component of it is the provision of Internet connectivity solutions, often generically called 'telecentres'.

These centres provide Internet-enabled information technology for people with currently no connectivity, embedded in a complete solution that generates economic and social value in ways that actually preserve and enhance the environment. The Internet is a tool that holds the promise of empowering people to make informed, effective choices for themselves about their economy, their society and their environment. In addition to providing information, access to financial resources (e.g. microcredit) and access to markets, it can assist people in acting effectively on that information: for example, in optimising agricultural yields with fewer resources; maximising efficiency of transport and other energy usage; and developing industrial ecosystems in which there is no waste (Hawken *et al.* 1999).

8.3 Information technology and sustainable development in rural villages

The discussion of how information technology (IT) can underpin profound improvements in resource utilisation in general was the subject of another recent article (Sheats 2001). Here I focus entirely on the developing-world aspects by examining the example of the telecentres, exemplified by the LINCOS project (www.hp.com/e-inclusion). While there is much more to developing-world connectivity solutions than remote telecentres, this is what we, at Hewlett-Packard, have developed to the greatest extent, and for which we have some experience on which to base conclusions. I concentrate substantially on sustainability themes here, while acknowledging that some important aspects of e-inclusion (such as microcredit) are given rather less attention.

LINCOS is a programme with the fundamental goal of improving people's standard of living and empowering communities. As stated before, if this goal is achieved without proper respect for environmental consequences, it would completely negate itself, since the improvement would self-destruct in the cataclysm of ecosystem collapse (associated with radical climate change, loss of ecosystem services and loss of species diversity). A *real* improvement in living standard, in other words, is only one that is based on sustainable solutions. The concepts of ecological sustainability, cultural sensitivity and economic profitability are built into the foundation of LINCOS.

Physically, the fundamental basis of the LINCOS 'digital town centre' is a standard ISO shipping container (2.4 × 2.4 × 6.1 m) remodelled and equipped with a set of IT and wireless communications equipment. It is Internet-linked via satellite, with a stand-alone power source and measurement capabilities for medical and analytical applications.

Variations on this theme are elaborated according to need. For example, a distributed computing model (with a high-capacity server and several very low-cost network-based computers or 'thin clients') is applicable in many cases (and will save a great deal of energy). Other models will be devoted exclusively to the provision of Internet access, to computer classes and education, to medical services, and a range of other applications. In some cases these units may be clustered; in others they will be separated by short distances with local wireless connections. As suitable local wireless-enabled information appliances become available, they will be distributed to users in a several-kilometre range around LINCOS centres to provide Internet connection and powerful computational resources to everyone, even those living in sparsely populated areas.

There are several general consequences that can be distinguished. First, the Internet provides access to a huge spectrum of information, enabling people to make informed decisions and to discuss these decisions among themselves. Land and water use practices, which are among the most critical for sustainability, could be greatly improved.

The second immediate consequence is the encouragement of commercial activities that actually encourage the protection of nature rather than its destruction. Eco-tourism, properly managed, can turn natural beauty and biological wealth into an economic asset that people will be motivated to preserve. The ability to sell crafts in the world market provides valuable income in a village setting, using minimal resources. Digital jobs (programming, data manipulation, etc.), the elements of the knowledge-based economy, can be accomplished anywhere in the world with a good Internet connection. A few additional physical appliances (providing direct feedback on environmental health) can substantially enhance the environmental consciousness of a locale, as well as providing unique economic value (by, for example, certifying organic food production, sustainable forestry, etc.).

Finally, and most importantly, this programme will result in the integration of quite sophisticated IT into the life of the community before the demand develops for high-impact products such as frequent transport, refrigeration, air conditioning, household appliances and out-of-season fresh food supply. With the proper use of IT these products and processes can be made far more efficient (as well as effective for the customer) than the current developed-nation norm. Developing nations may actually have an advantage in being able to install the best available practices without having to displace their legacy infrastructure. They can become true 'digital ecosystems': rural communities that are attractive places to live and which stem the migration of people into crowded, polluted and impoverished megacities.

There are many other ways in which Internet-enabled IT can be of value for sustainability. The Internet provides the craftsperson with direct knowledge of market demand, allowing her or him to optimise product design and quality. Farmers can realise immense benefits. Studies have shown variation of up to threefold or more in the yields of basic crops grown in the same vicinity, through relatively minor changes in soil treatment (irrigation, fertiliser and tillage). A system in which inexpensive soil sensors gather information that is transmitted to an agricultural college or government agency where it is analysed and the recommended optimal practices returned to the farmer would have obvious and dramatic value to the farmer. This can reduce impacts due to pollution, excess water use, resources used to make wasted fertiliser, and so on (Sheats 2001). This is just one example of 'precision agriculture' adapted to the needs of the poor.

Simple e-commerce can have a dramatic impact. Whether the subject is coffee in Central America, pineapples in Bangladesh or cashews in Tanzania, farmers in such areas usually reap only a tiny fraction of the price commanded by their product at its final destination, in large part due to lack of market knowledge. Today coffee growers in San Marcos, Costa Rica, have increased their return sixfold due to the LINCOS system there. Such economic changes can mean the difference between barely scraping by and feeling in control of one's destiny, able to take responsibility for the condition of the Earth that is one's home. People who live on the land generally have a strong feeling for it and can be, given the economic opportunity, its best protectors.

Industry can also benefit. Many industries in developing nations are modest in scale; communication with other industries is limited at best, and often non-existent. Opportunities for turning waste-streams into economically valuable products (the general theme of industrial ecology) may exist without ever being recognised in the absence of the information exchange made easier by the Internet. This leads to the potential to achieve true industrial ecosystems, which resemble natural ones in that each industry's waste is food for another.

The importance of easy access to information cannot be overstated. How does a person in the rural developing world obtain information about the best practices in energy-efficient (or natural hazard-resistant) building practices, community planning, public health, and so on? We are so accustomed to the availability of information on the Internet that for the most part we no longer notice the extent to which we use it. If it is not there, a quick call or e-mail to the library results in its delivery within hours or a few days at most. If we should actually want the original source (a book, for example), bookstores are minutes away and online booksellers a few clicks. None of this exists in large reaches of the world, and all can be put there long before those places have paved roads and shopping malls.

All of this innovation will benefit the highly developed world as well. As emphasised by Prahalad and Hart, the potential for developing innovation that can work in cash-poor environments will lead to products and processes that feed back to the currently much more wasteful developed world, to the betterment of all. We need not think in terms of developing nations learning to get along with a less desirable solution than we have had; on the contrary we may find ourselves emulating them in the future.

8.4 A sustainable Internet business strategy for the developing world

The physical infrastructure represented by LINCOS is a necessary component of delivering value in a sustainable fashion to the developing world. It is not sufficient, however. Technology by itself is never a true solution. This principle is generally well understood in business, where the customer's need drives business strategy and product definition. Nevertheless, in the developed world, where customers frequently know the technology details and can construct a solution package from the available elements, a company can often get away with offering a generic product, such as a personal computer, without regard to its application. This will not work in the developing world, where the nearest store with parts and advice may be hundreds of miles away, and no one in the village has ever used a computer before. Nor can pricing and delivery follow the conventional model when the per capita income is several times smaller than the price of a single inexpensive computer and monitor.

But HP's initiative is about people, and not primarily about technology. It is about people having access to information so that they can make important choices in their lives. It is about people having access to healthcare, education and income opportunities where they live, in their language, consistent with their culture.

As seen by Hewlett-Packard, the Internet-enabled world, today, is driven by the intersection of three vectors. These are: infrastructure, to deliver computing services, available at all times, everywhere; appliances, to provide the desired computational result, appropriate to the user's needs; and e-services, integration of the technology with content structure and dynamic tools to give the user results while the technology remains in the background.

This framework applies quite well to the needs of the developing world, but implies solutions for each element that will be unique. The lack of installed telephone lines means that satellite or microwave delivery is in general critical (and for practical purposes necessary anywhere not served by optical fibre). In many cases appropriate computing appliances will be quite different from those popular in the US and similar regions. Devices that are designed according to the need can be cheaper, smaller and longer-lasting and require less energy while being more effective in serving the needs of their users.

Finally, the services will have to be designed (co-created) with these needs in mind, and delivered via business models that are uniquely tailored to their circumstances. While the target audience may not be able to afford a computer (even a cheaper thin client), anyone can afford to pay for services that directly improve their economic effectiveness. The challenge of how to finance the hardware has been addressed, with dramatic success, by Grameen Phone, showing that this can be done on a for-profit basis in even the poorest regions.

In keeping with the principles mentioned earlier, many of these qualities are also relevant to the developed world, but market conditions fail to justify the necessary R&D and production investment. Introduction of the results in the developing world will almost certainly have major beneficial ramifications in the developed world.

By keeping the fundamental focus always on the service provided to the customer, one is led to a business structure that is appropriate to the developing world. The concept of e-services (any information, business process, computing resource or application delivered over the Internet to drive new revenue streams or create efficiencies) is central to this strategy. In order to deliver these services to end-users in the developing world, partners are needed just as they are in the highly developed countries. Currently HP sells software tools, equipment and processes to companies that provide the Internet-based functionality that the customer (business, government or individual) wants.

Similar relationships must be created in the developing world as well. However, in many cases the required service providers do not yet exist, and their potential customer base does not have the experience necessary to take good advantage of them if they did exist. The Internet will enable operations that were not possible before, and new businesses will have to be created. Thus there is a prominent role for entrepreneurial development and training, business incubation structures and mentors to nurture and support these new enterprises (often micro enterprises), and a wide variety of funding sources and mechanisms. Much of this may itself be delivered via the Net.

Within the next decade, we expect to see financially robust, environmentally friendly e-services-based economies thriving throughout the regions currently labelled 'developing', and providing a locus for the most dynamic sources of innovation in the world. Any company that fails to see this vision today will not only miss out on the opportunity to solve some of the world's most pressing problems, it will miss out on the opportunity to ensure its own survival.

THE ENVIRONMENTAL IMPACT OF THE NEW ECONOMY
Deutsche Telekom, telecommunications services and the sustainable future

Markus Reichling and Tim Otto
Deutsche Telekom AG, Germany

In discussions with environmentalists, information technology (IT) experts and other interested parties, we frequently hear that many telecommunications services and Internet applications contribute to reduced pollution, sometimes to a considerable extent. The reasoning is that this is an inevitable outcome as so many products are dematerialised that ultimately there has to be a positive environmental impact on production, transport, usage and waste disposal. It is often maintained that substitution effects could prevent a number of causes of pollution (e.g. through telecommuting) where people would no longer need to drive a car to work. Some people were understandably excited by the idea that the electronic transmission of data and information might virtually solve global environmental problems.

The rise in critical voices of various environmental experts in publications (Grießhammer 1997; Radermacher 1999) and also our own reflections have led us to be more circumspect about statements concerning the eco-benefits of telecommunications and IT sectors that we could not prove. In November 1998, at a conference[1] in which the environmental representatives from all large telecommunications companies worldwide participated, there were still virtually no critical voices to be heard regarding possible environmental hazards caused by telecommunications services. At this point it became clear to us that it is critically important to systematically investigate the potential positive and negative environmental impacts of telecommunications services.

Our commitment to achieving new and comprehensive results in this area soon led to the sobering realisation of just how thoroughly complex such an investigation would be.

---

1 '2nd European Conference on Telecommunications and the Environment', organised by the European Telecommunications Public Network Operators' Association (ETNO) in Turin, Italy.

We encountered many problems in trying to investigate the ecological dimensions of tele-communications services, including defining the scope of the investigation, overcoming the problem of data acquisition, and selecting the appropriate evaluation approaches. At the same time, we received some strong support for our project. To begin with, Deutsche Telekom established the business goal of becoming a sustainable enterprise in a sustainable society in 1999.[2] The principal concept underlying this vision is that our products and services are not formed by customer needs alone, but that telecommunications services have the potential to bring about significant change in our society and should contribute to human development.

This was the aim of the Board of Management when, in keeping with its vision, it committed Deutsche Telekom to an environmental programme in October 2000 that defines these concerns as a company objective to be achieved by the end of 2004. Another source of support for our research was our corporate environmental 'allies' at Swisscom AG. Swisscom AG arrived at a similar conclusion as our company and they also began to analyse the environmental impacts of various telecommunications services (see Chapter 10 for a detailed summary of the research carried out by Swisscom AG).

In Section 9.1, we present a critical discussion of and offer our view on how and whether telecommunications services can contribute to sustainable development and, in particular, reduce the environmental impact of companies and society. Section 9.2 details and summarises the results of our environmental impact studies. We describe our preliminary results as well as some of the relevant methodological and background issues.

9.1 Do telecommunications services contribute to the sustainable development of companies and society?

The far-reaching development of the information age is felt in all areas of private and public life in the so-called developed countries of the world. Many families now take mobile telephones and Internet access for granted as much as radio and television were 30 years ago. Nobody appears to seriously doubt the often-made claim that information technology will be one of the most important sectors in the future. From supermarket shelves to the stock markets of the world, the impact of this development is apparent everywhere. The 'new economy' has public life fully in its grasp as its participants already consider it completely normal. Or are you still amazed when a company invites you to visit its website?

But how sustainable is this development? It is easy to define 'sustainability' as a balance of economic, ecological and social considerations, but just a moment's thought reveals the complexity of the term. How much social change is ethically acceptable when products can create completely new needs? How much environmental damage is permissible before a company is charged with being irresponsible and how much latitude do companies have to remain successful in the marketplace? While it is impossible to pro-

---

2 Sustainable development is development that fulfils the needs of the current generation without putting future generations at a needs-fulfilment disadvantage (the 'Brundtland Report'; WCED 1987: 43).

vide definitive answers to these questions, we can make a valuable contribution towards answering these questions by taking a critical approach *vis-à-vis* the activities, products and services of our company.

One of our key assumptions is that telecommunications services have been instrumental in developing totally new 'needs'. The desire of many people to be reachable at all times and to have push-button access to nearly all kinds of information is today no longer uncommon. The possibility of this type of universal communication seemed more like science fiction to most people just a few years ago. Is the telecommunications industry furthering sustainability by awakening and satisfying these needs? Does the enormous consumption of resources necessary to research and develop new technologies responsibly take into account our planet's environmental resources and the needs of future generations? For the time being, all of us need to and must address these questions on an individual basis. Perhaps the most important conclusion from our research is that the 'sustainability' of many products and services depends to a great extent on the individual user.

For instance, a book purchased online from home can be seen as an environmentally friendly act if the user has substituted an online purchase for a pollution-intensive act of driving to the bookshop. However, if the customer usually rides a public bus for such purchases, the environmental burden is about the same as an online purchase (see Section 9.2.1 for additional details on a Deutsche Telekom study on this issue). It is easy enough to deduce that it is even more environmentally friendly to travel by bicycle or on foot to the bookshop than ordering a book via the Internet. This methodology yields similar results for a number of products (e.g. electronically ordering travel tickets and shopping for different items at a mail-order company). Our research did not, however, take into account the environmental links between online shopping and transportation options (e.g. will online shopping lead to greater pollution-intensive activities such as air travel?).

Consequently, Deutsche Telekom's T-Online home e-commerce activities can be seen as reducing the overall environmental burden only if shopping for comparable goods at bricks-and-mortar shops has more of a negative impact on the environment. Similarly, there is a positive environmental impact of using the T-Net-Box, a virtual answering machine in the Deutsche Telekom network (see Section 9.2.2 for details), only when customers consciously avoid using their telephone-linked answering machine. A third of the total energy output of a coal-fired power station or the equivalent of half a million tons of CO_2 may be saved if the virtual machines replaced all the conventional answering machines in Germany (Gensch *et al.* 2000). There is an environmental advantage only when a change in customer behaviour leads to a substitution of an environmentally less demanding activity. Without this substitution effect, there is no practical contribution to sustainability from the T-Net-Box or the T-Online telecommunications service.

Videoconferencing represents another potential for environmental contribution from the telecommunications sector. Our research shows that a videoconference between business partners at a distance of just a few kilometres can result in environmental savings if one takes into account the transportation that is necessary for a face-to-face meeting (see Section 9.2.3 for details). The type of transportation used (i.e. car, train or aeroplane) plays an important role, though it does not have a significant impact on the overall result. Although not every personal meeting can be replaced by videoconferencing, there may arguably be a number of situations in which videoconferencing can serve as a viable substitute for a conventional business trip and, at the same time, benefit the global environment. Again, reducing the overall environmental demand is likely to occur when the number of people using videoconferencing reaches a certain critical mass. The reservations many people have about using a videoconferencing system constitute the system's biggest barrier, which is the situation Deutsche Telekom finds itself in.

Nevertheless, it would be short-sighted for a company to blame consumer behaviour for the lack of its commitment to sustainable products and services. Large global corporations such as Deutsche Telekom can significantly influence the use of their required energy and material inputs. As shown in Section 9.2.4, the energy consumption of Deutsche Telekom's fixed network infrastructure comes to 248.5 GJ or approximately 14.5 tons of CO_2 per kilometre of data line. When multiplied by the total cable length of Deutsche Telekom's fixed network, the resulting value is equivalent to the accumulated primary energy consumption, or amount of resulting CO_2, needed for the production and operation of the network infrastructure for 15 years of serviceable network component life. To understand the scope of the environmental impact of the fixed telephone network, one needs to compare this to a comparable infrastructure network such as Deutsche Bahn's railway network or the German federal road network (see Section 9.2.4 for the comparison).

9.2 Selected studies on telecommunication services and sustainability

9.2.1 E-commerce (business-to-consumer) and book purchasing

9.2.1.1 Background

Using the so-called 'screened LCA' method,[3] the primary aim of this study (Otto 2000) was to investigate whether there is an environmental benefit of making purchases online compared to conventional sales channels. Books were chosen as the consumer item since they are one of the established and largest e-commerce markets in Europe.

9.2.1.2 Methodology

Because they account for about 85% of the market for transporting products (Benz 1999), trucks were selected as the primary transport for the delivery of products to the customer. We established various scenarios for the product group under consideration by assigning distance and type of transport to each link in the supply chain,[4] while the amount of energy consumed[5] was calculated for each means of transport based on the distance travelled. Altogether, a total of 11 different supply chains were examined. Primary energy consumption was selected as the key environmental indicator. A higher primary energy

3 Screening life-cycle analysis.
4 A supply chain is a sequence of technically and organisationally linked processes in which persons or goods are moved from a source point to a target point (according to DIN 39781).
5 Primary energy is energy gained from fossil fuels such as crude oil, coal, etc.

consumption for the particular mode of transport would imply a greater overall environmental burden.

Our research discovered that a fixed, predefined supply chain does not exist for conventional sales or for online book purchases. The selection of a supply chain for book distribution is more likely to be oriented to customer preferences (e.g. quick delivery) or cost-effective solutions. Our study placed emphasis on supply chains that reflected the conditions typical of German online and conventional book sales. The transport of books and the customer's shopping trip were recorded as one. Our analysis also did not take into account supply chain links in which no goods were transported or in which multiple delivery attempts were made.

In estimating the overall environmental impact, we assumed that a typical customer going to a conventional bookstore uses an automobile (petrol; 50% capacity, or 2 persons), and alternatively public bus (50% capacity, or 24 passengers). Also, we assumed that the shopping trip was not solely for the purpose of buying a book. Therefore, only one-fifth of the primary energy consumption for the shopping trip for each mode of transportation was calculated. For the online book purchase, we estimated that about half an hour of online time would be required to make the necessary purchase. The electricity needed for this purchase was calculated in terms of primary energy usage, while the primary energy consumption for the distance delivery vehicles travel was adjusted for the number of customer deliveries per trip. A critical point in the supply chain of an online book purchase is the delivery of the ordered goods by a parcel post service.

Conventional book purchase*

Supply chain 1:   Publisher – Wholesaler – Regional distributor – Bookshop – Customer

Supply chain 2:   Publisher – Bookshop – Customer

Online book purchase

Supply chain 3:   Publisher – Online seller inventory – Freight mailing centre 1 – Freight mailing centre 2 – Delivery basis – Customer

Supply chain 5:   Publisher – Wholesaler – Freight mailing centre 1 – Freight mailing centre 2 – Delivery base – Customer

* The journey to the shops was calculated in each case on the basis of a passenger car and a public bus.

Table 9.1 **Book purchasing supply chains: conventional versus Internet**

Source: Otto 2000

9.2.1.3 Results

There is a difference of 107% in energy consumption between a conventional book purchased using a private automobile (c. 3.60 MJ) versus an online purchase (c. 1.74 MJ). The most important factor is the energy consumption of the automobile, which contributes an average of 88% to the total energy consumption of the supply chain. However, if the customer uses public transport for shopping (in this case a public bus), a conventional book purchase uses only 6% more energy compared to an online purchase. Personal computer operation was responsible for 59% of the total primary energy consumption in the supply chain for the online book purchase (the biggest user of primary energy), while the goods transport accounted for 41%.

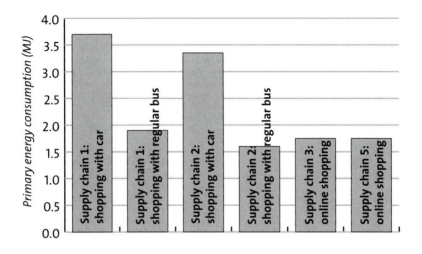

Figure 9.1 *Primary energy consumption of selected supply chains*

Source: Otto 2000

As discussed in Section 9.1, the overall environmental impact depends to a great extent on the transportation system customers use to go shopping. If the customer goes by bicycle or walks to shopping areas, conventional shopping may be environmentally superior. If on the other hand a customer uses an automobile to make his purchase, then there is an environmental advantage to the online purchase. In particular, the very high contribution of the PC to online orders and the contribution of the private car when shopping for goods represent environmental weak points and highlights the need to improve the environmental aspects of both conventional and online shopping.

9.2.2 The T-Net-Box

9.2.2.1 Background

As part of the 'Top Ten Innovations' project with the Oeko-Institut Freiburg, Deutsche Telekom commissioned a study (Gensch *et al.* 2000) to systematically investigate the ecological balance of the T-Net-Box, which is Deutsche Telekom's virtual call manager in its fixed network. Deutsche Telekom's T-Net-Box is a service invisible to the user and based on the so-called T-Net-Box platform in the telephone network. Compared to conventional answering machines, the T-Net-Box offers a number of unique features, including the **notification function**: the user is informed of incoming messages by a call and/or text notification and the message can be delivered to the user's own telephone or to any telephone of the user's choice; the **fax function**: it can receive and save faxes, while the saved incoming faxes can then be printed out on the user's own or another fax output device; and the **family box**: as many as nine personal message boxes can be set up with the T-Net-Box.

9.2.2.2 Methodology

The following 'functional units' were defined and compared for the purposes of the study: **T-Net-Box and answering machine**: provision of the service of automatically answering and storing calls, 1,000 units allotted for a period of one year; and the **T-Net-Box and fax device**: provision of the service of automatically storing incoming faxes, 1,000 units allotted for a period of one year.

Our analyses of T-Net-Box versus answering machine and T-Net-Box versus fax device were based on the following data and assumptions.

- **T-Net-Box.** A technical platform designed to be independent of the number of wired boxes for a maximum of 400,000 boxes; service life of 10 years was assumed for the technical platform for the T-Net-Box, which consists of 3.56 m^2 of circuit board and 5,997 microchips. The energy consumption of a technical platform is independent of the number of wired boxes. It is about 104 MWh per platform a year, and the specific end energy consumption is calculated at 1.3 kWh/box for 80,000 boxes per platform a year.

- **Answering machine.** A modern answering machine from Deutsche Telekom's current range of products was used as the basis of comparison. Its serviceable life is assumed to be 5 years; circuit board area: 8.78×10^{-3} m^2; number of chips: 8; standby power consumption: 4 W; standby end energy consumption: 35.04 kWh/a.

- **Fax device.** A modern fax machine from Deutsche Telekom's current range of products was chosen. Its serviceable life is assumed to be 5 years; circuit board area: 0.043 m^2; number of chips: 13; standby power consumption: 4 W; energy consumption: 35.04 kWh/a.

Our study took into account only the environmental impacts of circuit board and semiconductor chip production in our eco-analysis of the production phase of T-Net-Box, answering machines and fax devices, since circuit board and semiconductor production is much more resource-intensive than the production of other components (Strubel *et al.* 1999). They constitute more than 90% of the total production-side impact on the environment, whereas the other components have only a very slight impact on the eco-balance.

In the usage phase, only the energy consumption in standby operation for conventional answering and fax devices was taken into account. For the T-Net-Box, production-side applications for the ready spare parts were factored in as well as energy consumption. As for the post-consumption phase, only the waste potential based on amount was factored in.

9.2.2.3 Results

The environmental comparison between the T-Net-Box service and an answering machine reveals a significant advantage to the T-Net-Box service. In terms of the primary energy consumption and the greenhouse effect, the answering machine has a 27 times greater environmental impact than the T-Net-Box. In terms of the waste-stream, the differences are even more dramatic: the answering machine has a 66 times greater environmental impact than the T-Net-Box. The T-Net-Box also has an environmental edge over the fax device. In terms of primary energy consumption and the greenhouse gas emissions (associated with the manufacture and use of the fax device), a fax device has a 28 times greater environmental impact than the T-Net-Box.

However, T-Net-Box's potential to reduce the overall environmental burden depends a great deal on its future use in the consumer marketplace. Currently, about 40% of all German households (approx. 16 million) are equipped with an answering machine, which is typically in standby operation the whole day. Assuming an average standby power consumption of all answering machines at 5 W, the total power standby consumption in Germany is over 1,000 GWh a year or the equivalent of about 30% of the annual output of a large coal-fired power station. One hundred per cent use of the T-Net-Box service capacity translates into a net reduction of half a million tons of CO_2 or 8,000 TJ of primary energy.

9.2.3 Videoconferencing

9.2.3.1 Background

In co-operation with the Oeko-Institut Freiburg, Deutsche Telekom commissioned a study comparing videoconferencing to conventional meetings and conferencing (Quack and Gensch 2000). The videoconferencing system used in the study was the 'SwiftSite'[6] system made by PictureTel and marketed by Deutsche Telekom. A television set is needed to operate the system.

9.2.3.2 Methodology

The following 'functional unit' was defined and compared in the study: holding a four-hour talk-only conference with two participants who were at two different locations. Moreover, two specific calculations were made in the study. In the first calculation, only the primary energy requirements for operating the videoconferencing devices as well as the chosen means of transportation of the conferencing participants were computed. In the second calculation, the environmental impact of device production and transport were taken into account.

As in the T-Net-Box study, only the environmental impacts of circuit board production and semiconductor production were take into account. The eco-balance data for the television was taken from a study conducted by the Oeko-Institut Freiburg (Strubel *et al.* 1999) and was fully integrated into the environmental impact assessment of videoconferencing. The environmental impact of transportation was obtained on the basis of a

---

6 www.picturetel.de, February 2001.

person-based kilometre calculation.[7] The electricity required to operate the device and the energy consumed during the videoconference were also included in the final eco-analysis. Based on the assumption that the television and videoconferencing device required power only for the duration of the videoconference, the standby operation power consumption was not taken into account.

9.2.3.3 Results

Figure 9.2 shows that a videoconference—even over a short distance—is more environmentally friendly than a conventional meeting or a conference. As the distance between the participants increases, the environmental gap becomes even more dramatic. Using energy consumption as an indicator, a business trip using an automobile (i.e. petrol) has a 30 times greater environmental impact than a four-hour videoconference at a distance of 100 km. A key factor in the calculation is the type of transport used. If one compares a videoconference to a business trip via aeroplane at a distance of 1,000 km, videoconferencing has an environmental advantage by a factor of 500.

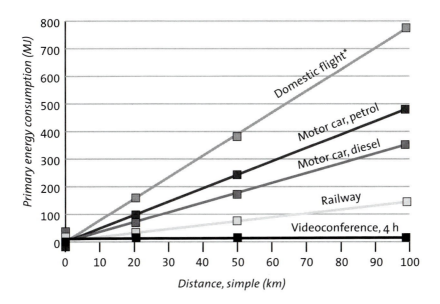

* Although air travel can be assumed to be irrelevant for distances of less than 100 km, it has been included here to indicate the basic trend.

Figure 9.2 *A comparison of primary energy consumption required to hold a four-hour videoconference versus various transportation options*

---

 7 This is the proportion of impact attributed to the production of the means of transport calculated on the basis of one person per driven kilometre.

Figure 9.3 takes into account the energy required to produce the videoconferencing equipment (videoconferencing device and television) and transportation (automobile and train) and it shows similar results as the information in Figure 9.2. Both figures show that the environmental and resource advantage of videoconferencing over traditional meetings or conferences increases exponentially as the number of travelling participants and the distances increase.

Despite its environmental advantage, videoconferencing does have its limitations. Videoconferencing may not be a viable alternative if (a) the participants have never personally met; (b) important topics better suited for face-to-face communication are to be addressed; and (c) the conference serves the goal of building or maintaining trust and understanding in a business relationship.

A critical factor in the diffusion of videoconferencing is the willingness of participants to work with this specific medium (e.g. a good deal of discipline regarding conversational behaviour may be required). Particularly for people in the business sector, videoconferencing represents an opportunity to make a positive contribution to the environment in the workplace. However, this environmental advantage can only be realised when it is used as a substitute for and not just as a supplement to traditional meetings and conferences.

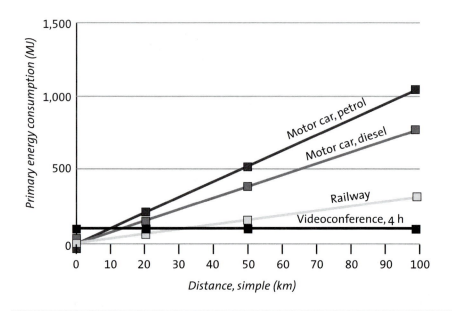

Figure 9.3 **Energy consumption needed for a four-hour videoconference compared to the energy required to operate and produce the particular transportation system**

9.2.4 Eco-assessment of Deutsche Telekom's network infrastructure

9.2.4.1 Background

What are the environmental and resource requirements to operate and maintain the company's vast network infrastructure? To find out, Deutsche Telekom decided to work with the University of Applied Sciences in Wiesbaden/Rüsselsheim in conducting an eco-evaluation of the company's fixed network infrastructure (Regner 2000).

9.2.4.2 Methodology

Using two of the company's network regions (one urban and one rural) as the sample group, the study carried out an environmental examination of the individual network elements (e.g. cable types, cabinets, switching equipment) and used this information to extrapolate the total environmental factors governing the entire network infrastructure. Based on the average service life of 15 years, the study tried to estimate the energy consumption and CO_2 emissions of Deutsche Telekom's network infrastructure and compare the results with other public networks such as road and railway systems. This study is only the first step and future studies need to take into account relevant environmental aspects of microwave systems, mobile communications and other tele-infrastructure systems, as well as the environmental impacts of installing the technology and laying the cable.

9.2.4.3 Results

Our study indicates that Germany's road and rail networks have between 30 and 35 times greater energy intensity level than Deutsche Telekom's fixed network. One may of course argue whether it is valid to compare the energy consumption of Deutsche Telekom's network infrastructure with road and railway networks, since one is used to transport data and information while the other two networks physically transport products and people. However, it may be a useful comparison as it shows the significant variation in energy consumption between telecommunications services and some of the traditional old-economy network infrastructure.

9.3 Telecommunications and the sustainable future

Very few people doubt the often-made claim that information technology will be one of the most important sectors in the future. From supermarket shelves to the stock markets of the world, the impact of this development can be seen everywhere. But, how sustainable is this development? How much social change is ethically acceptable when products can create completely new needs? How much environmental damage is permissible before a company is charged with being irresponsible? While it is impossible to provide definitive answers to these questions, we have hopefully made a valuable contribution by examining the environmental qualities of our company's products and services.

ENVIRONMENTAL IMPACTS OF TELECOMMUNICATIONS SERVICES
Two life-cycle analysis studies

Manfred Zurkirch
Swisscom Ltd, Switzerland

Inge Reichart
Swiss Federal Laboratories for
Materials Testing and Research

The explosion of Internet application usage and service access in recent years, through the World Wide Web, the Telnet or e-mail, has led to a vast increase in the amount of data transferred via this medium. Within Swisscom alone, there are on average 200 electronic mails sent per employee per week. At the same time, the traditional internal mail service has shown a strong decline in the number of documents delivered. Many claim that Internet services provide an important step towards the paperless office, which might imply a significant reduction in waste and environmental burden. The same holds true for telephone books that are being replaced by CD-ROMs and Internet directories. However, one has to bear in mind that considerable additional hardware is needed for these electronic services and that global paper consumption is not on the decline at the moment. This is an important area for study and provides the core of this chapter.

So far, only a few studies have been made of the environmental effects of non-physical, intangible and 'immaterial' services. The trustworthiness of these investigations has often been undermined by three aspects. First, the project sponsors have specific interests leading to a non-negligible influence on the results of the study. A typical example is a sponsor's influence on the setting of the system boundary (the inclusion or exclusion of what exactly is investigated): a very controversial topic. Second, studies often focus only on a specific scenario without considering the general framework. Hence, it is easy to attack the results and to disprove them. Third, the public expects black-and-white statements. In other words, rankings are generally preferred to conditional statements such as 'it depends'. However, this is often the frame in which results of such investigations are expressed.

In this chapter, particular emphasis is put on the setting of system boundaries as well as on checking for a wide range of parameters and their influence on the results. It is possible to adjust the way services are provided only if the effect of all relevant parameters is known.

The results of two such studies are presented here. The first study set out to compare two systems: e-mail and traditional postal services. The comparison covers the infrastructure needed to provide the services as allocated to the different modules such as printing, scanning and transmitting data. The impact assessment of each of these modules is then studied independently. Finally, all the modules are connected to reconstruct a complete system through which the service is provided.

The second study was a joint project between Swisscom and the Swiss Federal Laboratories for Materials Testing and Research (EMPA).[1] Here, 'a search for a telephone number' is taken as reference point in order to compare the following media: CD-ROM, the Internet, an ordinary phone book and the Teleguide. The last is an electronic appliance found in Swiss public telephone booths. The environmental impact was assessed by applying two methods: Ecoindicator 99 and Ecoscarcity. The methods themselves as well as the reasons for choosing them will be explained in the next section.

10.1 Choice of environmental assessment methods

The project sponsors requested assessment methods that are widely accepted in Europe and provide a complete aggregation of data. As a result of this, the CML method (Heijungs *et al.* 1992) was excluded. It was decided to use the European Ecoindicator 99 (Goedkoep and Spriensma 2000) and the Ecoscarcity method '97 (Brand *et al.* 1998). Ecoindicator 99 is an assessment method that has been updated and developed, based on the well-known Ecoindicator 95 (Goedkoep 1995). The Ecoscarcity method '97 (Brand *et al.* 1998) is less widely known, as it is an assessment method referring to the environmental situation in Switzerland. The description of this method is largely based on work by Braunschweig (Braunschweig and Müller-Wenk 1993).

10.1.1 The Ecoscarcity method: basic principles

The method is based on the 'environmental scarcity' approach. It is a quantitative, single-level method of impact assessment. The method was developed between 1988 and 1990 in collaboration with representatives from industry, universities and the government (Ahbe *et al.* 1990) and supplemented by Braunschweig and Müller-Wenk (1993) (see Fig. 10.1).

---

1 Further project sponsors were *Die Neue Zürcher Zeitung* AG (Switzerland), Ringier AG (Switzerland), the Association for the Promotion of Research in the Graphic Arts Industry (Switzerland) and the Commission for Technology and Innovation (Switzerland).

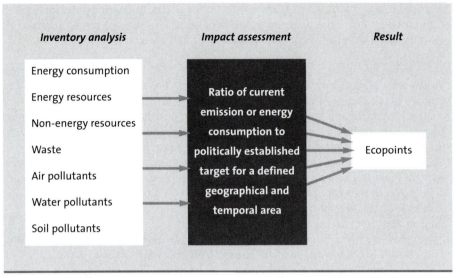

Figure 10.1 **Structure of the impact assessment using the ecoscarcity method**

10.1.2 *Ecofactors*

Calculation of ecofactors requires knowledge of the following flows:[2]

- Current annual flow of potentially hazardous substances
- Critical annual flow of potentially hazardous substances

The current flows are calculated using national statistics. To establish the critical flows, scientific data and legal requirements are used.

When using the formula in Box 10.1 to calculate ecofactors, normalisation, with respect to the critical flow, is first carried out and an impact assessment is made using the relationship between current and critical flow. Ecofactors are dependent on time ('in which year were the flows measured?') and space ('within which geographical area was

---

Ecofactor [1 / unit of environmental impact] = $(1 / F_c) \times (F / F_c) \times a$

F_c = critical flow (per year within a defined geographical area)
F = current flow (per year within the same geographical area)
a = factor without dimensions

Box 10.1 **Formula for calculation of ecofactors**

---

2 A flow is described as an emission (or consumption) within a particular time-span and geographical area.

the current flow measured and the critical flow established?'). Thus the calculation of ecofactors provides different values for different geographical regions, in both absolute and relative terms. This is because of:

- Different technological and economic situations (e.g. different relationship between current and critical flows)

- Different environmental situations (e.g. different data from which the eco-factors have been derived)

- Different social and political objectives for the environmental protection (e.g. different relationships between the various critical flows)

So far, ecofactors have been established for only a few countries, such as Switzerland and the Netherlands (Ahbe *et al.* 1990; Brand *et al.* 1997).

10.1.3 Emissions and energy consumption taken into account

The Ecoscarcity method takes into account pollutants into air, water and soil, and waste, as well as the depletion of scarce energy resources. The consumption of other resources such as metals has not been considered in this method, because they are not depleted, which is the evaluation criterion, but dispersed.

10.1.4 Calculation of ecopoints

The ecopoints (EP) are obtained by multiplying the ecofactors by the appropriate amount of materials and electricity used or substances emitted into water, soil and air.

10.2 Comparison of e-mail and traditional postal mail

This chapter presents results based only on the Ecoscarcity method.

10.2.1 Goals and functional unit

During the last two years, Swisscom started to evaluate some of the products it uses with the support of life-cycle assessment (LCA). The know-how gained from this work was used to discuss sustainable development issues with the main suppliers of products. These discussions have led to some positive environmental outcomes. Recently, for instance, Swisscom succeeded in presenting a prototype of an ecological cellular phone at a large IT fair.[3] The phone is lead- and bromide-free, its housing is made of recycled material and its charger is energy-optimised.

Based on this experience, Swisscom decided to move forward and investigate some of its services. A pioneering project was launched aimed at comparing Swisscom's internal

3   Orbit/Comdex in Basel, September 2000, in collaboration with Motorola.

e-mail service with the traditional internal mail service. The significance of the concept 'internal' is developed Section 10.2.2.

The prime goal of the study was to come up with an evaluation that could easily be applied to various scenarios. In this way it would be feasible to assess the environmental burden of services under a different set of assumptions and the effect of changing assumptions on final results. This would enable Swisscom to begin to assess the sustainability of telecommunication services in a transparent, quantitative manner.

It is important to note that clear analysis can only be developed for very specific scenarios. The method cannot answer the more general question of whether e-mail or traditional mail has the larger impact on the environment. In other words, while the study addresses a general functional activity, sending a message from A to B, each analysis is based on a scenario that defines parameters such as the size of message, distance to target, means of transport and so on. In order to conduct easy sensitivity analyses, these parameters have to be transparent and easily accessible.

10.2.2 *The system*

The offered services depend on an infrastructure that has to be well understood and taken into account when evaluating the environmental performance of the service. In the following paragraphs the internal mail delivery system of Swisscom and its e-mail infrastructure are briefly outlined.

10.2.2.1 Service A: traditional mail

The organisation of the internal carrier service is shown in Figure 10.2. The organisation is quite straightforward and does not need much explanation. However, it is worth mentioning that the internal mail service relies on the federal mail service for delivery to villages and cities. Within the same village the mail is transported by the internal postal service. At a quick glance, means of transport, distance and size of the mail have the most significant impact on the environment.

10.2.2.2 Service B: e-mail

The infrastructure needed to provide the e-mail service is shown in Figure 10.3. It is a little more complicated than traditional mail. One particular challenge was making an accurate definition of the hardware utilised per mail sent; as communication via e-mail is based on the Internet Protocol (IP), it is hard to tell which path the e-mail takes.

With IP every message is split up into different packets, each of which can choose a different path depending on traffic jams. Therefore, geographical distances are not correlated at all with the distances an e-mail really travels to reach the recipient. In other words, the definition of the number of switches, routers and servers that are, on average, involved in the transmission of an e-mail is not straightforward.

Within Swisscom, however, the situation is quite different. The network used for the internal transfer of data (e.g. e-mail, intranet) is called Infnet. This network is totally independent of the rest of the Internet and it is very dynamic (i.e. more bandwidth is rented if needed). The total traffic on this network, as well as the specific traffic due to e-mails, is well known. Hence an estimate of the traffic per e-mail is possible. Addi-

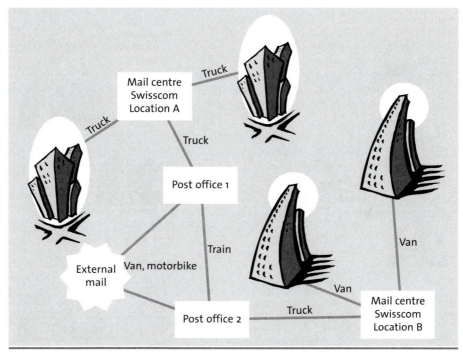

Figure 10.2 **Organisation of the swisscom internal mail delivery service (mail from external sources is excluded)**

tionally, it is convenient that the e-mail servers are strictly separated from the WWW servers for security reasons and that the exact number of servers and routers is known.

In this study we took into account the servers and routers but excluded the cables. This decision was taken for three main reasons. There is hardly any LCA data available on cables, the e-mail traffic is only responsible for 3% of the total traffic on the Infnet, and the assessment of a structure as complicated as the Infnet would have been far beyond the scope of this study. As such, it seemed an acceptable simplification.

10.2.3 System boundaries

Now that the two systems have been examined, the question arises as to how important sending an e-mail or a letter is compared with the other activities that take place in this system. Figure 10.4 shows a diagram of the electronic and traditional mail systems.

It is necessary to produce LCAs for each module included in the system. As some modules encompass different system elements, it does not make sense to choose them for establishing the system boundaries. The module 'Print document', for instance, includes the LCA of a printer and that of the paper used. Table 10.1 shows the most important system

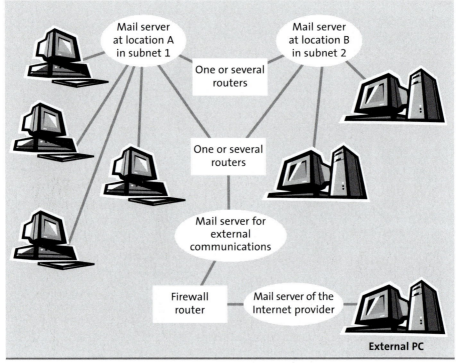

Figure 10.3 *Infrastructure required for the sending and storing of e-mails within Swisscom: a simplified diagram*

elements and provides a rough outline of the system boundaries chosen in this study in order to calculate the environmental impact of the modules as shown in Figure 10.4.[4]

Before presenting the evaluation, the definitions of the main terms used in the evaluation are given below:

- **System elements:** hardware evaluated using LCA (see Table 10.1)

- **Modules:** aspects of a whole system; contains one or several system elements (see Fig. 10.4)

- **Scenario:** combination of modules with fixed parameters (e.g. number of pages printed, distance covered); very specific application of a service

10.2.4 *Evaluation procedure*

In the evaluation procedure three steps are always followed:

---

4 Clearly, it was not possible to make a detailed LCA of all these elements. Most of the data has been taken from literature or assumptions have been made.

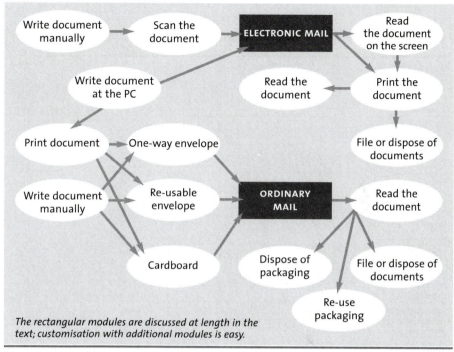

The rectangular modules are discussed at length in the text; customisation with additional modules is easy.

Figure 10.4 **Modular approach to the systems e-mail and ordinary mail**

1. Determination of the point of reference: that is, definition of the environmental impact per sheet, second, kilometre or byte. Definition of a user profile.

2. Collection of data from literature, manufacturers, inventories (e.g. Frischknecht *et al.* 1994; Maibach *et al.* 1995) and our own measurements (energy consumption in the use phase)

3. Evaluation utilising the Ecoscarcity method[5]

To illustrate these steps the evaluation of the system element 'PC' is set out below:

10.2.4.1 Environmental burden of a PC

1. As time is a crucial parameter when using a PC, the environmental burden per minute of operation is evaluated. A typical PC profile for a business user is 2,350 h/year, of which 20% is in standby mode and 80% in working mode.

---

5 As some of the LCAs found in literature have only been evaluated with the Ecoscarcity method and the inventories were not available, the assessment of some of the system elements could not be made with Ecoindicator 99.

System element	Raw material extraction	Production	Packaging	Trans-portation	Use	Main-tenance	End-of-life
Sheet (white)	✓	✓	✓	✓	–	–	✓
Sheet (grey)	✓	✓	✓	✓	–	–	✓
Envelope (white)	✓	✓	✓	✓	–	–	✓
Envelope (grey)	✓	✓	✓	✓	–	–	✓
Cardboard box	✓	✓	✓	✓	–	–	✓
Bulb (75 W)	✓	✓	✓	✓	✓	–	✓
Energy-saving bulb (15 W)	✓	✓	✓	✓	✓	–	✓
PC (including screen)	✓	✓	✓	✓	✓	✗	✓
Printer	✓	✓	✓	✓	✓	✗	✗
Scanner	✓	✓	✓	✗	✓	✗	✗
Air conditioning of servers	✗	✗	✗	✗	✓	✗	✗
Server	✓	✓	–	–	✓	✗	✓
Network/Infnet	✓	✓	✗	✗	✓	✗	✗
Truck (3.5 tons)	✓	✓	✓	✓	✓	✗	✓
Truck (28 tons)	✓	✓	✓	✓	✓	✗	✓
Train	✓	✓	✓	✓	✓	✗	✓
Buildings	–	–	–	–	–	–	–
Infrastructure for raw material extraction and production	✗	✗	✗	✗	✗	✗	✗
Production of software	✗	✗	✗	✗	✗	✗	✗
Office infrastructure (furniture, pencils, etc.)	–	–	–	–	–	–	–

✓ Considered

✗ Not considered (insufficient quality of data/system too complicated)

– Irrelevant

Table 10.1 **System boundaries for the essential system elements (some of these elements, obviously, are part of several modules)**

2. The data for the production of PCs has been taken from a detailed study (Soldera 1995). This study is based on a DEC (486 DX4, 100 MHz) and Panasonic monitor (15", VGA).[6] However, the power consumption data was generated from our own measurements. The results are as follows: Dell OptiPlex Gxi (Pentium II, 166 MHz): 50 W (sleep mode not activated); Dell Monitor (17"): 65 W (sleep mode 20 W).

3. The production, distribution and end-of-life burden of a PC gives rise to a burden of 300,000 EP.[7] If this number is distributed over the PC's assumed life-

6   There are also more recent studies on computers and screens that have been taken into account for the comparison of phone directories (Reichart *et al.* 2000 and references therein).

7   This is for the production of a cathode-ray-tube monitor and not a flat screen. Unfortunately, there is no detailed LCA on flat screens available. Recently, Jungbluth and Frischknecht (2000)

span of five years, we can calculate a burden of 0.53 EP/minute. For the defined user profile, the energy consumption adds up to 249 kWh per year, which results in 100,300 EP for a five-year period or 0.18 EP/minute.[8] In total, the PC is responsible for 0.71 EP/minute of use.

In the same way data can be collected for all the elements of the system. The most important results are presented in Table 10.2.

System element	Environmental burden	Source
PC	0.71 EP/minute	Soldera 1995; own energy consumption measurements
Scanner	0.23 EP/minute 0.13 EP/sheet*	Basic material list (Canon); own energy consumption measurements
Printer (inkjet)	0.125 EP/minute or 0.025 EP/sheet**	Basic material list (Canon); own energy consumption measurements
Server	3.50 EP/MByte[†]	Soldera 1995; own energy consumption measurements
Routers	0.114 EP/MByte[††]	Soldera 1995; own energy consumption measurements
Air conditioning (network)	1.65 EP/MByte[‡]	Own energy consumption measurements
Train	33.30 EP/tkm	Maibach *et al.* 1995
Truck	261 EP/tkm	Maibach *et al.* 1995
Car	190 EP/tkm	Maibach *et al.* 1995
Envelope	21.50 EP/envelope	Habersatter *et al.* 1998[‡‡]
Sheet (white)	5.10 EP/sheet	Habersatter *et al.* 1998
Bulb (for reading)	0.39 EP/minute (75 W) 0.08 EP/minute (15 W energy-saving bulb)	Mani 1994

*   User profile: 80% standby (4 W); 20% operation (8 W)—data from CanoScan FB620P
** Assumption: 5 sheets per minute; 50% standby (4 W); 50% operation (30 W)
†   It does not make sense to calculate the burden per minute because the time needed for saving and sending e-mails is irrelevant. As these servers are used for e-mails only, the hardware allocation per MByte of used disc space is logically stringent.
†† Based on an IBM Router (3 kg, 35 W); production data inferred from Soldera 1995
‡   This number corresponds to 50% of the energy consumption of the servers—an optimistic assumption because today it is still nearly 100% of the heat generated by the servers that has to be removed.
‡‡ In the source given there are values for all kinds of paper (also recycled paper).

Table 10.2 **Environmental burden caused by the different system elements that are needed for the two services based on the ecoscarcity method**

have conducted a basic comparison. However, as flat screens consist of many transistors, the production of which requires a lot of energy, it can safely be assumed that their environmental impact is not significantly smaller.

8   Assuming a Swiss electricity mix (40% hydro-energy; only about 8% fossil energy), which causes an environmental burden of 80.6 EP per kWh (Frischknecht *et al.* 1994).

10.2.5 *System elements and the complete scenarios*

After evaluating the various system elements, the final stage of the analysis involves assessing the environmental impact of specific scenarios. This is quite straightforward as shown in the two examples given below.

10.2.5.1 Scenario 1

A Word document with a size of 55 kilobytes (typically five pages) is sent over a distance of 20 km and has the following attributes:

- Weight of the document (including envelope): 40 g
- Time to write the document at the PC: 60 minutes
- Time to read the document at the PC: 30 minutes

In Figure 10.5, each module is represented by one bar. The bar 'printing', for instance, includes the burden caused by the printer as well as by the paper used.

10.2.5.2 Scenario 2

A colour photograph of 1 megabyte is sent over a distance of 300 km and has the following attributes:

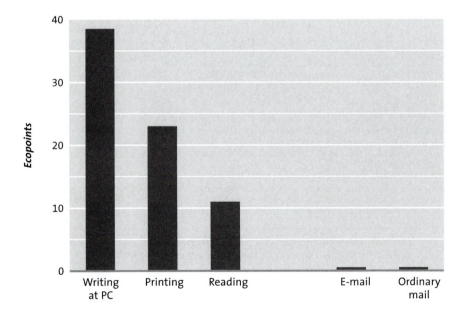

Figure 10.5 *Environmental impact of a specific scenario by means of the ecoscarcity method*

- Weight of document (including envelope): 10 g
- Time to process picture at the PC: 5 minutes
- Time to watch picture at the PC: 2 minutes

10.2.6 Conclusions: results of study 1

All the parameters chosen in scenarios 1 and 2 can be varied individually and the implications for the final results can be readily observed. Unfortunately, in this first study, there was no time to undertake a sophisticated sensitivity analysis. Even so, some interesting conclusions can be drawn.

First, it is often the case that the peripheral modules generate the largest share of the environmental burden rather than the transmission of an e-mail or the transportation of a letter. In other words, use of the PC and printing or scanning documents has a significant impact on the final results.

Second, there are situations where an e-mail contributes more to the overall environmental burden than ordinary mail (see Fig. 10.6). This might seem surprising, but looking at it in more detail it is not. It is a logical consequence of the assumption that the disk space of the e-mail servers is limited and that new servers have to be installed when the traffic increases.

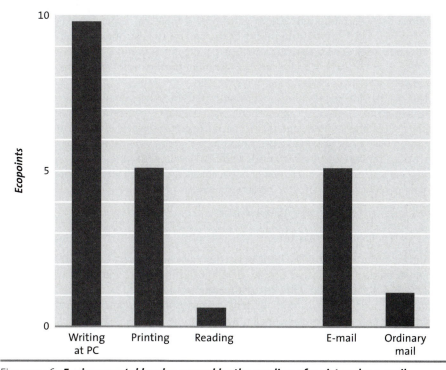

Figure 10.6 **Environmental burden caused by the sending of a picture by e-mail or via ordinary mail**

Using the evaluation derived from the various scenarios, we conclude that for small e-mails (without attachments and about 1 or 2 kilobytes) the break-even point between e-mail and surface mail is reached very quickly. For documents with a size of 15 pages (about 75 kilobytes in Word) the impact is roughly the same for distances up to 20 km. If we take documents that need a large disk space, such as photographs, but which are light after printing, the break-even distance might be as high as a few hundred kilometres. We have to be very careful with these conclusions as they only hold for the specified traffic data (Maibach *et al.* 1995), mails sent within Swisscom and the specified usage scenarios (printers, scanners and so on).

10.3 Comparison of different telephone directories

The second study was conducted together with EMPA St Gallen, a well-established institution in the area of environmental assessment with the expertise to yield more detailed results than the e-mail study discussed above. A report of the study has been published (Reichart *et al.* 2001). Here, only the most interesting results are discussed.

10.3.1 Goals and functional unit

The aim of the second study was to gain more knowledge about the environmental impact as well as to discover improvement options for the use of telephone directories. The research subject was a private search for a telephone number in different kinds of telephone directory, which again serves as a model for the use of shopping catalogues, dictionaries, etc.

There are five basic possibilities when searching for a telephone number in Switzerland: via Internet, CD-ROM, the phone book, the Teleguide—an electronic appliance found in public telephone booths—and the telephone operator (information number 111). The last option has not been taken into account in this study. All of the services mentioned are provided by Swisscom; some are also offered by competitors.

In order to assess the environmental impact of a single search for a telephone number, two parameters need first of all to be determined:

- The length of time needed for a search

- The frequency of inquiries

In contrast to the e-mail study within Swisscom, these parameters cannot be determined without defining a specific user profile. Here, the user is a Swiss adult with average intellectual abilities and the capability to use the Internet.

The length of time for a single search was determined empirically by a number of employees at EMPA, who are assumed to represent the average Swiss adult. A variety of simple and complicated addresses had to be checked in the different media. The resulting small differences in time between the media (see Fig. 10.7) are due to differences in handling the various keyboards, the retrieval times of electronic media, etc. In the case of the phone book, it is assumed that reading takes place during daylight hours. Thus, it is

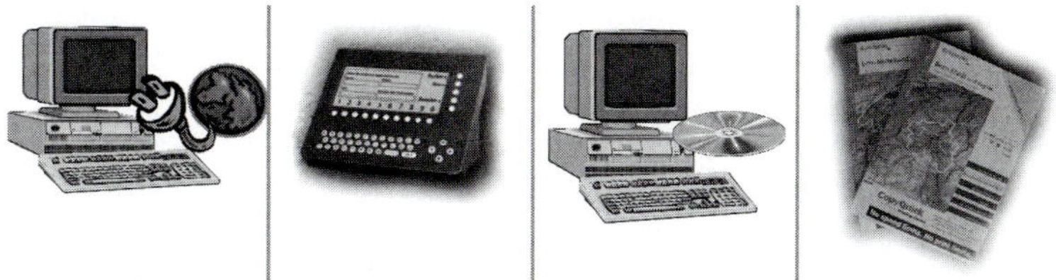

	Online	Teleguide	CD-ROM	Phone book
Time per search	59 seconds	55 seconds	45 seconds	Irrelevant
Frequency	Irrelevant	12/day	2/week	2/week

Figure 10.7 **Functional unit or reference object of 'a search for a telephone number'**

not necessary to know the length of time needed for a single search, as the environmental impact of an inquiry can be determined by frequency alone.

The second parameter, the average frequency of looking up a telephone number, is only definitely known for the publicly used Teleguide, which averages 12 inquiries per day.[9] As the average rate of searching for a telephone number at home is not known, it was assumed to be two inquiries per week (see Fig. 10.7). This parameter will be varied later.

For the phone book, the CD-ROM and the Teleguide, it is essential to know how many times they have been used during their life-span. Only then can the environmental burden caused during production and disposal of the medium be allocated accurately to a single search. If, for instance, a phone book is used only once in its 15-month life, the environmental load of this inquiry would be tremendous.

In the case of the Internet search, it is sufficient to know the length of time needed for a single search, because that time-span is set in relation to the overall active use of the computer. That way the environmental impact caused during production and disposal of the computer can be allocated correctly to an online search as well as to a CD-ROM inquiry.

10.3.2 The system

The above-mentioned user is a typical adult living in an average household in Switzerland,[10] which has a computer, a CD-ROM of telephone numbers and, on average, 1.5 phone books. The computer is used in an average way: i.e. also for other purposes.

The media investigated are specified as follows:

- **Computer:** mid-range desktop computer; state of the art; four-year life-span; switched on for two hours per day (145 W); off for the rest of the time

- **CD-ROM:** includes manual and cardboard packaging; 15-month life-span

9   Internal source, Swisscom.
10 There are, on average, 2.3 people per household in Switzerland.

- **Teleguide:** there is only one type of Teleguide installed in phone booths; seven-year life-span

- **1.5 phone books:** average size in relation to all the 25 Swiss phone books available

As well as the media mentioned, power consumption for the running of the electronic telephone directory as well as for the data transfer in the Internet have been taken into account. Figure 10.8 shows the system boundary in a simplified way. Only the updating of the telephone directory has not been included. The media investigated are taken into account from 'cradle to grave', i.e. from the extraction of raw materials to disposal, including all transportation processes. Furthermore, the recycling of the paper for the phone book has been considered.[11] In the case of paper products, part of the waste paper is incinerated. A credit[12] is given for the generation of heat and power through the burning of paper, which is assumed to partly replace oil heating as well as power generation in Switzerland.

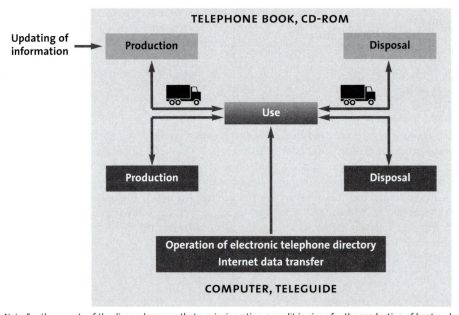

Note: For those parts of the disposal process that are incineration, a credit is given for the production of heat and power generated from waste.

Figure 10.8 *System boundary*

---

11   As standard allocation procedure, the 'allocation based on the number of subsequent uses', also called 'co-product allocation', has been used. This implies that the environmental impact for paper production and recycling is summarised taking the average number of life-cycles per fibre in Switzerland. The environmental impact is then divided by the average number of cycles. This gives the average environmental impact of each life-span of the paper.
12   The credit is the 'negative' environmental impact shown in Figs. 10.9 and 10.12.

The assumed electricity mix requires further explanation. During the production phase of the media, the relevant national electricity mix was used depending on the country of production: i.e. the average European electricity mix for the production of electronic goods and the Swiss electricity mix for the production of paper products. As the use of either media is presumed to take place in Switzerland, the Swiss electricity mix was assumed for the use phase of electronic media. However, a sensitivity analysis was conducted for the use phase, whereby the Swiss electricity mix was replaced by the average European electricity mix.

10.3.3 Evaluation of the environmental burden

All the processes within the system boundary were modelled and assessed for their environmental impact. The project team used the 'Umberto' software and the two assessment methods Ecoindicator 99 and Ecoscarcity. Results will be shown here only for the Ecoscarcity method, as application of the other method does not offer much new insight.

Data for the production processes was, in the case of paper media, mostly collected from manufacturers and, in the case of electronic media,[13] based on literature. Transportation and disposal processes were based completely on existing inventories. Much of the data for the use phase was gathered by EMPA.

LCAs are nearly always hampered by the fact that no calculation of error is made and, as a consequence, the error bar of the result is not known. In order to—at least partly—account for this, we will only claim a difference in the environmental impact of media if that difference is greater than 100%.

10.3.4 Results

The environmental burden of a single inquiry is much lower for the online service and the Teleguide compared to the phone book and the CD-ROM (see Fig. 10.9). This holds true under the assumption that the average frequency of inquiries is twice a week in the user's household. The high environmental impact shown for the online service and the Teleguide is due to the production of pulp and paper for the phone book, and the manual and the cardboard packaging for the CD-ROM. Roughly a third of the environmental impact of the CD-ROM could be reduced by replacing the present manual with a file on the CD-ROM itself and the omission of the cardboard box.

The question remains: what influence has the assumption about the user's frequency of inquiries on the result obtained? The relationship between environmental burden and frequency of use is shown in Figure 10.10. At low frequencies, we find the difference already seen between phone book and CD-ROM on the one hand and online service and Teleguide on the other. Once telephone numbers are looked up more than eight times a week, the environmental impact of all media is the same. There are three reasons for this. First, the environmental impact per search in the phone book and CD-ROM depends mostly on frequency. Second, as the Teleguide is used by the public, a behavioural change of a single person has only marginal influence on the way the appliance is used overall.

---

13   In the case of the computer, there is a significant data gap for the production of about 40% of the weight of the electronic parts.

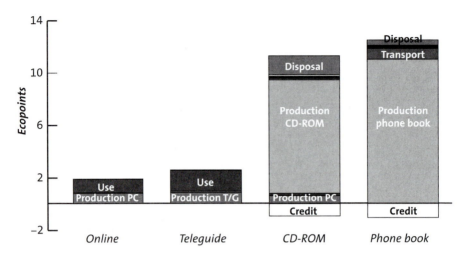

This evaluation holds true under the condition that the phone directories are used twice a week, except for the Teleguide, where there are 12 requests per day.

Figure 10.9 *Environmental impact of a inquiry for a telephone number: assessed using the ecoscarcity method*

Third, the environmental impact of the online service depends only on time per search, not on frequency (see Section 10.3.1).

As the environmental impact of the online service and the Teleguide becomes increasingly relevant at higher frequencies of use, closer investigation is indicated. As can be seen in Figure 10.9, nearly half of the environmental burden is due to the production of the computer or the Teleguide, while over half is due to use phase. Figure 10.11 shows the environmental impact of that use phase, i.e. the power consumption. The biggest energy 'consumers' are the Teleguide itself, the running of the telephone network, data transfer in the Internet and, finally, the running of the private computer. The high amount of energy consumption of the Teleguide is mostly due to standby losses.

In order to acquire greater insight into the way individual parameters influence the result, many sensitivity analyses were conducted. Only those sensitivity results will be presented that had a major influence on the result previously shown in Figures 10.9 and 10.10.

An example of a significant finding is the situation where the results of an inquiry are printed on a private printer. If this happens, an extra amount of roughly seven ecopoints has to be added to the environmental impact of a single inquiry. Hence, the environmental advantage of, for example, the online service, at low user frequencies, disappears if the inquiry results are printed. The additional impact is mostly due to the production of the paper.[14]

14 Assumption: wood-free, uncoated paper.

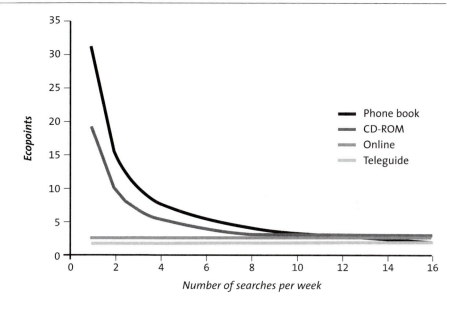

Figure 10.10 *Relationship between the environmental burden caused by one inquiry and the frequency with which telephone numbers are looked up by the user*

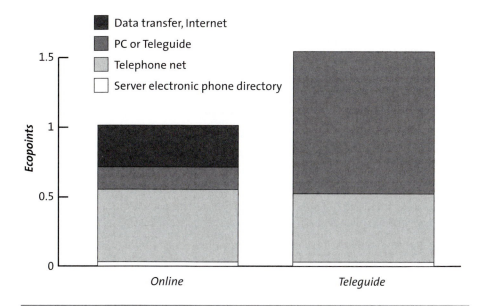

Figure 10.11 *Environmental impact of the online service and Teleguide during use phase*

Further, the influence of the assumed electricity mix during use phase was tested. We replaced the Swiss electricity mix with the average European electricity mix. This exchange is presumed to represent the use of the investigated media in a country elsewhere in Europe, where electricity is generated to a much larger extent from fossil fuels relative to Switzerland, which has a rather high proportion of energy generated by hydropower. Figure 10.12 shows the significant influence of the electricity mix. The increase in the environmental impact caused by changing the electricity mix is shown on the top of each of the electronic media, within the dotted lines. Here, as a reference point, the initial frequency of two inquiries per week is taken. As a consequence, any environmental advantage seen in the online service or the teleguide is lost, even at low use frequencies, if the electronic media are consuming energy that is produced by a large proportion of fossil fuel instead of renewable energy sources, as is the case in Switzerland.

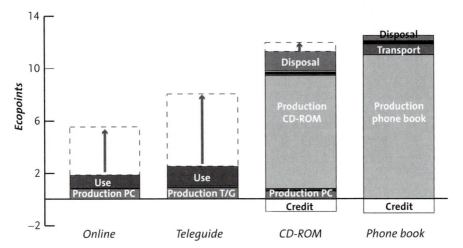

This evaluation holds true under the condition that the phone directories are used twice a week, except for the Teleguide, where there are 12 requests per day.

Figure 10.12   **The environmental impact of a single inquiry and the influence of the electricity mix assumed during use phase**

10.3.5 Conclusions: study 2

Summarising the results, the online service and the Teleguide offer an environmental advantage in comparison to a CD-ROM and a phone book as long as:

- The directories are used at low frequencies, which is typical for private use.

- The inquiry results are not printed.

- The electricity consumed by the electronic media is generated to a large extent from renewable energy sources.

If the phone book is used eight or more times a week, the environmental impact of all media is the same (under the assumption of the Swiss electricity mix during use phase).

10.4 Final remarks on the methodology

The Ecoscarcity method and Ecoindicator 99—like all quantitative assessment methods—are supposed to provide exact results. However, this is not the case. In fact, even in detailed LCA studies a large number of assumptions are made to compensate for the lack of input data. For example, it is nearly impossible to collect all data on the production of electronic parts used in the system because their supply chain is very complex. In the case of PC production there are hundreds of suppliers involved in the final product. Therefore, data requests often cannot be answered accurately. The assessment methods themselves are a second source of inaccuracy as they are based on fragmentary statistics and assumptions. In fact, the author uses the following rules to interpret LCA data:

Differences between two scenarios

< 50 %	equal
50–100%	trend
> 100%	clear difference

Although there are uncertainties, the methodology has the advantage of clarity and transparency. Sensitivity analysis for the various modules can easily be accomplished and provides a sound understanding of the relationship between telecommunications services and the environment. In fact, each scenario can be adjusted to represent a specific use of a service in order to find out which parameters have the most significant effects on the overall environmental burden.

EXPLORING THE GLOBAL–LOCAL AXIS
Telecommunications and environmental sustainability in Japan

Brendan Barrett
United Nations University/Institute
of Advanced Studies, Japan

Ichiro Yamada
NTT Lifestyle and Environmental
Technology Laboratories, Japan

An increasing number of policy-makers and researchers around the world are currently trying to link local information and decision-making with global sustainability trends. They are reflecting on the pressing global problems facing modern society and examining ways in which local measures can contribute to understanding and amelioration of environmental problems. This tendency is clearly evident in recent efforts to deal with climate change where bottom-up initiatives have been accompanied by complementary efforts to downscale both science and policy (Kates and Torrie 1998).

Correspondingly, Ulrich Beck, in his recent work entitled *What is Globalisation?*, highlights the need for our institutions and organisations to reorganise themselves along a global–local axis (Beck 2000). In this so-called 'second modernity' typified by globalisation, Beck argues that no event on our planet can be seen as purely local since 'all inventions, victories and catastrophes affect the whole world'. Echoing the visionary works of Marshall McLuhan on the emergence of the 'global village' brought about by our electronic interdependence (McLuhan 1962), Roland Robertson stresses how widely and deeply the awareness of the world as a single place has become part of everyday reality (Robertson 1992).

He also argues that global and local are not mutually exclusive and indeed local must be understood as an aspect of the global. To put it simply, globalisation implies the coming together of local cultures, or more precisely a process of 'glocalisation'. This is not an entirely neutral development and as Bauman (1998) so clearly explains both globalisation and localisation can be understood as expressions of new polarisations and stratification in society. Nowhere is this more apparent than with respect to the emergence of the information society and the Internet.

The contemporary 'digital divide' at the global level is clear to all observers but what remains uncertain is the potential impact on the distribution of power, wealth, privileges and freedoms. Social projects that seek to bridge the digital divide by providing greater community access to information society technologies (ISTs), while fundamentally important *per se*, must be critically scrutinised in the context of the motivations of the stakeholders involved in project promotion.

At the time of writing, Japan appears to have one foot firmly planted on the wrong side of the global digital divide. Most recent statistics for 2000 indicate that around 20% of Japanese are currently online, which represents some 27 million citizens.[1] However, a large proportion (figures vary) is accessing the Internet via mobile phones, mainly for e-mail and travel/entertainment information.

The degree of Internet penetration into other sectors of society (e-commerce and government services such as health, education and environmental protection) is far behind that of the United States and other leading countries. This may all change in the near future especially with the adoption by the government of Japan of the November 2000 Basic Information Technology Strategy which seeks to turn the country into an IT leader within five years through four basic measures:

- Development of an ultra-high-speed network infrastructure and competition policies

- Facilitation of electronic commerce

- Realisation of electronic government

- Nurturing high-quality human resources

For Nippon Telegraph and Telephone Corporation (NTT) these proposals represent both a significant opportunity and a threat. As the largest telecommunications carrier in Japan,[2] NTT has been blamed, perhaps unfairly, in some quarters for dragging its feet and in some respects hindering the spread of the information society within Japan (Low *et al.* 1999).

However, these recent moves on the part of the national administration firmly place the burden of responsibility on NTT to perform competitively on the global market while at the same time provide services that enhance local capacities and meet local needs. We can see, quite clearly, that NTT must embrace the above-mentioned global—local axis while at the same time ensuring that the policies and projects it pursues do not create a new socially unacceptable stratification. This is no simple task.

In this chapter we explore these new challenges for NTT within the context of a very specific theme: environmental sustainability. In particular, we focus on the local—global dimension by examining a collaborative project currently under way in the north of Japan entitled the Iwate Environment Network (IEN).

This project includes participation from an international agency, the United Nations University/Institute of Advanced Studies, and a local government, Iwate Prefectural Government. It highlights the new environmental and social responsibilities that major

---

1   The data is taken from the Nua Internet Surveys website: www.nua.com.
2   Telecommunications is used broadly to include the basic infrastructure supporting the information society. The so-called information industries are more extensive and include computers, entertainment/content and equipment.

telecommunications corporations need to assume and the new forms of partnership arrangements that appear to be awakening in support of this social function as part of the sustainable transformation of the information technology industry.

11.1 Telecommunications and the environment: a global movement

In the post-1992 Earth Summit world, it is worthy of note that the global telecommunications sector has paid considerable attention to the environmental implications of its activities through the leadership of the International Telecommunication Union (ITU). Environmental sustainability was a key theme at both the 1994 World Telecommunication and Development Conference (WTDC) held in Buenos Aires and the Plenipotentiary Conference of the ITU in Kyoto in the same year. It is interesting to note that the Japanese delegation to the WTDC submitted a study on the role of ISTs in alleviating urban congestion.

They argued that online banking and teleworking could reduce the need for travel contingent on three factors: (a) the level of development of the telecommunication infrastructure; (b) existing dominant means of transport; and (c) social and business circumstances. Other delegations indicated the role of these new technologies in support of the monitoring of greenhouse gas emissions or as a means to promote sustainable and integrated rural development.

In Kyoto, delegates went further with the adoption of Resolution 35 stating that telecommunications technologies have an important role in protecting the environment through monitoring, reducing paperwork, promoting rural development and reducing congestion, and by facilitating rapid decisions in support of environmental protection. In addition to seeking greater information dissemination on the environmentally friendly role of these technologies, the delegates called on the ITU to undertake further studies, organise seminars and training programmes as well as exhibitions.[3]

At the regional level, the first European workshop on ecodesign in the telecommunications industry was held in London on 3–4 March 1994. Moreover, the European Institute for Research and Strategic Studies in Telecommunications (EURESCOM) based in Germany has undertaken several projects on the theme of telecommunications and the environment. Project 518 specifically deals with this thematic area and includes participation from 12 European telecommunications carriers including Belgacom, British Telecom, Deutsche Telekom and France Telecom. One major outcome from this project was the preparation of a 'Charter of Environmental Commitment' which the project participants have adopted.

From September 1995 to March 1997 EURESCOM systematically explored the commercial opportunities arising from sustainable development and the possibility of identifying common areas of environmental improvement for public network operators.[4] The

---

3 For more information see the website of the International Telecommunication Union: www. itu.int.

4 A pre-study (project 501) was also undertaken from January to September 1995 to, among other things, identify the possibilities for telecommunications to support sustainable development.

first project research report was published in November 1996 entitled *Calling for a Better Tomorrow: Environmental Improvement through the Use of Telecommunication Services* (EURESCOM 1996).

The report highlighted six areas where societal/environmental benefits could ensue from more extensive use of telecommunications, namely: energy, materials consumption, communication/knowledge, data transfer, travel/transport and culture/leisure. Specific examples are quoted. For instance, the potential energy efficiency of telecommunications was illustrated through comparison between the 1994–95 CO_2 emissions of British Airways flights at 13 million tonnes with the 2 million tonnes emitted from the entire BT network. Other studies have been undertaken on the potential for improved waste management in the telecommunications industry, benchmarking on network energy consumption, ecodesign of equipment, utilisation of renewable energy and energy conservation, and need for environmental training programmes.[5]

Many of the proposals arising from these studies have been incorporated in the operations of the European telecommunications carriers; BT offers perhaps the most comprehensive coverage of environmental issues and provides a comprehensive set of environmental performance reports from 1994 onwards.[6] The environmental activities of BT are extensive and include life-cycle assessment, ISO 14001 compliance and contribution to the environmental initiatives of other bodies including local government and Local Agenda 21 specifically.

Elsewhere in the world, we can note that interesting work has been undertaken in Latin America that culminated in an assessment of the impact of telecommunications in sustainable development presented at the Summit of the Americas on Sustainable Development held in Bolivia in December 1996. Commenting on the huge economic power of the global information industry, which was estimated in 1995 to have a revenue of nearly US$2 trillion, the summit highlighted the potentially significant environmentally beneficial impacts from the telecommunications sector and linked it to liberalisation and privatisation reforms.

A similar interest in these issues can be found in North America with discussions taking place mainly in the US Telecom Association, which has an active environmental committee and runs major environmental conferences every two years. The May 2001 conference dealt specifically with the 'Impact of the Telecom Industry on the Environment' including themes such as managing environmental liabilities, environmental reporting, environmental impacts of e-commerce, teleworking and emerging network technologies.[7] A hard edge is added to this activity through the direct intervention of the US Environmental Protection Agency, which, in January 1998, began inviting the telecommunications companies to take advantage of the unique self-policing measures on the discovery, disclosure, correction and prevention of environment-related hazards instituted in 1995.

Moreover, two leading telecommunication/Internet-supporting companies, AT&T and Nortel Networks, have introduced comprehensive programmes to reduce paper consumption through the use of information technologies, heightened employee awareness

5   For more information see the EURESCOM website: www.eurescom.de.
6   Complete information on the environmental aspects of BT's activities including performance reports from 1997 to 2000 can be found at www.bt.com/world/environment.
7   For more information see the USTA website: www.usta.org.

and increased use of electronic mail. For instance, between 1997 and 1998, Nortel Networks' intranet resulted in paper use reduction of 1140 metric tons, a 17% cut (and a 25% reduction in tons per dollar of sales) (Romm *et al.* 1999).

Quite clearly from the above examples, we can note growing international interest in the links between this important growth sector and the environment as well as national pressures to reform the industry and to ensure enhanced environmental performance. This situation also applies in Japan where in May 1998 the Ministry of Post and Telecommunications published a report entitled *Addressing Global Environmental Preservation through Information Communications Systems* (MPT 1998).

The report was prepared by the Telecommunications Council and estimated that this sector could assist Japan in reducing its CO_2 emissions by over 4 million tons by 2010–12 in line with the requirements of the Kyoto Protocol.[8] This would be achieved through expansions in teleworking,[9] integrated (intelligent) transport systems, and paper reduction through local area networks utilisation, Internet, intelligent buildings, electronic publishing and distance learning. As shown in the next section, a large part of the responsibility for implementing measures proposed in the above report was placed on the shoulders of NTT. Other institutions encouraged to take action include the Japan Federation of Economic Organisations (Keidanren). Environmental monitoring (particularly of air pollution) was also seen as an important goal and reference was made to the area-wide environmental observation AMeDAS that was developed by NTT.

11.2 **NTT and environmental sustainability**

NTT was restructured in 1999 but remains the dominant domestic telecommunications carrier.[10] The NTT Group, as it is now called, employs around 200,000 (with just over 3,000 working at various research institutes) and in 1998 had a consolidated operating profit of ¥9,729 billion. In the immediate future, the Group's goals are focused in three areas:

- Developing information-based commerce

- Innovative group financial management (leveraging R&D capacities to support all NTT units)

- Enhancement of international operations

---

8   Under the Protocol, Japan is required to reduce emissions by 6%. This has been calculated as approximately 56 millions tons of CO_2.

9   In 1996, the number of regular white-collar employees in Japan who carried out teleworking more than once a week was estimated by the MPT as approximately 680,000 (4% of the total regular white-collar employees in Japan). The MPT also estimated that the number would increase to 2,480,000 in 2001 (MPT 2000).

10   NTT was reorganised in July 1999 into a new system as a holding company. It includes five major operating companies: NTT East, NTT West, NTT Communications, NTT DoCoMo and NTT Data.

Environmental considerations are also a central part of NTT's activities and in 1991 the Group adopted a Global Environmental Charter that places emphasis on paper resource management, prevention of global warming, reductions in environmental load through waste management, establishment of an environmental management system and disclosure of environmental information.

The Charter also mentions the need for NTT to make a social contribution through environmental measures developed in co-ordination with citizens and government agencies. The IEN project discussed in this chapter is one example of the implementation of this objective and illustrates NTT's efforts to bridge the global–local axis highlighted above. In 1999, in order to adapt existing corporate environmental protection activities to the new organisational structure, a basic strategy was prepared entitled 'The NTT Group Ecology Programme 21'. The three interlocking pillars of the programme are shown in Figure 11.1.

Of particular relevance to this chapter is the emphasis placed on the contribution to area-wide ecological communities (which in essence evolved out of the IEN and other related initiatives) and the establishment of Ecology Community Plazas (the first of which was set up in Morioka, Iwate, in May 2000). These centres are being implemented on an experimental basis in order conduct various environmental protection activities determined by the needs of each local community. The Plaza in Morioka provides infor-

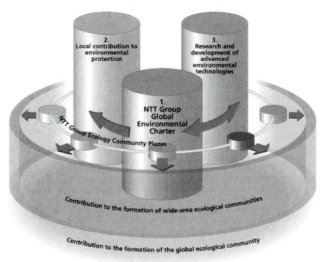

Environmental preservation activities for the future of the Earth
NTT Group Ecology Program 21

In recognition of the importance of environmental preservation as a challenge to be tackled on a global scale in the 21st century, NTT Group is determined to concentrate on the basic policy we call 'NTT Group Ecology Program 21', in order to contribute to the formation of a global ecological community by starting from each locality.

Figure 11.1 *Utilising R&D to transform the NTT Group and creating links with the local community*

mation on the environment derived from the IEN project as well as space and facilities (including teleconferencing) to support NGO networking on the environment and education for local schoolchildren. If the Plazas prove to be successful then NTT plans to create a nationwide network.

Considerably more information on the environmental activities of the NTT Group can be found in the 1999 Environmental Protection Activity Report.[11] Concerning the major goals related to the global environment, NTT has set targets for 2010 to reduce consumption of virgin pulp by 20% compared to the 1991 level, CO_2 emissions to 1990 levels, and ceasing the use of CFCs. The targets for pulp and industrial waste reduction have already been achieved (even surpassed for the latter) but technical difficulties have been encountered with the control of CO_2 emissions mainly due to the rapidly increasing demands for telecommunications.[12] In 1994, NTT terminated first-time CFC use and is now working on the replacement of CFC-reliant turbo refrigerators.

Perhaps most relevant to this chapter is the work of the Group in relation to the promotion of environmental conservation of which the IEN represents a flagship project. Other projects in this area include:

- **Environmental monitoring/sensing technologies.** Initiated in 1991, NTT has developed technologies to monitor air and water quality. This includes testing in Iwate and Kochi prefectures.

- **AMeDAS.** The Automated Meteorological Data Acquisition System was established in 1993 and includes continuous environmental monitoring at 1,300 observation stations across Japan. The Meteorological Agency, local governments and the media utilise the data.

- **Regional air pollution monitoring.** In 1997, local governments in Japan operated 2,135 fixed-point observation stations for air pollutants such as SO_2 and NO_x. In 1995, NTT Saitama branch began connecting 50 monitoring stations in the prefecture utilising an ISDN link enabling rapid collection and assessment of data. When smog incidents occur, warning messages are distributed by fax to local municipalities, schools and residences. Similar projects are under consideration in Nagasaki, Mie and Akita.

- **Teleworking.** NTT is undertaking research on 'information-intensive' home environments and corporate information systems employing ISDN and optical fibre networks.

- **World Nature Network (WNN).** Established in 1995, this online information source covers issues such as nature conservation around the globe, leisure, society and environment. This is an important resource for the Kids' Eco-Club system of Japan.

- **Kankyo (Environmental) Goo.** In 1999, NTT established 'Kankyo Goo' as an online environmental information service that employs the use of sophisticated

---

11   The report can be downloaded from the NTT website at www.ntt.co.jp.
12   It is estimated that, without comprehensive measures, electricity consumption (and associated CO_2 generation) by NTT activities could reach 10 billion kWh in 2010 which compares with 3.4 billion kWh in 1990.

information query and retrieval services. The site is very popular with over 800,000 hits per month.

What do all these initiatives exemplify? In part they highlight the ongoing institutional transformation that has been stimulated by the need to respond to environmental problems. This is the subject of much scholarship in the social sciences (and environmental sociology) under the meta-theory of ecological modernisation (Mol and Sonnenfeld 2000). This theoretical perspective offers five basic driving forces behind this transformative process that can be linked to the strategic directions employed by NTT as follows:

- Technologies (and science) are valued for their actual and potential role in curing and preventing environmental problems. NTT's approach to environmental issues is very much technology-driven but includes efforts to add a social dimension.

- Increasing importance of market dynamics and economic agents such as producers and consumers. NTT is seeking to provide environmental services for its consumers and develop environmental projects with multiple stakeholders, keeping in mind long-term market dynamics ensuing from the shift to an information society.

- Transformation of the role of the nation-state with the emergence of more decentralised and consensual styles of governance. NTT is enhancing its links with local communities and experimenting with the use of the Internet as an information dissemination tool. A future direction could include greater involvement in local consensual policy formulation along the lines of Local Agenda 21, perhaps following the model from BT.

- Modifications in the position, role and ideology of social movements. NTT is opening up increasingly to social movements through information disclosure, although progress is slow. Greater opportunities do exist for NTT to further explore these links through projects such as IEN.

- Changing discursive practices and new ideologies. Businesses such as NTT are no longer allowed to neglect the environment completely. Nor is it acceptable to counter-position economic and environmental interests. Instead we note how NTT and other telecommunications companies around the world are adopting and participating in the environmental discourse and the associated ideologies (zero emissions, ISO 14001, industrial ecology, factor 4, The Natural Step, and so on). Put simply, responding to environmental issues has become an ideological driving force for business opportunity.

Social theories such as ecological modernisation provide a useful framework by which to understand the changing global patterns of the telecommunications industry and place this transformation process within the context of broader social change (the impact of the so-called global modernity) in Western industrialised countries (Spaargaren *et al.* 2000). The IEN project, although never actually conceived with these goals in mind, provides a convenient experimental space to explore some of the themes outlined above. It represents one platform whereby we can investigate the implications of the global–

local axis in considering issues such as the environment, information and institutional change in a social learning context.

11.3 Iwate Environment Network: a collaborative project

The Iwate Environment Network (IEN) is a collaborative effort between government, academia and business founded on a partnership between NTT, Iwate Prefectural Government (IPG) and the Institute of Advanced Studies (IAS) of the United Nations University (UNU).[13] Through this initiative, multimedia and information technologies (mainly the Internet) are utilised to gather information on environmental conditions in Iwate.

The project provides environmental information that is relevant to people throughout their entire lives with the support from local schools and universities. Special events have been organised for the general public and sub-projects implemented to promote community participation as well as to provide ideas and approaches (mainly zero emissions and The Natural Step) to green entrepreneurs and decision-makers. The environmental education and social dimensions of this project are particularly important (although this was not initially the case).

It is envisaged that as the project evolves in the future it could become a case study for the UNU/IAS Virtual University[14] by examining the roles of local universities, museums, schools, public education centres, various stakeholders and the community in the development and utilisation of knowledge (Grove-White 1996). Consideration is also being given to how best to use this knowledge to develop local solutions to pressing environmental problems.

Interestingly, compared with many locations in Japan, Iwate Prefecture is relatively free from significant environmental problems. Located in the north of the main island of Honshu, Iwate has a small population of around 1.4 million but is the second-largest prefecture in terms of land area with over 15,000 km². It can be described as a periphery region with respect to its proximity to the main economic development areas of Japan, and with a small manufacturing sector the growth of the local economy has been sluggish.

The local administration, and the young and energetic Governor Hiroya Masuda in particular, are keen to create a new model for the development of the prefecture. They face numerous structural problems including a rapidly ageing population (18% of the

---

13 The original idea for the establishment of the network developed out of an earlier collaboration between UNU and NTT to co-organise a forum on Multimedia and the Global Environment in October 1997. Following that collaboration, NTT submitted a proposal to UNU/IAS for a project entitled 'The Ecology Network'. In subsequent negotiations the project design was modified and IPG was invited to participate as the field for the research activity. The first project meeting between the three parties took place at UNU on 11 December 1997. The three parties signed an agreement in September 1998 and the project was officially launched at UNU/IAS in March 1999 and will continue until March 2002.

14 The Virtual University Initiative at UNU/IAS explores the utilisation of information technologies and the Internet to provide distance-learning opportunities to an extensive global community of scholars.

local citizenry is over 60 compared with 14% for the rest of Japan). A number of policies are being developed under the banners of Information–People–Environment. These policies seek to promote Iwate as the 'Environmental Capital' of Japan (IPG 1999). The IEN is one project contributing to this overall goal and also matches the information society policies currently being promoted by the prefectural authority.

Recent data on the number of Internet users around Japan indicates that Iwate Prefecture is placed 17th with respect to the percentage of the total population that has used the Internet in the past year. On average 20% of the Japanese population has access to the Internet. However, as shown in Figure 11.2, the regional distribution is very uneven from a high of 30% for Kanagawa to a low of 2% for Yamaguchi. Iwate is below the national average at 14% of the population: about 100,000 persons. Officials from Iwate Prefecture believe that home usage of the Internet is much smaller at around 3% of all households.

A major concern therefore is how best to stimulate the shift to an information society so that Iwate is not left on the wrong side of the digital divide. A major plan to tackle this issue head-on was developed in 1998 by the prefectural authority and includes provisions for the development of a fibre-optic network linking key focal centres (prefectural

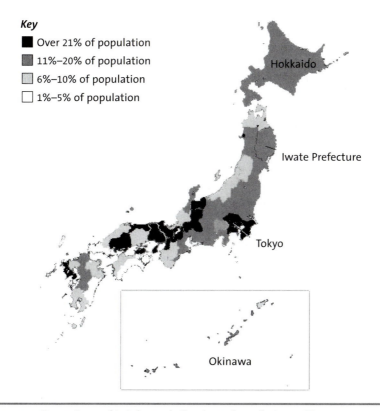

Key

- ■ Over 21% of population
- ▨ 11%–20% of population
- ▧ 6%–10% of population
- ☐ 1%–5% of population

Hokkaido

Iwate Prefecture

Tokyo

Okinawa

Figure 11.2 ***Percentage of total population in each prefecture of Japan using the Internet in 1999***

regional offices, hospitals, universities, etc.) by 2005 (IPG 1998). The main concerns, however, relate to the type of information that is likely to become accessible via this new infrastructure—hence the attractiveness of pilot projects such as the IEN. However, this type of pilot project has required significant investment for the collaborating partners. NTT alone has invested about ¥300 million (US$270,000) on equipment and content development in the past two years and roughly US$45,000 on maintenance of the equipment. Personnel expenses are not included. Furthermore, inclusion of all expenses (salaries, etc.) for IPG and UNU/IAS could take the total costs for the project to date to over US$0.5 million.

11.4 **Approach and achievements**

The IEN project adopts an action-oriented research method based on field-testing and experimentation. A multidisciplinary research team has been established bringing together practitioners and researchers from a variety of fields including education, social sciences, information and environmental technologies. In addition, an environmental education advisory group composed of local teachers and professors, NGOs and business representatives was set up to propose and evaluate sub-projects with an environmental education component.

The first task in the project development and the initial priority for NTT's participation in the project was the establishment of a prototype Web-accessible information system, incorporating the environmental monitoring sensors (for air and water) supported by information databases. This involved the field-testing of new monitoring technologies developed in NTT laboratories.

Second, the information collection, management, processing and delivery component of the project involved the placement of sensors, transmission, storage and processing of environmental data. A decentralised system was established utilising three NTT research centres located throughout Japan and linked seamlessly via the Internet. Japanese and English websites were established and efforts made to ensure that data is presented in a format that is easily understood by prefectural residents and business.

Third, once the monitoring and dissemination components were fully functional, the project team and the advisory group began to explore how best to use the data in an educational context. The local teachers proposed a number of sub-projects that involved the use of Internet technologies to enhance the classroom setting through the use of teleconferencing. These provide real-time access to local environmental experts ('Open Lesson') with the teachers providing lessons in the environment, broadcast to the students at more than one school (Sanriku Dive).

The following achievements have resulted from this project since 1998:

- Periodic water quality monitoring with community participation on Kitakami River has taken place on three occasions to automatically measure water quality levels (including pH, dissolved oxygen, water temperature, deoxidised electric potential and salt concentrations).[15] This data, and images obtained by digital

15   Monitoring took place in August, September and November 1998.

camera, were transmitted over portable telephone lines for release on the Internet as real-time environmental information. The results are still accessible online as a virtual environmental tour of the river.

- Long-term, automatic monitoring of water quality at five locations on the Mabechi River covering pH, dissolved oxygen, water temperature, salt concentration, deoxidised electric potential and water levels

- Monitoring of acid rain levels by students at 90 schools in the Iwate[16]

- Automatic monitoring of CO_2 concentrations at three locations: (i) a forest area (East Japan Recreation Centre); (ii) a residential area (Takizawamura Sugo); and (iii) an urban area (Iwate Prefecture Pollution Centre)[17]

- Automatic monitoring of NO_2 at four locations around Morioka and suspended particulate matter concentrations in air at three locations near Kitakami City

- A Japanese version of the project web page became operational in August 1999 providing access to real-time environmental information (http://ecology.mcon. ne.jp). The English version of the web page came online in January 2000 (www. ias.unu.edu/ecology).

- The first environmental education pilot project was undertaken on 29 September 1999 involving the use of the Internet to provide a class in real time (http:// sanriku.mcon.ne.jp). A teacher member of the Environmental Education Advisory Group dived off the Sanriku coastline and his class was accessible real-time to students in the local primary schools. Local television companies and the press covered the event extensively.

- An international symposium on Environment, Information and Education was held on 11 November 1999 in Morioka, Iwate. The symposium was broadcast live via the Internet and included the second pilot environmental education experiment entitled 'Open Lesson', involving a multipoint video conference between three local schools and experts at various environmental installations in the prefecture. The schoolchildren undertook a range of environment-related experiments and contacted the experts regarding points of clarification and concern.

- In April 2000, primary and middle schoolchildren in Iwate participated in the development of a cherry-blossom map for the entire prefecture. The children monitored the timing of the first blossoms as they spread from north to south, indicating when the blossom season ended. All the information was collated in one location and presented on an animated map accessible via the Internet. The children and teachers were encouraged to consider the potential impacts of

16 Initial discussions on the design of this survey took place in September 1998 between NTT and IPG. A sample homepage was developed in October 1998 and is accessible via the Internet. The sub-project was officially launched by the Governor of Iwate Prefecture on 24 November 1998. In December 1998, a mobile exhibition of the acid rain monitoring project toured the prefecture.

17 After testing, official measurement of CO_2 levels began on 4 December 1998 and the web page was developed in April 1999.

environmental change (e.g. global warming) on this culturally significant event for the Japanese.

■ Also in April 2000 an environmental attitudes survey was undertaken of over 1,000 high-school students in Iwate asking them about their attitudes towards the environment, the types of conservation activity they have been involved with, how they get information on the environment and so on. Not surprisingly, only 8% obtained environmental information from the Internet.

■ From May to July 2000, the third environmental education pilot project was implemented. This involved utilisation of the Internet to allow children at three schools to observe remotely the nesting of the black-headed gull in a nature conservation area.

■ In November 2000, a major conference was organised entitled the 'Iwate Environment Millennium 2000 Forum' and, because environmental education is the main activity of the IEN project, one panel discussion during the Forum dealt with the role of information technologies in support of environmental education. This included presentations from NTT, UNU/IAS, the Japanese Ministry of Education, Culture, Sports, Science and Technology (MEXT) and from local teachers and NGO representatives. Over 700 local citizens attended the Forum.

The IEN Project has attracted considerable local attention since its launch in 1998 and was the subject of a television programme by NHK (the Japan Broadcasting Corporation) aired on 25 August 2000. In the remaining period of this pilot project it is envisaged that greater emphasis will be placed on higher education and community participation through the Virtual University. In addition, consideration will be given to the possibility of developing similar projects elsewhere in Japan. It is hoped that IPG will continue to build on its experience with the IEN project in the years to come.

11.4 Concluding remarks

In this chapter we have highlighted the move on the part of major telecommunications carriers around the globe to integrate issues of sustainability into their operations. While the focus of much of their action has been on tackling global environment-related problems such as the need to reduce CO_2 emissions and the institutionalising of environmental management systems based on ISO 14001, there is also a significant focus on projects that contribute to society.

The IEN project forms part of this bigger picture whereby a globally competitive business such as NTT needs to re-engage local communities in order to exemplify some form of social responsibility. It also corroborates some of the theoretical perspectives raised by the ecological modernists in their interpretation of new roles of technologies, market dynamics, decentralised governance and emergence of new ideologies.

The IEN project illustrates how these tendencies are now intimately linked with the new information society technologies, which represent powerful tools to potentially accelerate an ecologically inspired transformation of society. At the same time, the opportunity to field-test monitoring technologies is invaluable for NTT from a marketing standpoint and to explore the potential as a future business opportunity.

The IEN project is an excellent example of how a technology-driven initiative can be redirected towards fulfilling an important social function. Although not part of a preconceived plan, there are a number of elements of this project that embody important developments for NTT as a telecommunications carrier keen to contribute to the resolution of environmental issues. In particular, the partnerships created through this project work to both legitimise (with the participation of the UNU) and to tap local knowledge/resources (through participation of IPG).

Rather than merely providing basic infrastructure provision, NTT as a service provider is focusing on the 'software' function of the Internet. In this way it is gaining experience and expertise that will enable it to become more closely connected, by being in better 'touch' with members of communities involved with the provision and use of environmental information. Local teachers and NGO representatives have praised the work of the team involved in the IEN project indicating that they felt it had contributed successfully to the partial bridging of barriers between local institutions such as government, universities, schools and business.

Unfortunately, in some respects the IEN project has proved disappointing. While attracting considerable local and national media attention, the actual usage of this potentially very powerful Internet-based network and infrastructure has been lower than hoped. To some extent this reflects the limited number of people currently online in Iwate and the region as a whole. It may also be a problem more of the 'curiosity divide' than of the digital one. The monthly Web statistics for the IEN site are shown in Figure 11.3 and

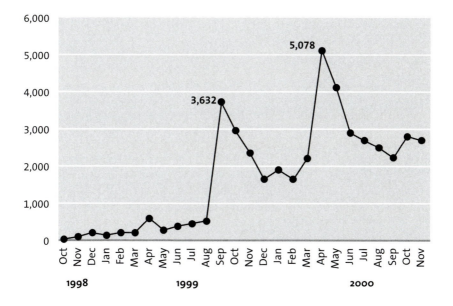

Figure 11.3 ***Monthly access statistics for the IEN website***

indicate that, since September 1998, roughly 44,000 people have visited the site. The number visiting the site has gradually increased with an average of 2,600 visitors per month in 2000.

The project may actually be premature for the locality and more work may be required to raise awareness of the potential of these kinds of tool for local environmental governance and democracy. For instance, at the municipal level there is only an average ratio of 0.4 computers per government official and the prefecture only just attained a 1–1 ratio in 2000 (jumping from a ratio of 0.47–1 in 1997). Only 63% of local teachers have access to a computer. In addition, only 36% of primary schools and 46.5% of middle schools have access to the Internet.

With plans under way to rectify this situation, it is reasonable to predict that in the future there could be new associations, projects and formal groups arising in Iwate and extending the work into other regions. Information technology could help to create and maintain a sense of cohesion within the organisations and help to bridge the local–global axis. However, the future of environmental conservation and the Internet depends more on changes of sociocultural values than simply on technological innovations and new infrastructure.

New ISTs enable us to handle more information, which forms the basis for our decisions, but these decisions will continue be made within the framework of the existing social culture. If they are to go further towards improving human understanding of how to improve the interaction between natural and societal systems at the local level, projects such as IEN need to increase their efforts to examine more effectively the interactions between technology, environmental knowledge and the transformation of sociocultural values. The most exciting feature of the IEN project, however, is that it exemplifies a desire to reflect on these themes on the part of a major business such as NTT, government, academia and the community.

PRODUCT-ORIENTED ENVIRONMENTAL MANAGEMENT
The case of Xerox Europe

Frank de Bakker
Vrije Universiteit, the Netherlands

David Foley
Xerox Europe, UK

Environmental characteristics of products are receiving increasing attention in the process towards sustainable development. Hart (1995), for instance, distinguished between three interconnected strategies: pollution prevention, product stewardship and sustainable development. Pollution prevention concerns the reduction of pollution during production processes, product stewardship aims at broadening environmental concerns towards products, and sustainable development includes negative links between economy and ecology within the firm's scope. According to Roome (2001), sustainable development can be seen as a normative, systemic, multidisciplinary, future-oriented and transformational process.

To understand the possibilities for making a transition from product stewardship to sustainable development strategies, it is useful to obtain a better insight into the way in which an individual company can organise the management of its products' environmental characteristics. Over the last few years, many related concepts have been proposed to address the environmental impact of products, such as extended producer responsibility, integrated product policy, and product-oriented environmental management (POEM). This chapter focuses on the organisational implications of POEM, which can be defined as 'a management tool in which by taking a systematic approach all processes and activities in a company can be organised such that the environmental impact along the product chain can be constantly controlled, minimised and avoided wherever possible' (Brezet et al. 2000: iii).

There are several reasons for the increasing emphasis on 'products and the environment', including greater awareness of products as sources of environmental burden; environmental policies are increasingly focusing on products; and many stakeholders in the product life-cycle, including manufacturers, can have a significant influence on a product's environmental characteristics (Kärnä 1999). To date, much of the emphasis on products' environmental characteristics has focused on issues related to product development such as design for environment and ecodesign (Roy 1994; Brezet and van Hemel 1997; Zhang *et al.* 1997), and product take-back and asset recovery (Thierry *et al.* 1995; Ayres *et al.* 1997), and related methodologies and instruments. Unfortunately, there has been less attention on the organisational aspects: that is, the way a firm can manage its products' environmental characteristics in an integrated manner (Lenox and Ehrenfeld 1997).

To understand such organisational implications of POEM within a large, proactive firm, this chapter examines Xerox Europe, a large multinational producing and selling document-processing products and services throughout Europe, Asia and Africa.[1] This company provides an interesting case study to explore the organisation aspects of POEM because Xerox is leading the development of new and innovative solutions to document production, management and distribution. How Xerox implements and integrates environmental concerns into its business model can provide some valuable insights into the enablers and barriers of sustainability for modern electronic and communication technology companies.

The chapter is divided into the following sections. Section 12.1 explores the theoretical dimensions of our research, while Section 12.2 discusses some of the methodological considerations. Some of the enablers of and barriers to POEM at Xerox Europe are then discussed (Section 12.3) followed by a description of the important organisational elements surrounding the POEM concept (Section 12.4). Section 12.5 presents some of the key lessons from this case study and finally some concluding thoughts on POEM and Xerox Europe are offered (Section 12.6).

12.1 Theoretical background

As Roome (1998b: 271) noted, 'Researchers have a responsibility to construct bridges between theory, concept, method and practice.' To understand the implications of organising POEM at the level of an individual firm, three key theoretical areas need to be explored: a stakeholder focus to determine which interests are to be served; continuous improvement to emphasise the enduring character of POEM; and a capability perspective to consider the development of the capabilities required to manage products' environmental characteristics (de Bakker *et al.* 1999; de Bakker 2001).

As the scope of a company's environmental management broadens, POEM can be seen as imposing new demands on a firm. Greater emphasis on products' environmental characteristics implies a more extensive examination of the product life-cycle and greater involvement of stakeholders such as suppliers, customers and regulators. If POEM is to be seen as part of the process towards sustainable development, a firm needs to be able to address the different stakeholder interests *vis-à-vis* a product's environmental characteristics. In this process of identifying and balancing different stakeholder interests, the role of managerial decision-makers is important, since the perception of stakeholder

---

1 This chapter is partly based on de Bakker 2001.

interests can influence a firm's organisational response to environmental issues[2] (Fineman and Clarke 1996; Henriques and Sadorsky 1999).

To respond to the different stakeholder demands, a firm needs to develop and maintain specific organisational capabilities, which can be defined as 'complex bundles of skills and accumulated knowledge, exercised through organisational processes, that enable firms to co-ordinate activities and make use of their assets' (Day 1994: 38). Since stakeholder demands and product characteristics can change frequently, the organisation of POEM has to be a dynamic and continuous process. Sharma and Vredenburg (1998) suggested in their work that the capability perspective, stakeholder integration, learning and continuous innovation can all be related. The process of organising POEM can be considered a 'capability-building process',[3] in which the continuous balancing of different stakeholder interests is required (de Bakker 2001). A closer examination of this complex process within a company setting may therefore deliver some useful insights into how a company is able to balance different if not conflicting stakeholder interests.

Considering environmental management as a capability-building process has been proposed earlier, but attention mainly focused on strategic aspects of environmental management (den Hond 1996). We think it is necessary to address both the strategic and operational implications of POEM in order to get an insight into the organisation of POEM. Again, focusing on the position of managerial decision-makers is useful, as these decision-makers play an important role in the process of balancing and addressing different stakeholder interests, and in developing an organisational response. They are important in this specific capability-building process, both at a strategic and an operational level, as they do not only influence a company's environmental strategy, but see to its implementation at an operational level as well. In the next section, some methodological issues are discussed.

12.2 Methodological issues

The goal of our case study is to look at the way POEM has been implemented and managed within Xerox Europe. An important emphasis of the research is to examine the organisational aspects of POEM: that is, the way capabilities to organise POEM are developed and maintained at the firm level, and the way different stakeholders are involved in the process. Selected interviews with nine company personnel from a variety of company functions were conducted at different Xerox facilities in the UK and the Netherlands. The work responsibilities of these nine people directly involve product-oriented environ-

---

2   One should note, however, that stakeholder requirements (especially customers' requirements) can also drive developments in the opposite direction from environmental improvement. Balancing different inputs to the decision-making process therefore needs to be done in line with strategic goals.

3   A useful view on the capability-building process is provided by Iansiti and Clark (1994), who distinguish between a concept development and an implementation phase, seeing capability-building as a form of problem-solving. Their approach is based on product development, and has also been applied in environmental management (den Hond 1996), making it useful for application to the POEM concept (de Bakker 2001).

mental issues, including remanufacturing and asset recovery, marketing, environmental management and product development. Also, they all participate in the Xerox Europe Environmental Network, a group of managers representing the various business and geographical units within Xerox.

The interviews were conducted in April 2000 and were returned to the interviewees for verification. The interviews were supplemented with additional information, such as annual reports, environment, health and safety (EHS) reports and information acquired from literature or through the Internet. Additional insights were gained by ongoing research on Xerox's approach to sustainability, particularly the setting and monitoring of progress towards sustainability targets has been investigated (Foley *et al.* 2000). After describing some of the important barriers and enablers to POEM at Xerox Europe, we will then discuss some of the key organisational aspects of implementing and managing POEM.

12.3   Enablers of and barriers to POEM at Xerox Europe

Xerox Europe, which is the European subsidiary of Xerox Corporation, provides solutions to help manage documents (e.g. paper, electronic and online) and markets high-value hardware, software, services and solutions for small businesses, global enterprises and home offices. The interviews and research were conducted in the first half of 2000, at a time when Xerox Corporation was undertaking a radical business turnaround programme to return to business success. The case study reveals useful insights into the organisational and cultural dimensions of managing POEM in what may be described as a turbulent business environment.

12.3.1 Enablers of POEM

An important enabler of POEM at Xerox Europe is regarded to be the company's 'solutions' approach (e.g. the development of software and systems to optimise the management of documents within an institution or group) as well as its well-known reputation for knowledge management. A number of interviews cited the company's involvement in business networks and partnerships as a plus, as well as its emphasis on R&D, devotion to human resources and quality management, and its own business procedures and processes (e.g. Xerox Management Model [XMM]) as key enablers of POEM.

With the ability to manage environmental issues becoming an important component of doing business in the global marketplace, there is a growing awareness and consensus within the company that Xerox should have the most stringent and efficient compliance system in the world, since the company uses one set of compliance criteria worldwide. One important enabler related to this is the belief that POEM is consistent with Xerox's existing environmental policy and strategy as well as with its general corporate philosophy of putting the customer first. POEM is also consistent with Xerox's drive to be more energy- and resource-efficient (i.e. saving money, being more efficient—both for Xerox and its customers) and to be a good corporate citizen ('doing the right things').

With an increasing number of customers requiring their suppliers to have environmental management systems and environmental issues being incorporated into bids and tenders, environmental concerns along sustainable production and consumption are becoming business competition issues (Zint and Frederick 2001). While some interviewees observed that customers might be more motivated by short-term business factors than by a sense of responsibility towards the environment or society, there is a strong sense that POEM is a 'value-added' management tool because it fits so well with Xerox's existing business strategy, environmental policy, corporate culture and brand image

12.3.2 Barriers to POEM

One barrier was that Xerox did not always publicise externally what had been achieved with POEM (both financially and environmentally) and some interviewees felt that the company could do more to publicise the results of the POEM programme. Another barrier to implementing POEM is the lack of understanding of environmental issues in the financial community. Despite a lot of research activity in this area, it remains difficult to translate environmental issues into shareholder value. Some of the barriers mentioned in the interviews include the problem of conceptualising POEM as a business operational concern, the difficulty of implementing an environmental management programme while the company is in the middle of corporate restructuring, and the possibility that some customers may take issues with remanufactured products as being 'not new'.

In general, POEM was viewed as an important concept for the company and its customers. To organise and implement POEM, a number of interviewees suggested a need for a small internal team whose members come from all functional areas of the company, and emphasised the importance of internal and external communication. As one interviewee commented, 'we need to continue'—not viewing POEM as a one-time project but as a *process*. The potential for POEM to develop within a firm may be best when a pragmatic approach—that is, through cost avoidance in service and recycling—is used in its implementation. POEM is becoming more important, but it can only truly develop when people understand and accept the relevant issues. Knowledge and understanding therefore are regarded as crucial elements in the successful adoption of POEM.

12.4 Organisational elements of POEM at Xerox Europe

12.4.1 Products

Xerox's main products are copiers, printers, fax machines and multifunctional devices, with increasing emphasis on providing document solutions. The products facilitate the efficiency of handling data and information. According to the people interviewed, important characteristics of the company products are advanced technology and high quality. Some of the notable features of the products are the shift towards digital products,[4] Xerox's asset management operations, the product range, the firm's stability

---

4 The office product industry has undergone a rapid shift from analogue (light lens) technology to digital technology. In light lens products the image is captured by reflecting light through a

and longevity, and the total service coverage. Product reliability, ease of use and longevity are also mentioned as product strengths.

The primary customer demands include cost, reliability, service quality, provision of supplies, and, for digital machines, functionality. Quality, cost and the availability of the latest features are key demands. Some attention also is paid to chemical emissions and effects, and to safety. Within Xerox, 3R+V (reliability, responsiveness, relationship and value) is the standard answer to the question of what the company's key product demands are.

12.4.2 Environmental management

Xerox has a long-standing tradition of environmental management[5] and interviewees acknowledged that there is a high awareness of environmental issues within Xerox. Important elements of the company's environmental management strategy are asset recovery, zero landfill and the '3R programme' (reduce, re-use and recycle). Increased attention to the environmental characteristics of products fits in very well with the firm's aim to provide value to its customers, employees and society at large.

Remanufacturing has historically played an important role in allowing Xerox to remain competitive and to reduce costs, and it builds on the product stewardship background that originated from its lease tradition in its business. Due to the transition to digital products, colour printing and networks, light lens products are currently in a declining market stage in life-cycle terms. This implies that more hardware is returning than is being put out. Xerox has to maintain service obligations for these products, and is able to do so in part through its asset recovery programme. New digital technologies bring new opportunities in paper and energy savings, upgradability and remote diagnosis, but there is only limited experience in remanufacturing and recycling of these products.

According to the people interviewed, quality management and environmental management are closely related. Within the company, there is a tendency for environmental management systems (EMSs) to be implemented by quality groups and supported by environmental groups. EMS is increasingly seen as a marketing issue due to the growing awareness among customers as well as increasing requirement for a certified EMS. Co-operation between different functional units and partnerships with other industries are becoming more relevant. The POEM concept appears compatible with several business processes within the company including the Xerox Management Model (XMM) or the time-to-market (TTM) process. However, determining the effectiveness of environmental management still remains difficult. Consequently, some interviewees indicated that environmental metrics need be incorporated into financial and operational performance indices to gain the support of management.

series of lenses. In a digital device, the image is captured by a charge-coupled device (CCD) array. The advent of digital technology has allowed a considerable change in the functionality of these machines. For a further comparison between analogue and digital copying, see Kerr and Ryan 2001.
5   For an overview of environmental management at Xerox, see Maslennikova and Foley 2000.

12.4.3 Senior management

XMM is an important instrument in the way Xerox manages its operations. Environmental and social responsibilities are a part of the 'management leadership' section of the XMM, while managers in all functions have responsibilities that are outlined in this model. Active management support for POEM-like initiatives is created through dialogues with senior management, who commit themselves to the results of such a dialogue and provide support for the company's commitment. Mainstreaming environmental issues as a general management concern is an important component of this dialogue process. For instance, design for environment (DfE) initiatives can be directly integrated into product development processes. Moreover, environmental concerns can be discussed in 'operating review meetings', while environmental affairs can be incorporated into the business strategy processes.

By defining requirements, understanding risk management and getting these insights across to the company's product development section, the corporate EHS department can have a major influence on POEM by emphasising the importance of making customers aware of the environmental benefits of Xerox's products. In organising POEM, the effective communication of environmental benefits is critically important. Most interviewees think that there is sufficient knowledge within the company to organise POEM, but some people feel that this knowledge does not permeate sufficiently throughout the company.

In addition, there is some doubt as to whether there is sufficient time and/or interest in the POEM concept. Regarding their own role in implementing POEM and in the environmental management arena, the interviewees repeatedly used terms such as 'facilitating', 'informing' and 'being aware and making aware'. Other roles mentioned in the interviews include identification of emerging areas of interest and helping to shape and prioritise relevant legislation.

12.5 Lessons learned

A number of conclusions and lessons can be derived from this case study of Xerox Europe's experience with POEM. These points cannot serve as a generic 'recipe' as the implementation of any programme is often determined by the internal structure and culture of an individual company. However, they are likely to provide a useful roadmap. The people interviewed identified many capabilities required for organising POEM, ranging from senior management commitment (to provide a drive and impetus) to have recognised environmental champions in key functional areas of the company.

In addition, a committed workforce, established best practices and processes, as well as an effective communicated plan on specific environmental issues were acknowledged as important. Also, a dedicated group such as an EHS department is useful to look at all the changes, to keep track of, and possibly influence, legislation, and to maintain an overview of the entire product life-cycle. Direct involvement from cradle to grave is needed, including participating in the design stage, soliciting good customer feedback and monitoring developments in technology and measurement methods.

POEM focuses on products across their entire life-cycle. Therefore interactions within the product chain, involving many different stakeholder interests, are important. Xerox is in a good position to influence its suppliers on environmental issues and the POEM concept provides the basis from which to establish partnerships with these suppliers. POEM as an issue needs to be elevated to senior management level, since top-management support is essential for the development and diffusion of POEM within a company.

POEM is a continual process and its continuity needs to be enhanced through the targeting, measuring and reporting of goals and objectives. The consensus of the people interviewed is that there are no short quick fixes to environmental issues: it takes sustained commitment, effort and time. Some interviewees remarked that the people involved in environmental activities should be those who see a long-term career in these issues. Otherwise, you may end up with gaps. If necessary, environmental considerations should be put above financial considerations when, for example, legislation and ethical considerations are involved.

12.6 Conclusion

To conclude, we turn once more to the notion of sustainable development. POEM decreases the environmental impact of products, thereby minimising risks and hazards.

Managerial decision-makers are crucial players in the process of organising POEM by balancing which stakeholders' interests to address and through the framing of problems according to these interests. In this respect, Henriques and Sadorsky (1999: 97) noted that if a firm 'wishes to make environmental issues a priority, it may want to hire managers who react positively to stakeholders who represent the values the company wants to espouse'. To that statement we could add that these managers also would need to possess an ability to build 'capabilities'.

Stakeholder involvement and communication is an increasingly important issue in the POEM concept. 'The exchange of information and opinions with selected target groups, provides companies with an opportunity to widen their perspective on potential and desirable product improvements' (Weterings 1998: 194). Such dialogues with relevant stakeholders are likely to improve the quality and create better awareness of POEM as a management tool.

Xerox, a leading company in the global information and communications technology sector, is continuing to integrate environmental concerns to its overall business strategy. The key to the success of this process will be the drive toward a waste-free company. Xerox, for instance, aims to have 'waste-free factories producing waste-free products for waste-free offices'. Product stewardship has been Xerox's traditional strength and will continue to play an important part in the company's environmental management strategy. The company's vision of environment, health and safety leadership is constantly evolving as it strives to maximise value to its customers, employees and society, while maintaining relevance and consistency with changing business strategies and product lines. To relate this vision to POEM, taking a process view, developing and maintaining the required capabilities and addressing the stakeholder interests perceived relevant are important. POEM is then likely to play an important role in helping Xerox to strike this delicate balance.

Part 3
OLD-ECONOMY CONCERNS IN A NEW-ECONOMY WORLD

INFORMATION AND COMMUNICATIONS TECHNOLOGIES
Boon or bane to sustainable development?

Josephine Chinying Lang
Nanyang Technological University, Singapore

In today's world, the communication infrastructure is fast becoming as fundamental to the proper functioning of an economy as physical infrastructure. Information and communications technologies (ICTs) have made people around the world more connected to one another in a manner that was not possible before. In the initial euphoria of the Internet age, ICTs were quickly touted as being a godsend for the environmental cause. Unlike the industrial revolution, which brought great pressures to bear on natural resources, the ICT revolution was perceived as being light in material demands but heavy on information processing. ICTs appeared to promote continued economic growth with minimal environmental impact, since new wealth was going to be created through intangible assets, while helping to reduce the movement and processing of tangibles.

This chapter argues that ICTs represent a double-edged sword for economic development that is 'sustainable', defined by the United Nations World Commission on the Environment and Development to mean meeting the needs of the present without compromising the ability of the future generations to meet their own needs (WCED 1987). The basic rationale is that ICTs do not necessarily disengage the flow of information from the flow of tangible things. For example, instead of a much-heralded paperless environment, the advent of computerisation raised the demand for paper. Global paper consumption is estimated to have tripled over the past several decades and to grow by about 50% by 2010. Asian countries will see even larger increases of up to 80% (WRI 1998–99).

Similarly, rather than reducing demand for transportation of people and products through telecommuting, the growth in car usage and ownership shows no signs of abating. If there are 750 vehicles per 1,000 persons in the United States, and only 8 vehicles per 1,000 in China or 7 per 1,000 in India, China and India will see rapid growth in vehicle ownership. While the OECD (Organisation for Economic Co-operation and Development) countries will still account for 60% of global motor vehicle emissions by 2050, China and India will account for the bulk of the rest, if the 20-year linear growth in emissions continues (WRI 1998–99). Not coincidentally, global warming and urban pollution problems are also expected to worsen.

This chapter discusses new environmental challenges arising from the widespread use of ICTs. Section 13.1 discusses the negative impacts of ICTs resulting from the changing nature of wealth generation, global economic integration and regulatory arbitrage. The flipside is discussed in Section 13.2, where ICTs promote corporate environmental transparency, the development of industrial ecology, and online communities. Section 13.3 offers some concluding thoughts on the overall impact of ICTs on sustainable development.

13.1 New environmental challenges of ICTs

Initially, the new economy was heralded as being environmentally friendly because wealth would be derived from the better management of information. But the virtual value chain that generates any economic rents in the tangible world is inevitably grounded in some material value chain. Thus, the bursting of the dot.com bubble the world over from April 2000 involved start-ups that were not grounded in business models with any real world value. That burst bubble suggests that information flow uncoupled from the flow of material things has little economic value.

Increased information flow that augments a real-world value chain must mean a higher flow of products of a materialistic culture, which suggests an increase rather a decrease in consumption. ICT capabilities are enabling customers to gather information quickly and effortlessly about products, prices, quality and inventory. This promotes and facilitates an increasingly ravenous consumption, which translates into unprecedented stresses on the environment.

ICTs also promote unsustainable globalisation pressures. According to Saurin (1993: 48), 'Increasingly we produce what we do not consume, and we consume what we do not produce.' The consequences of poor environmental policies could further be exacerbated by trade liberalisation. With greater economic integration, it is difficult for governments to adopt optimal environmental policies unilaterally as the globalisation of the world economy may reduce their regulatory autonomy somewhat, making it more difficult to adopt more stringent environmental standards without concerted effort among nations (Charnovitz 2000).

13.1.1 The changing nature of wealth creation

Even though developing countries are rapidly increasing their share of trade in labour-intensive products as well as capital- and skill-intensive ones, these countries are encountering falling profit margins due to the tremendous downward pressure on prices of many of their products (Lall 1998; Kotabe 1998). In the knowledge age, resource extraction and ownership of industrial production capacity will not generate the superior economic rents of the industrial age. As other less-developed countries start to industrialise, Asian countries will face dwindling cost advantages over other regions of the world.

Competitive pressures may motivate firms to try to circumvent environmental regulatory controls and for governments to under-regulate environmental harms. As a result, the environmental status of countries with 'comparative advantages' in hosting polluting industries may deteriorate. In these countries, it will remain true that economic development will not prioritise sustainability. With intense global competition, there is product proliferation, compressed product life-cycles and accelerated product obsolescence. Product proliferation is evident in many diverse industries judging by the number of new product introductions, the available product varieties and long product lines (Bayus and Putsis 1999). Besides moving more products to market faster, companies are also rushing to compress their product life-cycles and hasten product obsolescence (Rosenau 1988; Vesey 1992; Griffin 1997; Bayus 1994).

In the automobile cycle, for example, development of new models used to take a seven-year development cycle. Now, new models are being produced every two years. Then there are new electronic gadgets products churned out every year. The manufacturing of these products involves the use of new hazardous materials and generates waste-streams that regulators may find difficult to incorporate into regulatory structures. Not surprisingly, the Pilot Environmental Sustainability Index of all developing Asian nations languish in the third, fourth and fifth quintiles. In order to remain competitive, many developing countries will not only increase the volume of raw material extraction but also ratchet up industrial output, even though the proliferation of low-cost manufacturers and producers around the world has made the delivery of volume less effective as a competitive tool (Kotabe 1998).

13.1.2 Global economic integration

The drivers of globalisation, especially that of the services sector, include the spatial reorganisation of production to international trade and the integration of financial markets (Mittleman 1996). First, advances in production made it possible to locate different parts of the value chain in various locations around the world depending on host-country advantage. The latter may include not only low wages but also lax environmental regulations and so on at one extreme, and well-established industry–university collaboration for R&D at the other. There is a huge academic literature on multinational corporations (MNCs) which I do not have time to review, but suffice to say that an international economy based merely on the exchange of tangibles—that is, trade—has been transformed into one based also on transnational production (Cox 1997).

For this discussion, the important point is that the extent and pace of this transnationalisation of production processes has led to the internationalisation of supporting services. This is what is bringing pressure on national governments to (a) liberalise their home markets not only in commodities but also in services and (b) incorporate services into new trading arrangements, as is evident in the current round of negotiations on investments and services in the World Trade Organisation (WTO).

Critically, it was the rise of enabling electronic technology in information processing and telecommunications that transformed international finance, making it possible for the frictionless transfer of huge amounts of capital across borders at the click of a button. By the late 1980s, the value of foreign exchange trading was exceeding the value of international trade by a factor of 40 times, topping US$1.2 trillion daily (UNCTAD 1995). And, by the late 1990s, the extended ICT industry, including Internet technologies, was drastically ratcheting up the quantity, quality and speed of information transfer, promoting what would with hindsight be called the dot.com bubble.

ICTs represent a key component in the rapid integration of the global economy. ICTs deepen the integration of national economies by moving beyond traditional trade-based linkages to ever more complex and deeper raw material sourcing, production linkages, market linkages and financial flows. Essentially, globalisation is leading to an increasingly dense network of economic interactions.

In sum, the transnationalisation of production and of finance comprise the key processes that permitted the compression of time and space in globalisation. This technologically driven process of globalisation places a premium on information- and knowledge-intensive activities. As wealth creation is increasingly linked to knowledge creation, future distribution of economic wealth is expected to favour ownership of intangible knowledge assets rather than ownership of raw materials and production capacity. Almost by definition, this means that services will be impacted greatly. The growing policy focus on and political rhetoric about the knowledge-based economy are being driven precisely by the need to specialise in knowledge-intensive sectors given production structures that are increasingly defined by technological advantages.

But this globalised economic integration leads to ever-greater demands on the Earth's ecosystems. Even a quarter of a century ago, Bennett (1976) saw that such an enlarging system would change the relationships between human beings and nature with two detrimental effects: *viz.*, the irrevocable tendency to use ever-larger quantities of energy, and the breakdown of the local sufficiency of human/natural subsystems.

13.1.3 Regulatory arbitrage

Under globalisation, activities that used to take place under one roof may now be distributed around the globe. The advent of ICTs has made the establishing of close ties among buyers, suppliers and other strategic stakeholders easier. This has resulted in greater efficiency: production costs are lowered by co-ordinating and integrating business activities across jurisdictions as ICTs enable and facilitate the formation of international networks for fabrication, assembly, distribution and servicing.

As a result, manufacturing and assembly value chains are not situated in the same jurisdiction but frequently away from each other in separate countries. For example, American dominance of the hard disk drive industry depends on the effective integration of its technological cluster in Silicon Valley and its manufacturing cluster in Singapore. Today no hard disk drive assembly occurs in the United States, yet 85% of the industry remains in American hands (McKendrick *et al.* 2000).

ICTs make the sourcing of supplies from different firms in multiple jurisdictions possible, including countries with lower environmental standards. With international networks for the fabrication, assembly and distribution of goods and services, firms may find it worthwhile to unbundle its value-adding processes to arbitrage between varying environmental regulatory standards in different countries. The unbundled components of the value chains can reappear as new businesses under different SIC (standard industrial classification) codes in jurisdictions that have different environmental regulations.

As the value chain remains integrated in virtual space, the co-ordination of activities proceeds unhindered. The low-cost sourcing of materials and products from small and medium-sized firms in different locations spreads out the pollution, which is made even easier with small-scale machines used in multiple localities. These small machines impose relatively minor health hazards on small groups of people. Even though the aggregate environmental damage may be considerable, local environmental authorities will not have the incentive to monitor or regulate such 'tiny' polluting firms. Likewise, individual victims will not find it worthwhile to sue culprit firms as the cost of litigation may exceed the harm suffered by each individual. This strategic blurring of industry boundaries makes the enforcement of industry-based and media-specific environmental standards extremely difficult.

The upshot is that ICTs facilitate the selection of geographical localities on the basis of how non-stringent their environmental regulations are. This regulatory arbitrage means that firms can circumvent unfavourable regulatory regimes more easily by using sophisticated supply-chain software to reduce transaction costs involved in co-ordinating and integrating value chains across borders. The net effect of this regulatory arbitrage is that environmental regulations designed in the 1970s and 1980s are ill equipped to protect local communities, particularly in the developing world, in the 21st century.

13.2 Harnessing ICTs for sustainable development

It is important to keep in mind, however, that ICTs can also be used to promote sustainable development. With the use of ICTs, environmental concerns can be magnified and made relevant to the business world. First, ICTs can facilitate in harmonising environmental regulations, standards and procedures globally. This helps in levelling the 'green' playing field. ICTs can also increase the transparency of how production practices impact the environment. Reducing information asymmetry between producers and regulators puts pressure on businesses to make sustainability a desirable feature of their operations. Second, ICTs can promote environmentally friendly industrial ecology. Finally, ICTs can promote online environmental communities that cut across national boundaries, industry borders and institutions.

13.2.1 Promoting corporate environmental transparency

If the current economic system leans too far towards favouring private commercial interests and reduces the possibilities for public control over environmental degradation, the application of ICTs can help remedy this bias. Information is essential in improving the quality of corporate governance with regard to issues related to sustainable development.

Environmental information asymmetry between firms and the community enables firms to act opportunistically. This information asymmetry exists because the community does not have information regarding the environmental impact of a firm's products, processes and waste management. Firms tend to withhold or omit such information or sometimes even manipulate environmentally sensitive information about its products and processes (Kulkarni 2000). When this informational asymmetry prevails, the likelihood for opportunism to generate rents increases, opportunism being the seeking of self-interest with guile (Williamson 1985).

The development of ICTs creates new opportunities for non-governmental organisations (NGOs) and local communities to exploit the power of sharing information. The Internet has become an extensive source of information on environmental issues. It allows instantaneous and inexpensive access to environmental information provided by environmental experts, NGOs, environmental agencies and local communities.

ICTs can also be deployed to increase the cost for environmentally opportunistic behaviour. Just as the Internet has made cost transparency a reality by making price comparisons easy with readily accessible information, it can also be used to provide environmental information that goes towards green transparency and ecological scores to empower environmentally conscious customers who will make informed product and service choices. Empowered stakeholders such as these can influence business policy decisions.

There are several notable policy and business initiatives that encourage this type of green business transparency. For example, the Green Index, developed by CALSTART, is a tool designed to measure the environmental image of global automobile makers (Amburg and Gage 2001), while the Global Reporting Initiative (GRI) is trying to forge a consensus among businesses, environmental groups, accounting firms and others on guidelines for a set of common environmental management and sustainability reporting elements. From the private sector, the Dow Jones joined forces with SAM Sustainability Group Indexes to launch a special sustainability index to track the environmental performance of industries. Dow Jones's reputation in the financial sector affords increased credibility to environmental performance metrics of various industries.

One important policy initiative that helps to reduce environmental information asymmetry is the toxic release reporting requirements that were established in 1986 under Title III of the Superfund Amendments and Reauthorisation Act (SARA), otherwise known as the Community Right-to-Know Act. As a consequence, data on actual emissions and releases has become accessible to public scrutiny. The US Environmental Protection Agency (EPA) maintains a national inventory of toxic releases to the environment in a computerised database known as the Toxics Release Inventory (TRI). Free access to such data has given some communities leverage to demand corporate accountability and to put pressure on industry to curtail emissions (Pezzoli 2000).

The extent to which sustainable development goals can be advanced in this networked age may be largely dependent on which interested parties acquire, organise, retrieve and disseminate environmental information effectively. The public's heightened awareness of polluting activities due to information disclosure increases the possibility that regulatory agencies establish stricter or more comprehensive regulatory requirements.

13.2.2 Facilitating industrial ecology

Environmental problems encountered by industry arise primarily from the use of a strictly linear production process: extracting raw materials and fossil energy, processing the material using that energy, and disposing waste back into natural ecosystems. Industrial ecology is a new approach to the industrial design of products and processes by implementing sustainable manufacturing strategies so that the waste of one production process becomes the feedstock for another. This seeks to optimise the total materials cycle from virgin material to finished material, to component, to product, to waste product, and ultimate disposal (Jelinski *et. al.* 2001). In light of today's complex webs of economic activity, an equally intricate web of players in an industrial ecology is needed to replicate the ecological footprints of material flows in order to optimise re-use, recycling and recovery.

High-quality, interactive information systems can enable scientists, regulators and other stakeholders to act in concert to address ever more complex environmental problems. ICTs can facilitate the tracking of products and processes from cradle to grave, and allow distributed knowledge creation driven by problems arising in the real economic and social world rather than embedded in disciplines. This flexible structure of knowledge creation encourages collaboration among diverse groups of individuals not located in the same institution or sited in the same geographical location. New knowledge in the development of industrial ecology can be generated, validated and accomplished with reference to broadly based groups of stakeholders. Connectivity and interactivity afforded by the Internet attenuate spatial and temporal constraints and can hasten the formation of an effective global industrial ecology.

Individual manufacturing processes cannot be considered in isolation. Instead, inter-organisation collaboration on a global scale that promotes a sustainable system of production using ICTs to facilitate global product analysis from resource to recovery is necessary. ICTs not only bring buyers and sellers of recyclable waste and recycled materials together but also allow firms involved in collection, separation, transportation, treatment and recovery to collaborate across national boundaries. Consequently, ICTs can facilitate the development of cross-boundary environmental regulatory systems that speed up worldwide acceptance of International eco-management standards such as ISO 14000 and hasten global harmonisation of eco-labelling and life-cycle assessment among nations.

An example of this inter-organisation collaboration is the world's first eco-industrial park in Kalundborg, Denmark. Steam, gas, cooling water and gypsum are circulated among the partners at Kalundborg, a partnership evolved over the last 20 years between the Asnaes Power Company, a Novo Nordisk pharmaceutical plant, a Gyproc wallboard producer, and a Statoil refinery. The partners created the inter-firm arrangements for a variety of reasons: cheaper materials and energy, minimisation of disposal costs, income generated from production residue, and greater environmental responsibility (Center of Excellence for Sustainable Development 2001).

The 1998 round table on the industrial ecology of pulp and paper conducted by the editor of the *Journal of Industrial Ecology* is a good illustration of advancing knowledge mediated by ICTs. This round table through e-mails spanned two continents, from Los Angeles to Vienna, and lasted for nearly three weeks, involving authors of three published articles, a moderator and some invited observers. Only authors and moderator were allowed to 'speak'. The asynchronous nature of e-mail gave participants the opportunity to think and respond carefully to the dialogue. The low cost of Internet communication made the project financially feasible, substituting electronic communication for air travel (Lifset 1998).

13.2.3 *Promoting online environmental communities*

The Internet is efficient for conveying information written in hypertext: that is, information organised in a way that makes accessing it far less time-consuming than traditional linear methods of reading. In contrast to the traditional reading of a text in a linear fashion, websites permit readers to jump around the body of a text, and from one distinct text to another through the use of links. This ability opens up new possibilities for intertextual reading and community-building.

The Internet facilitates the development, growth and maintenance of distance-transcending relationships. In addition to one-on-one relationships, computer-mediated communication promotes both real-time and asynchronous communal relationships. Rheingold (1994) has defined such communities as social aggregations that emerge from the Internet when enough people carry on certain public discussion long enough, with sufficient human feeling, to form webs of personal relationships in cyberspace. It has been suggested that imagined communities emerge from the sharing of myths and knowledge and stories regardless of geographic proximity (Anderson 1983).

Policy-making in the field of ecology can no longer be a strictly national affair. Therefore, policy-makers and citizens who share common concerns must be capable of forming a constituency and mobilising support across borders and regions. Individuals interested in promoting sustainable development can now create virtual communities by establishing a virtual community through timely news items, useful databases and interesting environmental stories. To perpetuate a true sense of community, it is important that participants be incorporated into the process of community-building.

NGOs have played a critical role in the development of many green virtual networks and online communities. Enhanced communication capacities permit the formation of international alliances for a range of purposes, from monitoring raw material extraction and harvesting techniques to creating a campaign to ban landmines. No less than seven major international NGO law organisations communicate frequently on the Internet. Using advanced information and communication technology tools, NGOs can now be involved directly in a policy-making role and not just trying to impact environmental policy. For instance, the World Resources Institute's Forest Watch programme has developed a global Web-based monitoring system to verify whether timber is being harvested in a sustainable manner. Local NGOs can use the Web-based information to check to see if companies are living up to their green forestry commitments. Importantly, the money behind this initiative was given by furniture companies anxious to verify the commitments of their suppliers (Salzman 1999).

One example of a virtual community used to augment a real-world inter-organisational network can be seen in the experience of the US EPA. The EPA has laid out a comprehensive infrastructure for a virtual environmental community that complements the real face-to-face one. The main feature of both the real and virtual communities is the promotion of partnership with stakeholders, especially those in the private sector. Many corporate green teams have been working co-operatively with the EPA in physical and virtual space to achieve goals set in various environmental programmes, including the 33/50 initiative, Waste Wise, Climate Wise, Green Lights, Energy Star and others. Such a voluntary approach to environmental protection stimulates greater environmental creativity and innovations that achieve measurable results faster and with lower costs than with traditional 'command-and-control' regulatory approaches (Lang and Ho 1998).

Finally, ICTs can speed up learning by environmental agencies in developing countries. Many components of a developed country's regulatory programmes are available either in hard copy, facsimile, CD-ROM or via the Internet. Such a prodigious arsenal of regulatory weapons grew slowly over time in developed countries. But environmental regulators in developing countries can now access voluminous material with which they can make policy decisions. Several Asian and Mexican regulatory agencies subscribe to and follow the US Federal Register and its litany of environmental regulation (Prince and Nelson 1996).

13.3 Conclusion

On balance, whether ICTs ultimately help or retard sustainable development efforts will depend on the aims of those who use such technologies. One must not, however, assume that the forces for and against sustainable development will necessarily balance each other. Small-scale but widely distributed environmentally destructive behaviour may not capture the attention of regulatory agencies or NGOs because they may not be politically salient. This means that there is the possibility of a threat of distributed pollution that accumulates into non-negligible dimensions.

Hence, environmental policy mechanisms that are piecemeal, industry-specific and nation-bound may create constraints and pose a barrier to sustainable development. What is urgently needed is a global and an integrated approach towards environmental governance. For example, an atmospheric dispersion model that predicts the impact of emissions from all sources and monitors ambient pollution levels at various receptor points is needed if meaningful ameliorative measures are to be taken. Such holistic efforts will be needed as the environmental benefits of ICTs are to become truly globalised.

INFORMATION AND COMMUNICATIONS TECHNOLOGIES AND BUSINESS TRAVEL
Environmental possibilities, problems and implications

Peter Arnfalk
Lund University, Sweden

14.1 Introduction

Whether we call it a shift in paradigm, an information or knowledge society, or the new or Internet economy, we cannot help but notice the drastic changes the world is currently undergoing. The 'digitalisation' of our lives is becoming increasingly apparent as the use of information and communications technology (ICT) products and services changes the way we work, live, communicate, socialise, travel and so on. Amid such drastic societal changes, it may be a smart move to take the opportunity to alleviate some of the drawbacks of our industrialised society.

One of the more devastating drawbacks is the environmental deterioration we have generated through extensive resource depletion. Great expectations have been expressed in that moving from atoms to bits (Negroponte 1995) could lead to dematerialisation, a reduction in material and energy consumption, and substitute travel. In this chapter I will discuss the potential and limitations of substituting travel with various means of ICT-based communication, and the implications for the global environment. I will then discuss the future outlook of, and some of the barriers to, holding virtual meetings using ICT-based communication tools in business enterprises. However, some background information on travel and its environmental impact needs to be highlighted.

14.1.1 *Travel: an overview*

According to the World Tourism Organisation (WTO), the total number of international arrivals[1] has grown in the last 50 years from 25 to nearly 700 million, corresponding to an average growth rate of 7% per annum. Business travel accounted for 18% of total arrivals. Not only has it grown in terms of numbers, it has also expanded geographically. Air transport remains the dominant means of international travel (43%), followed by road transport (42%), rail transport (7%) and sea transport (8%) (WTO 2000).

One explanation for this trend is that travelling is becoming more accessible and affordable to an increasing number of people. Another key factor, particularly for business travel, is the general trend towards **globalisation**. The marketplace is expanding to an international level, with customers often located in distant corners of the world. Companies are merging into multinational conglomerates with factories and offices distributed worldwide. Consequently, this development generates an increased need for business communication between remote units in a company: for example, between a design department in the US and a production facility in Manila.

A globalised market also creates a need for international salesperson–customer interaction, contact between wholesalers and retailers, and so on. These communication needs generate a lot of meetings, of which many, in turn, require people to travel long distances to attend. A similar increasing trend is found in domestic business travel. This is a rational and straightforward explanation of what generates business travel, but it is probably only part of the story behind business travel's massive growth. Other less tangible drivers may also be contributing factors.[2]

The classic German expression 'Wenn jemand eine Reise tut, so kann er was verzählen'[3] ('the one who travels has got something to tell') indicates the kind of respect and interest that a traveller experiences. Being a cosmopolitan globetrotter is often considered to be positive and thrilling, and legendary travellers such as Marco Polo, Christopher Columbus, Dr Livingstone, Scott and Amundsen, and even Phileas Fogg, enjoy a place in history for their travelling escapades.

Because of the prestige of global travel, a number of companies use business travel as a selling point in recruitment. Business travel is still surrounded by an aura of status and glamour even though travelling in business class has become increasingly commonplace and is no longer the privilege of top management alone. That a company considers you and your work to be important enough to spend thousands of dollars to send you to some remote part of the world is enough to boost most people's egos, and signals professional success. However, in companies where most of the staff travels, the motivation is less, and travelling is considered hard work that you would happily reduce.

1   International arrivals refer to international travel by all commercial transportation modes: air, train, road transport and boat.
2   After the terrorist attacks on 11 September 2001, travelling has decreased, including business travel. Many companies restrict their employees' travel; and the security risk, as well as fear (and sometimes the argument 'my family won't allow me'), has become an acceptable excuse for many not to travel for business purposes. At the same time, the audio- and videoconferencing market has experienced a dramatic increase.
3   From the poem 'Urians Reise um die Welt' written in 1786 by Mattias Claudius (set to music by Ludwig van Beethoven).

14.1.2 *Travel: environmental, social and business implications*

Transportation has become one of the major contributors to a number of global environmental problems: climate change, acidification, eutrophication, local air pollution, loss of biodiversity and noise. Greenhouse gas emissions from the transport sector in the European Union (EU) are expected to increase by 39% by 2010, compared to 1990 levels, making transportation the single largest contributor to the EU's greenhouse gas emissions. This would seriously jeopardise the possibilities of achieving the reduction target in greenhouse gas emissions agreed under the Kyoto Protocol (a total *decrease* in CO_2 emissions of 8% during the same period) (EEA 2000). Moreover, stabilising atmospheric CO_2 concentrations at safe levels will require a 60%–80% cut in carbon emissions from current levels (Brown *et al.* 1999).

Despite its obvious environmental threat, mobility has long been considered a necessity for society's growth and welfare, for company sales and competitiveness, and for personal development and success. The OECD (Organisation for Economic Co-operation and Development) policy meeting on 'Sustainable Consumption and Individual Travel Behaviour' concluded that:

> The individual's right to unlimited, motorised personal mobility has emerged as an important measure of progress in modern, democratic societies. As a result, many governments have been hesitant to expressly seek to change people's behaviour to achieve less environmentally harmful travel patterns. It has become clear that technical solutions alone will not be sufficient to mitigate transport's negative impacts (OECD 1997).

Interestingly enough, aviation has long enjoyed an exemption from tax on all jet fuels used on international flights since 1944 and 'slipped through the net' again when the CO_2 emissions reductions were adopted as part of the Kyoto Protocol in 1997 (IPPR 2000). However, it is becoming clear that the transport sector will have to internalise a larger share of its environmental and social costs in the future,[4] resulting in higher prices for freight transport and travelling.

In the business sector, there is also a growing awareness of the environmental and financial impact of travel. One illustrative example of this is the telecom company Ericsson, which estimates that 73% of the CO_2 per capita emissions of its Swedish employees originated from their business travel (Ericsson 1998). The cost of travel is another emerging business concern. The average annual travel cost per US business traveller is about US$9,000. Business travel-related activities (including entertainment) in 1999 amounted to US$396 billion and accounts for the third-largest controllable expense in US corporations after payroll and information services. In many non-manufacturing firms, the total expenditure of corporate travel has become the second-largest item in the expense budget (Gibbs 2000).

Yet another strong incentive to reduce the volume of business travel is the time it requires and therefore displaces from both professional and personal activities. This may lead to travel-related stress, something that one in every four business travellers in the US experiences. The predominant causes of such stress include spending time away from their family and worrying about work piling up at the office (Infocom 1999).

---

4 Society's expenses for transport infrastructure and usage amounts to 1%–2% of GDP in OECD countries, while the total social cost, which traffic would have to pay for in order to internalise all external costs, amounts to 4%–8% of GDP.

14.2 Virtual meetings and the ICT-based communication medium

One way to tackle this growing problem is to replace travel with virtual meetings. I will briefly describe the concept of a virtual meeting and elaborate on the possibilities and consequences of shifting some of the business communication to the ICT-based medium.

14.2.1 Virtual meetings: what are they?

Virtual meetings have been around ever since Alexander Graham Bell invented the telephone in 1876. Since then, we have been able to communicate with each other at two or more locations in real time. The virtual communication toolbox has expanded rapidly over the years, with a number of new communication tools and users. The telephone system has been described as the 'world's largest machine' (Karlsson and Sturesson 1995: 286) with more than one billion stationary telephones (POTS—plain old telephone system), mobile phones, faxes, modems and other communication tools connected in a literal World Wide Web. The cost of telecommunications is constantly declining, while availability and reliability is increasing.

Most telephone conversations take place between two people. If a meeting with more than two people is scheduled to take place, a **multi-user audioconference call** can be used to connect three or more telephones at the same time. Another option is to connect via a **conference telephone**, a type of telephone with a speaker function that allows a group of people to communicate via the phone with one or several people at the other end. These two options are called **audioconferencing**. The big drawback of audioconferencing is that you cannot see the person or people with whom you are talking. This problem is overcome by **videoconferencing**, in which two or more places are connected via special equipment that allows the participants to both listen and to see each other.

There are two main types of videoconferencing system: desktop systems and group systems. A group system typically consists of a big television and a camera along with such accessories as electronic whiteboards, document cameras and computers. Using this system, several people can participate at each end. Desktop or personal videoconferencing usually consists of a computer equipped with a small camera, a microphone, a video and audio circuit board, and special software. With this equipment one to two persons can communicate from each computer. Multi-user conferences are possible as several computers can be connected simultaneously.

Computer links also offers the possibility of online collaboration, making it possible for a group of people to simultaneously and remotely edit the same document, draw pictures, give oral and visual presentations and so on. Communication via the Internet offers a nearly unlimited range of options, and this technology is developing very quickly (Halme *et al.* 2001).

14.2.2 Virtual meetings and their environmental implications

The electronics industry is generally considered to be a 'clean' industry with a limited environmental impact. This may be true compared to many other industries. However, the size and growth of the electronics industry makes its environmental impact potentially very significant. Materials production and manufacturing require large amounts of resources, including a number of heavy metals. End-of-life systems for electronic goods currently exist in only six countries,[5] leaving the vast majority of countries in the world with a minimal or non-existent system in place for take-back and recycling of electronics.

Consequently, an important question needs to be asked: do virtual meetings have an eco-advantage over business travel once the environmental impacts of the necessary communication technologies have been factored in? British Telecom (see Table 14.1) tackled this issue in 1991 when the company compared the energy used to make a telephone call with that of a journey, either by car, rail or air (BT 1991).

Type of call	Mode of transport	Distance (km)	Length of time on phone to use equivalent amount of energy
Local	Car	10	21 hours
Trunk	Rail	320	33 days
Trunk	Car	320	7 days
International	Air	5,000	5 weeks

Table 14.1 **Comparison of the energy used for transportation and a telephone call**

Source: BT 1991

A more comprehensive approach is to examine this question from a life-cycle analysis (LCA) perspective. In one Swedish LCA study, the environmental impact from a video-conference between two offices in Stockholm and Gothenburg was compared with the impact of one person travelling by high-speed train and by air (Östermark *et al.* 1999). The study took into account seven different ecological impact categories (resource depletion, global warming, acidification, eutrophication, photo-oxidant formation, toxicity and eco-toxicity) using two different possible scenarios. In scenario 1, the equipment was used 5 hours per week and left in standby mode for the rest of the week, while in scenario 2 the videoconference was used 30 hours per week and left in standby mode only during office hours.

The LCA study found an environmental advantage for the videoconference, though not in all circumstances. The environmental impact of the virtual meeting was at least five times less than flying. In scenario 2, when the equipment was used 30 hours per week, the environmental impact was comparable to that of a train trip. However, when the equipment was used as little as in scenario 1 and left on all the time, the train trip had less environmental impact in several impact categories.[6] The frequency and type of use is

5   Norway, Switzerland, the Netherlands, Taiwan, Japan (March 2001) and Sweden (July 2001).
6   The system boundaries set up for the LCA were intentionally chosen to be unfavourable for the videoconference as compared to the two means of transport. The construction, use and scrapping of the telecom equipment and networks were included in the comparison, but this was not the case for the two transportation modes. For the train and aeroplane, only the use of electricity/fuel was included. When only the use of the electronic equipment was included, the impact from videoconferencing was a hundredfold less.

obviously a very important factor in garnering an environmental benefit (as well as economic benefits) from the use of ICTs.

14.2.3 Virtual meetings as a replacement for travel

Does the use of virtual communication technology reduce travelling? This question has been the subject of numerous research studies, focusing mainly on the use of teleconferencing. In one of the first studies of its kind (1983–86), David Bennison found that 87% of the respondents in the UK were convinced that the use of the videoconference had led to a reduction in travelling, while no one claimed that it had caused an increase in travel (Bennison 1988). According to a 1993 Yankee Group study, *Fortune* 1,000 companies were asked about their use of videoconferencing and how much travel it had replaced. One third of the respondents said that it had had little impact on their companies' travel; 16% said that video meetings had replaced travel a lot; and 51% said it had replaced travel 'somewhat' (Feldman 1993). A comprehensive review article in the *Transportation Journal* concerning the effect of videoconferencing on business air travel concluded that 79% of corporate travel managers think that videoconferencing reduces travel costs, audioconferencing more commonly replaces travel than videoconferencing, and that the meetings that most often are replaced by virtual meetings are internal business meetings (Bender and Stephenson 1996).

In 1999, I conducted a number of studies on the use of videoconferencing and its impact on business travel in Swedish companies and organisations (Arnfalk 1999). Figure 14.1 show the conclusion of the surveys that ask respondents to state how the use of video-

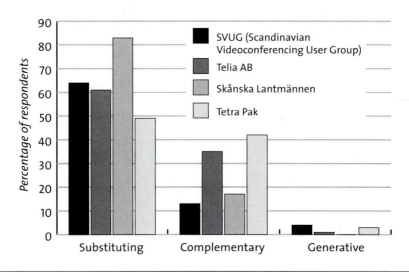

Figure 14.1 **Respondents' impression of the effect that their use of videoconferencing has had on their own business travel. Personnel in four Swedish organisations were surveyed: the Scandinavian Videoconferencing User Group, the companies Tetra Pak and Telia, and the farmers' association Skånska Lantmännen**

Source: Arnfalk 1999

conferencing had impacted their travelling. The results from these studies support the findings from the previous research that **substitution** (i.e. the technology is used to replace an in-person meeting that would have required travelling) of trips is the dominant effect. To a lesser extent, videoconferencing was also found to be used as a **complement** (i.e. virtual communication used as a complement to ordinary in-person meetings—the applications do not affect travelling) to an unchanged number of business trips.

But in very few cases, the survey showed **generation** (i.e. the use of virtual communication makes it possible to initiate and maintain more geographically distant contacts, leading to a net increase in travelling) of additional travel. The savings in travelling differed between the surveyed organisations, and depended on such factors as frequency of equipment usage, the number of participants in a meeting that would have had to travel, the geographical distribution of the organisations studied, and the types of meeting substituted.

14.2.4 The limited use of virtual meetings

As the virtual meeting format is a relatively new phenomenon and relies on technology that has been developed over the last few decades, it may take some time before conference telephones and videoconference equipment become standard office technologies. However, the promise of improved efficiency, increasing demand for 'quality' time, cost–benefit savings and so on associated with virtual meeting technologies may never be realised unless there is an increase in the number of users in companies and organisations. To find out why people were so reluctant to switch to virtual meetings, I conducted a comparative study of users and non-users in 1999 using a group of employees from two Swedish organisations: the Scanian Farmers' Association and the telecom company Telia (Arnfalk 1999).

14.2.4.1 Non-users

Employees from these two organisations were asked why they had never used the videoconferencing equipment and their responses are shown in Table 14.2. The two most common responses were 'never been asked to try' and 'never felt any need to use it'. These two answers indicate that there is a lack of basic awareness of these technologies, and that the employees have little or no knowledge of what videoconferencing can be used for. It is noteworthy that the telecom company Telia has employees that do not know how to locate or how to use the videoconference equipment.

Very few respondents asserted that not being able to take advantage of tax-free goods (at airports, on ferries, etc.), frequent-flyer credits and travel allowances have influenced their decisions. However, when people in this group were asked what they consider as the major obstacle in the efforts to reduced travel, a majority of the respondents agreed that these factors are important or very important. An interesting anecdote illustrates the importance of the frequent-flyer programme. Given a choice between an immediate departure with an airline that did not provide any bonus points or waiting an extra hour for an airline that did, 18 out of 20 employees at a major Swedish company on a flight between Oslo and Stockholm chose the later flight (Kogg 2000).

Reasons for never using videoconferencing	Telia (%)	Skånska Lantmännen (%)
Don't know where the equipment is; don't know how to do it	30	17
Never been asked to try	77	70
No access to the equipment	23	11
Never felt any need to use it	41	52
Can't replace a physical meeting	4	5
Too few/no meeting partners with access to videoconferencing equipment	9	11
Nicer to travel	2	0
Miss out on travel expense compensation, on tax-free goods and frequent-flyer points	2	0
Other reasons	7	6

Table 14.2 **Reasons for not using videoconferencing given by respondents in the organisations Skånska Lantmännen (Scanian Farmers' Association) and the telecom company Telia**

Source: Arnfalk 1999

14.2.4.2 Users

Figure 14.2 shows the responses from the employees who use the videoconferencing equipment and they indicate that they are far from satisfied with how the technology works. Technical problems can eventually be overcome, but issues such as the lack of socialising and bonding with colleagues and business contacts and doing away with the discomfort of the new forms of meeting are much harder to resolve.

One key problem with virtual meetings is that they do not fully replace in-person meetings. A large part of communicating and getting an impression of somebody is through eye contact, facial expressions, gestures, handshakes, scents, the way they dress and so on, and much of this kind of information unfortunately gets lost in a virtual meeting setting. A videoconference studio with good sound and picture transfer, combined with the possibility of viewing and sharing documents, is probably the closest (commercially available) alternative to a real meeting today. But how much of an in-person meeting does this actually manage to replace? This question was posed to the employees at four organisations and the responses are noted in Figure 14.3. The average 'degree of substitution' was 61%, varying from 50% to 68% between the different organisations, with more than 15% of the respondents believing that 100% of the meetings could be replaced (Arnfalk 1999)

A more common form of virtual meeting is audioconferencing. In a recent study at the Swedish telecom company Telia, employees were asked about their use of audioconferencing, videoconferencing and Netmeeting (an Internet and PC-based conference system). Audioconferencing was by far the most frequently used, with more than 90% of

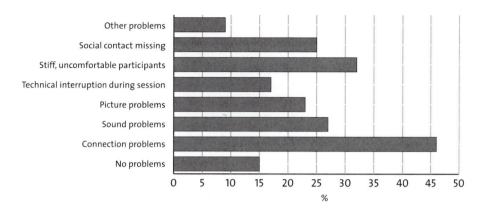

Figure 14.2   ***Main problems experienced during videoconferences. The results shown are the average figures from surveys at the Scandinavian Videoconferencing User Group, the companies Tetra Pak and Telia, and the farmers' association Skånska Lantmännen***

Source: Arnfalk 1999

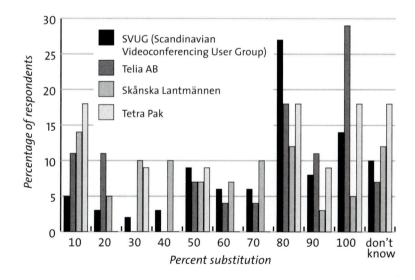

Figure 14.3   ***Respondents' impression of the 'degree of substitution' that videoconferencing had in relation to an in-person meeting. Results are collected from surveys at four organisations: Scandinavian Videoconferencing User Group, the companies Tetra Pak and Telia, and the farmers' association Skånska Lantmännen***

Source: Arnfalk 1999

the respondents using telephone conferences for business meetings (on average eight times per month). This can be compared to the use of Netmeeting (71% on average once per month) and videoconferencing (14.5% on average three times per year). The respondents were also asked if they felt as comfortable having a virtual meeting as when they had an in-person meeting. In the case of audioconferencing, 9% fully disagreed, as compared to 22% for videoconferencing. Concerning both types of meeting, a majority of the respondents agreed that they were disturbed by other participants' lack of skills in how to act in the meeting and how to use the equipment.

14.2.5 The future outlook for virtual meetings

How can we overcome the deeply rooted travel and in-person meeting culture and make the transition to a more sustainable work environment? An important step may be for companies and organisations to acknowledge and understand the environmental dimensions of business travel. If the environmental angle does not get the necessary attention, then bringing greater awareness of the financial cost of travel expenses may help convince senior management as to the importance of this issue.

Another important step is to have easily accessible and well-functioning virtual alternatives to in-person meetings. Common facilities such as conference telephone rooms or video studios to hold a virtual meeting are essential as is a person within the organisation with responsibility for ensuring that the communication technology and equipment is in good working order. In too many cases people have had bad initial experiences with the technology and are scared away forever. It should be as simple as booking a flight with a travel agent.

Moreover, employees need to know and understand the different options available. They should be encouraged to try the videoconference equipment and learn what kind of meeting it can be used as a substitute for. The initial resistance in trying out and learning something new can be a powerful discouraging force. If top management 'walks the talk' and acts as a vanguard, this shift has a greater chance of being successful in the long run.

Once the basic technology and human resources infrastructure is in place, an organisation needs to make a firm commitment in facilitating and supporting a shift away from the traditional business travel system. To move away from thinking just in terms of travelling and instead focusing more on actual meetings and communications, an organisation may wish to devise a common booking system for both virtual meetings and traditional business trips. A meeting bureau may be retained instead of a travel bureau to help suggest and set up the optimal form of meeting for each type of occasion.[7] Furthermore, the budget allocation for travel can instead be targeted for meetings, and a travel allowance may become a meeting allowance. Making these kinds of shift can be a major challenge, as they disturb systems that are well established in people's minds and in organisational culture. The important thing is to develop awareness and acceptance of the alternatives to travel, throughout the entire organisation.

---

7   The construction company Skånska and the travel bureau Bennet BTI are currently building a joint system for this kind of meetings management.

HOW FABULOUS FABLESSNESS?
Environmental challenges of economic restructuring in the semiconductor industry

Jan Mazurek
Progressive Policy Institute, USA

In 1965, Intel Corp. founder Gordon Moore accurately predicted that the semiconductor industry's focus on continuous innovation would double the power of a computer chip every 18–24 months. Such advances have been powered in part by the industry's use of chemicals that rank among the most toxic in industrial production (LaDou 1986). From the onset, the US semiconductor industry's focus on rapid innovation has confounded attempts to evaluate the environmental and human health effects of microchip manufacture. More recently, large-scale shifts in how and where US firms produce or 'fabricate' chips, has made tracking and evaluating the environmental impact of semiconductor manufacture even more complicated.

The ability of microchip companies to build 'fabs' (free-standing production plants) anywhere and/or subcontract with third parties obviously makes environmental problems harder to identify, understand and manage. The following case study shows how the leading US chemical registry, the Toxics Release Inventory (TRI), fails to account for the effects of globalisation and economic restructuring in the US semiconductor industry. The TRI is based on the increasingly outmoded assumption that one firm, under one factory roof in the United States still conducts production. Although TRI data shows a decrease in toxics released and transferred off-site by the semiconductor industry since 1988, it is likely that organisational and geographic shifts have contributed to the declines.

Another problem with relocation is that, although US environmental laws help to ensure that states follow uniform environmental standards, not all jurisdictions possess the same level of resources, industry-specific expertise and even political will to administer and enforce federal laws. The case is even more pronounced at the international level. The uneven capacity among countries to administer environmental programmes may help to heighten controversy associated with industry expansion. Although there is insufficient evidence to show that US semiconductor companies build new fabs in regions where environmental regulations are weak, it appears to be the case that some localities most anxious to lure microchip fabs often possess the fewest public resources to protect human health and the environment.

15.1 Sources and types of restructuring

Restructuring may be understood as an effort among US semiconductor firms to improve long-overlooked weaknesses in production methods (Angel 1994). As long as US semiconductor firms faced few foreign competitors, there was little need to focus on product quality and manufacturing methods. US firms instead largely pursued a strategy of continuous technological innovation. Increased international competition, coupled with the complexities and spiralling cost of constructing fabrication facilities (a new fab may cost up to US$5 billion), have prompted some firms to pool the construction and operating cost of microchip fabs and others to abandon manufacturing entirely.

Table 15.1 illustrates three ways in which US semiconductor firms have restructured. 'Fabless' companies are firms that design and sell chips but do not fabricate them. Others have entered into strategic alliances to pool the cost of fab construction. Free-standing firms such as Intel find it in their interest to maintain control over production. However, improvements in design and manufacturing allow free-standing firms increasingly to locate production outside Silicon Valley in other parts of the United States and the globe. Whereas microchip design, fabrication and assembly once took place under a single company roof, a chip engineered and sold by a Texas firm may now be crafted by a competitor in Phoenix, New York or Taiwan, assembled in Singapore and sold in Los Angeles.

15.2 Misleading toxic release and transfer trends

Although many of the environmental effects of chemicals used to fabricate microchips remain undocumented, a few notorious substances have been linked to spontaneous abortion among women who work in microchip fabrication facilities. Some health experts believe that chemicals used to manufacture microchips can cause more serious health problems, such as cancer. And, as the legacy of Silicon Valley shows, the industry has generated large quantities of hazardous waste. In addition to housing the single highest density of high-tech electronic firms, Santa Clara County boasts 29 of the US Environmental Protection Agency's Superfund sites: the largest collection of toxic contamination spots of any county in the United States.

Restructuring, including the attendant shift of chip fabrication out of Silicon Valley, complicates even further efforts to evaluate industry and corporate environmental performance. For example, in the firm's annual report for 1995, National Semiconductor pointed to an 88% reduction in chemicals reported to the TRI since 1988 as an example of environmental progress (National Semiconductor 1995). The Semiconductor Industry

Company headquarters	Partner	Fab locations			
		United States	Asia	Europe	Middle East
FABLESS COMPANIES					
SEEQ Technology, California	American Microsystems Inc. (AMI) Hualon Microelectronics International Microelectronic Products Ricoh Rohm Samsung	Idaho	Korea Taiwan Japan		
Cyrix Corporation, Texas	IBM Microelectronics SGS Thomson	New York New Jersey Vermont Arizona Texas		France Italy	
STRATEGIC PARTNERS					
Advanced Micro Devices, California	Sony Microelectronics Fujitsu Ltd	California Texas	Japan	Germany	
National Semiconductor, California	Intel Corp. National Semiconductor Sunrise Ltd Synaptics Inc. Integrated Information Technology	Maine Texas Utah		Scotland	
FREESTANDING FABS					
Intel Corporation, California	National Semiconductor Advanced Micro Devices	California Arizona New Mexico Oregon Puerto Rico		Ireland	Israel
Cypress Semiconductor, California		California Texas Minnesota			

Note: Cyrix Corporation purchased by National Semiconductor in 1997.

Table 15.1 **Three production types**

Source: SEC 1997

Association (SIA) similarly cites TRI data since 1988 as an indication that toxics released and transferred off-site by the industry are declining (SIA 1997a). However, what National Semiconductor and SIA fail to discuss is whether the declines are due to superior environmental performance or to other factors. As the following case study makes clear, at least some of the declines are due to globalisation and economic restructuring.

The chief reason that the TRI reports fail to account for the effects of globalisation and restructuring is that organisational change in the industry has outpaced federal record-keeping methods. In a supplement on Silicon Valley, *The Economist* (1997a: 19) observed: 'It is hard to exaggerate how far ahead of the American government Silicon Valley has moved. Even the statistics are a quagmire.'

Established in the 1930s, the nation's standard industrial classification (SIC) fails to reflect some of the most basic features of high-tech sectors. For example, software publishers in California are ineligible for research and development tax credits because the SIC fails to classify the companies as 'manufacturers' (Hamilton 1996). The SIC is currently undergoing an overhaul to make it more accurately reflect the US business landscape. Yet it remains unclear whether the revised codes will precisely reflect the new industrial configuration of chip making. In the absence of correct statistics, information to help chart economic alignments among designers, foundries and manufacturers is best obtained through trade press articles and reports filed annually by public companies with the Securities and Exchange Commission (SEC).

The weaknesses of the SIC system are incorporated into federal environmental tracking tools such as the TRI, which identifies sectors, industries and individual facilities with two-digit and four-digit SIC codes. Congress created the TRI as part of Title III of the Superfund Amendments and Reauthorisation Act (SARA), to avoid the type of contamination that arose from Union Carbide's accident in Bhopal, India. Title III develops emergency response provisions in order to avert similar tragedies. The US Environmental Protection Agency (EPA) developed the TRI to provide the public with continuing information on firms' emissions and transport activities.

The TRI is a useful tool for people who use the database to track chemical emissions at facilities that produce products designed and sold by one company. Interested individuals may use the database to track the 343 chemicals (expanded to roughly 650 in 1994) on which firms must report. For example, a Silicon Valley public-interest coalition staged a protest at a Santa Clara IBM plant in 1989 after learning from the TRI that the facility was responsible for emitting the largest quantity of chlorofluorocarbons (CFCs) in the United States. The group demanded and received from IBM a pledge to reduce and eventually phase out the use of the ozone-depleting substances (EPA 1990: 323).

Although the database helps individuals to track and monitor progress at facilities owned and operated by a single firm, it is a less useful measure of industry progress in reducing TRI emissions and transfers off-site. For example, the TRI cannot be used to hold accountable a fabless company that merely designs and sells microchips but contracts their fabrication out to third parties. In addition, the TRI is not a useful tool with which to compare performance among firms that continue to own and operate microchip fabrication plants. Fab closure, strategic alliances and the increasing ability of chip-makers in recent years to build new fabs abroad further limit the TRI's usefulness as a measure of industry performance. Trade press articles and company shareholder reports help to plug some data holes, but notable gaps remain. The gaps are more glaring for product identity and output data: information necessary to evaluate environmental performance among different facilities and firms.

To gain further insight into the possible sources of the TRI declines, the following discussion pairs economic information developed for six US companies with the data reported by the companies to the TRI. The six companies appear in Table 15.2. They range in size from small (e.g. SEEQ Technology) to giants such as Intel as measured in terms of revenue. In fiscal year 1996, SEEQ's revenues were US$31,338,000 (SEEQ 1997: 2). In contrast, Intel's sales in 1996 came to US$20.8 billion. The distinction is important because it is generally the case that smaller companies report that they are less able than Fortune 500 firms to devote resources to environment, health and safety issues (EHS). Combined, the six companies represent between 5% and 12% of all releases and transfers reported to the TRI by semiconductor firms operating in the United States between 1988 and 1995, respectively.

Company	Revenues (US$)	Primary products
Intel	20,870,000,000	Microprocessors
National Semiconductor	2,623,100,000	System-level products for fax machines, local and wide-area networking and telecommunications
Advanced Micro Devices	1,953,019,000	Microprocessors
Cypress Semiconductor	528,400,000	Memory chips and programmable logic devices
Cyrix	183,825,000	Microprocessors
SEEQ Technology	31,338,000	Local area network (LAN) chips

Table 15.2 **Firm size, by revenue, fiscal year 1996**

Source: SEC 1997

Table 15.3 shows emissions and transfers off-site of toxic chemicals for the six firms. SEEQ filed TRI reports up to 1990. However, no TRI data is available for SEEQ in 1995 because the company by then had permanently closed its California fab. Likewise, Cyrix is a 'fabless' chip company that relies entirely on third-party suppliers to manufacture its chips.

Company	Reporting year (pounds)	
	1988	1995
Intel	523,692	2,618,082
National Semiconductor	580,861	209,917
Advanced Micro Devices	442,246	308,670
Cypress Semiconductor	19,123	579
SEEQ Technology	2,950	n/a
Cyrix	0	0
Total	*1,568,872*	*3,137,248*

Table 15.3 **TRI releases and transfers, 1988, 1995**

Source: EPA 1997b

Overall, between 1988 and 1995, releases and transfers fell for three of the firms for which TRI data is available for both years. Only Intel's total TRI amounts increased between 1988 and 1995. Intel's increases are likely to be the result of significant expansion at the company's reporting facilities such as those in New Mexico. The increase may also be due to EPA's decision to nearly double the number of chemicals on which firms are required to report.

To help account for TRI declines, Table 15.4 illustrates changes during the same period in the number and location of facilities operated by five of the six companies for which TRI data is available. Recall that Cyrix is a fabless producer which most recently con-

Company	1988	1995
Cyrix	n/a	n/a
AMD	California (5) Texas (2)	California (1) Texas (1)
Cypress	California (1) Texas (1)	Texas (1) Minnesota (1)
Intel	Arizona (2) California (3) New Mexico (1) Oregon (2)	Arizona (1) New Mexico (1) Oregon (1) Puerto Rico (1)
National Semiconductor	Arizona (1) Connecticut (1) Maine (1) Texas (1) Utah (1)	Maine (1) Texas (1) Utah (1)
SEEQ Technology	California (1)	n/a
Total	23	11

Note: A TRI 'facility' does not necessarily denote a microchip fab.

Table 15.4 *TRI facilities reporting, 1988, 1995*

Source: EPA 1997b; SEC 1997

tracted manufacturing out to IBM Microelectronics and SGS Thomson. The most obvious trend among the five firms is the shift of manufacturing facilities away from California to other parts of the United States. The number of AMD California facilities reporting to the TRI dropped from five to one over the period. Intel's dropped from three to one. SEEQ closed its California fab in 1992 and California-based Cypress opened fabs in Texas and Minnesota. The remaining AMD and Intel facilities in California are primarily used for research purposes rather than high-volume production and thus are not likely to trigger TRI reporting thresholds.

With the exception of Cypress Semiconductor, which experienced no net change in the number of reporting facilities during the period, the number of facilities reporting to the TRI also declined. For all five firms, the number of facilities that filed TRI reports fell from 23 to 11 from 1988 to 1995. AMD's fell from seven to two and Intel's from seven to four. National's dropped from five to three.

There are a number of possible explanations for the TRI declines. One is that the facility continued to operate but did not use any of the 650 chemicals in sufficient quantity to trigger a report. Another is that the facility was temporarily idled or converted to another use. Finally, facilities may simply have been closed. In the case of National Semiconductor, some of the TRI declines are clearly due to the closure of manufacturing facilities. According to annual reports and features in the trade press, in 1988 National Semiconductor announced plans to phase out its Santa Clara microchip production lines and shift production to Arlington, Texas. National also sold, then leased back, its Texas fab and Santa Clara microchip development centre in 1990. The firm's Danbury, Connecticut, and Tucson facilities were idled by 1994. During the period, National also sold its Puyallup, Washington, fab to Matsushita, a Japanese microchip manufacturer. Whereas National closed, sold or idled some facilities in the United States, the company also expanded and constructed new microchip manufacturing facilities overseas. National, until 1998, operated three fabs in Scotland's 'Silicon Glen'.[1]

According to company reports, National has maintained a manufacturing presence in Scotland since the 1970s.[2] However, the company also significantly expanded production there during the reporting period. National reported that production at its Scotland facility increased by 85% in 1994.[3] Although the company is obviously not required to report to the TRI on emissions from its overseas facilities, National Semiconductor reports that emissions at the Greenock, Scotland, fabs in 1994 declined by more than 18% and water usage by 25% (see footnote 3). National also operates manufacturing facilities in Malaysia. More recently, National Semiconductor launched the company's first joint venture called National Semiconductor Shanghai Sunrise Ltd in China (see footnote 2). Located in Shanghai, the joint venture includes manufacturing and testing facilities.

AMD similarly shut down all manufacturing facilities in Silicon Valley, retaining only its advanced manufacturing facility. AMD also sold two of its Texas fabs to Sony Microelectronics. AMD currently operates a fab in Japan in conjunction with Fujitsu and is constructing another fab there, as well as in the former East Germany.

Whereas National and AMD still operate fabs, SEEQ announced in 1991 plans to phase out production entirely at its California facility and close the plant in 1992. SEEQ now obtains chips from a changing set of suppliers, known as 'foundries'. Foundry suppliers focus exclusively on manufacturing and not on design or sales. In 1996, SEEQ's manufacturing partners included American Microsystems Inc. (AMI) Semiconductor, Ricoh, Rohm, Samsung and Taiwan Semiconductor Manufacturing Corporation (TSMC). According to its company reports, Ricoh lists manufacturing facilities in California and Georgia. Samsung operates microchip fabs in Korea and Portugal and recently announced plans to construct a new fab in Austin, Texas. TSMC operates two fabs in Taiwan's version of Silicon Valley, the Hsin-chu region, and has announced plans to add two additional facilities in Taiwan.

SEEQ's foundry partners in 1995, the most recent year for which EPA has released TRI reports, included AMI Semiconductor, Hualon Microelectronics, International Microelectronic Products (IMP), Ricoh, Rohm and Samsung (SEEQ 1996). According to an e-mail reply from a SEEQ representative, the company is too small to mount an active programme to monitor the environmental performance of microchip suppliers. However,

---

1   In 1998, National announced plans to consolidate manufacturing from three fabs to one in Scotland and sought investors to purchase its remaining fab. The company's 1998 decision to seek investors for its remaining facility was reversed in 1999; however, National did proceed with its consolidation.

2   National Semiconductor (1997) list of worldwide manufacturing facilities. Available at www.national.com/company/index.html.

3   National Semiconductor (1996) Greenock, Scotland, available at www.national.com/environment/momentum/location05.html.

'SEEQ works under the assumption that local laws and ordinances in suppliers' respective jurisdictions govern day to day factory discharge and disposal.'[4]

It is not possible to use the TRI to gauge emissions for SEEQ's overseas suppliers. However, releases and transfers in 1995 do appear on the database for SEEQ's US supplier, AMI. That year, releases and transfers for AMI's Pocatello, Idaho, facility came to 8,256 kg. Nonetheless, it is impossible to determine what proportion of AMI's releases and transfers were due to production for SEEQ. It may be SEEQ's other foundry partners have facilities in the United States as well but either failed to use TRI chemicals or used TRI chemicals in insufficient quantities to trigger reports. Another possibility is that TRI reports are listed under another SIC code. For example, SEEQ supplier Ricoh also makes photocopiers and other electronic equipment that appear under other parts of the SIC 36 designation and possibly also parts of SIC 35. In any case, it is impossible to use the TRI to identify what proportion of releases and transfers from SEEQ's third-party suppliers were due to production of SEEQ products. If revenues are a proxy for output, however, it is likely that environmental impacts from SEEQ are relatively small compared with companies such as Intel and National Semiconductor.

Similarly, no TRI reports exist for Cyrix because, like SEEQ, the Texas-based microprocessor firm is a fabless company. Before the company was purchased by National Semiconductor in 1997, Cyrix primarily obtained supplies from IBM Microelectronics and SGS Thomson. IBM Microelectronics reported emissions and transfers to the TRI for its US facilities in 1995, but it is impossible to determine how much of IBM's emissions are due to production for Cyrix. According to an e-mail reply from IBM's Corporate Environmental Affairs department, it is not possible to segregate TRI release and transfer data for Cyrix's product because IBM manufactures the product in the same buildings, using the same equipment as it does for the manufacture of IBM's own product. According to the company: 'If IBM performed foundry work in a building on production lines dedicated solely to Cyrix production, segregating TRI data would be relatively simpler.'

Presently, however, IBM representatives report that implementing a scheme to segregate releases and transfers from its own products and those of Cyrix would be costly because the amount of chips that the company manufactures for Cyrix's products represents a small portion of IBM's overall production from the facility. Since IBM's production for Cyrix forms a relatively small proportion of output and TRI releases and transfers, IBM believes that environmental health and safety resources are better invested 'in producing real environmental benefits'.[5]

In terms of industry-wide trends, it is possible that a proportion of the TRI declines since 1988 result from firms shifting production to newer, more efficient fabrication facilities outside California. In other words, emissions fell because one new fab can do the same work as two or three older facilities. However, in order to compare emissions among fabs, adjustments must be made for output, microchip type and chemical use, data that for the most part is impossible to obtain.

4 Personal communication with James Middleton, Director of Operations, SEEQ Technology Incorporated, 29 October 1997.
5 Personal communication with Edan Dionne, Corporate Environmental Affairs, IBM Corporation, 14 October 1997.

15.3 Tracking global emissions

Whereas some firms merely shifted production away from California into other parts of the United States, three of the six firms examined also constructed new or expanded existing microchip fabs abroad since 1988. Because firms with operations outside the United States and its territories are not required to report to the TRI, such geographic shifts of both production and pollution may contribute to the appearance of improved environmental performance. For example, by 1995 Intel had expanded fab operations to Ireland and Israel. Similarly, National expanded production at its Scotland fabs. Finally, AMD in conjunction with Fujitsu constructed a new facility in Japan.

In 1993 IBM Corporation modified its internal reporting requirements in order to help the public to track emissions from its non-US facilities engaged in computer and microchip manufacture. Although EPA does not require US firms to report on emissions from overseas facilities, IBM voluntarily applied the TRI format to report on emissions from facilities abroad. The data, which does not distinguish between computer and microchip facilities, is available in the firm's 1996 annual environmental report for emissions from IBM facilities in the United States and abroad during 1995 (IBM 1996). That year, IBM's US sites, which manufacture chips as well as products such as computers, used 27 chemicals in sufficient quantity to trigger reporting. Combined, the facilities released or transferred off-site as waste 5.64 million kg. That same year, total SARA Section 313 and reportable quantities from IBM's non-US sites, including chip fabs, was 10.61 million kg (IBM 1996).

Between 1988 and 1995, three of the six firms studied here also sold or leased manufacturing facilities to foreign companies. For example, AMD sold two Texas fabs to Sony; National sold a Washington fab to Matsushita; National sold its Arlington, Texas, facility to an unspecified company and then leased the site back.

It is possible to use the TRI to track changes in facility ownership that result from lease or sale because EPA supplies each reporting firm with a facility identification code that does not change when a plant is sold. For example, while emissions from National's Puyallup, Washington, fab ceased in 1990, it is possible to use the facility identification code to determine that Matsushita now operates the facility. The TRI facility identification code also makes it possible to monitor emissions from the Texas fabs sold by AMD to Sony. While it is possible to use the TRI to continue to track emissions, the ownership transfers nonetheless contribute to the appearance that National and AMD's company-wide (as opposed to facility) TRI emissions and transfers declined.

Given the increased complexity of production relationships among chip firms, the TRI is an inaccurate measure of industry and company trends. As the six firms show, the development of the TRI coincides with the idling, closure and geographic shift of fabs to other parts of the United States and abroad.

In addition to serving as a tracking device, interested citizens and regulatory agencies also use the TRI to promote industry's environmental performance. When a fabless company has foundry partners in the United States, it is possible to use TRI reports to examine emissions and transfers from foundries. However, few foundries make chips exclusively for one partner. Some, such as IBM, also produce chips for firms such as Cyrix, as well as for IBM machines. Since fabless companies seldom pinpoint where foundries produce chips and in what amount, it is impossible to use the TRI to track most emissions due to US foundries. Foundry agreements and the location overseas of new US fabs further complicate efforts to assess environmental performance because US firms are not required to report on operations of overseas facilities. IBM's move to adopt the TRI format to report on its non-US facilities is a notable and promising exception. National Semiconductor and Intel supply information on the environmental performance of their overseas facilities but not in a format identical to TRI. It must also be noted that, while these three companies have elected voluntarily to report on some aspects of environmental performance of their foreign facilities, the data is impossible to verify in an independent way. What is clear is that, in the case of four of the sample firms examined here, declining TRI numbers may be due in part to the expansion both of US-owned fabs overseas and fabless partnerships with offshore foundries.

15.4 Accountability issues

As production relationships among chip companies become more complex, so do the associated environmental issues. One problem is that fablessness may reduce incentives for US companies to promote better environmental results from their constantly shifting sets of foundry suppliers.

The rising prominence of suppliers is not confined to the semiconductor industry, but occurs everywhere from the automotive to the entertainment industries. To promote the environmental performance of suppliers, some firms, academics and environmental managers have endorsed the adoption of voluntary worldwide environmental standards. Among the most prominent is the 14000 initiative by the International Organisation for Standardisation (ISO), a private, non-profit organisation that seeks to develop more uniform international business methods. The certification is predicated on the idea that attention to environmental concerns may become a source of advantage for suppliers and sellers.

To date, companies must obtain certification through third-party audits for one part of the series, ISO 14001. ISO 14001 describes in general features that a firm's environmental management system must contain. For example, companies should be committed to 'continual improvement and prevention of pollution' (ISO 1995: 8) and develop procedures and plans to identify the environmental aspects of different corporate operations.

Whereas the European Union (EU) lobbied for performance standards, the United States and others successfully countered that standards on pollution levels could impose trade barriers (Milliman 1995: 8). ISO 14001 could become a way for customers in one country to compel suppliers in another to adopt more uniform environmental management systems. Indeed, some EU countries seek to give preference to suppliers that have obtained ISO certification (Milliman 1995: 10).

15.5 Supplier selection

It is premature to evaluate the efficacy of ISO 14000 and 14001 because implementation is still largely under way. However, a growing number of studies have attempted to examine methods such as ISO 14001 to improve the environmental performance of suppliers in the electronics and computer industry (Bérubé 1992).

The studies identify the factors that promote firms to employ environmental concerns when selecting suppliers, as well as during supplier partnerships (Bérubé 1992; Sarkis *et al.* 1995). In a survey of 50 of the largest US computer companies, Bérubé found that, while firms' interest in integrating environmental concerns is growing, for most companies environmental concerns still are the least important factor when selecting a supplier. Among the few proactive companies that do use environmental criteria to select suppliers, Bérubé found that large companies are much more likely than smaller ones to consider environmental issues when selecting suppliers.

Related to Bérubé's findings is a study that shows that strategic partnerships that are long-term, information-intensive and forged from a small, rather than large, set of potential suppliers have a better chance of minimising materials use and waste generation (Sarkis *et al.* 1995).

In contrast, most fabless semiconductor companies such as SEEQ are relatively small, as measured in terms of staff size and sales. Recall that, in 1996, the company employed around 74 people and had slightly over US$31 million in revenues. In contrast, that same year Intel's revenues exceeded US$20 billion and the workforce worldwide was near 40,000. Another factor discouraging better supplier relationships is the extremely fluid nature of contracts, most of which are under five years. SEEQ, for example, does not maintain long-term, non-cancellable contracts with its microchip suppliers.[6] Consequently, suppliers could choose to prioritise manufacturing facilities for other uses or reduce or eliminate chip deliveries to SEEQ at extremely short notice.

Foundry partnerships may also discourage environmental concerns by providing few incentives for firms to enhance manufacturing methods. Producing microchips free of defects requires a high degree of technical skill, the latest equipment and close co-operation between microchip foundries and the circuit designer. However, short-term, variable partnerships and the often great geographic distance between fabless firms and overseas foundries diminish opportunities for designers and foundries to resolve production problems (Mazurek 1994). Though partnerships among producers require information exchange between product designers and manufacturers, technology licensing and co-operative technology development may provide greater opportunities to incorporate environmental concerns into product and process design. However, Angel (1994: 135) found that most agreements by chip design houses are for fabrication, as distinct from technology licensing or co-operative technology development.

That fabless production may fail to fit the criteria for the promotion of environmental concerns is not surprising, given that the current emphasis of fabless companies is on design, rather than manufacturing. Though fablessness does reduce expenditures associated with fab construction, the diminished focus on manufacturing carries risks for fabless companies as well. For example, it is not uncommon for foundries to experience manufacturing problems that result in delivery delays, or for partnerships to dissolve in less than five years as a result of recurrent supply or product performance problems. As Cyrix reports:

---

6 Personal communication with James Middleton, Director of Operations, SEEQ Technology Incorporated, 29 October 1997.

> The company's reliance on third-party manufacturers creates risks that the
> company will not be able to obtain capacity to meet its manufacturing require-
> ments, will not be able to obtain products with acceptable yields, or will not
> have access to necessary process technologies (Cyrix 1996: 15).

The experience of SEEQ illustrates what happens when a foundry partnership ends in divorce: 'In the second half of '95 our revenues were adversely affected by the unexpected phase-out of one of our foundry sources.' The company reacted by quickly establishing ties to two additional sources.

It is possible that the current set of conditions that discourage environmental concerns among foundries will subside as third-party suppliers mature and gain the ability to invest in equipment and upgrades. Indeed, TSMC, one of the largest and most established foundries, is currently constructing two new microchip fabs in Taiwan that the company pledges will deliver state-of-the-art environmental performance. The TSMC case suggests that, as chip firms increasingly search for methods to differentiate products from the competition, ISO 14001 certification may serve as a way for chip manufacturers to distinguish themselves in highly competitive markets. Currently, TSMC prominently features its Taiwanese fabs as meeting ISO 14001 management standards. National Semiconductor similarly advertises the ISO 14001-certified status of its Scotland facility on the company's website (see footnote 3; TSMC 1997).[7]

Bérubé finds that firms may eventually find it in their interest to incorporate environmental concerns if permitting or compliance problems lead to repeated product delays (Bérubé 1992: 1). However, such a scenario assumes that foundries are located in places with sufficient resources to scrutinise permits and conduct routine inspections. A recent analysis of 22 computer and electronics companies, including semiconductor firms based in five countries, found that, even though all the companies are based in advanced capitalist countries, half of their manufacturing and assembly facilities are in developing countries (Plazola 1997).

By all accounts, the majority of developing countries simply lack comparable resources to inspect and, when necessary, bring enforcement actions against firms that violate standards. Taiwan, home of TSMC, is perhaps the most notorious example. The large island suffers from serious air and water pollution, as well as a growing number of contaminated industrial sites due to its rapid economic growth during the last two decades (Arrigo et al. 1996: 765-77). As environmental conditions in Taiwan have continued to deteriorate seriously, the government has recently passed a flurry of environmental laws and introduced an enforcement agency patterned after those in the United States and Japan. Despite the proliferation of laws, Arrigo et al. (1996) report that there is little effective enforcement against polluters due primarily to fears that more stringent environmental protection will retard economic growth.

In the context of Taiwan's weak regulatory climate, efforts such as ISO 14001 could provide additional assurance that a company is meeting environmental goals. As the shortcomings of the TRI illustrate, the presence of voluntary international standards such as ISO 14000 may eventually help to make environmental management practices around the globe more uniform.

---

7   www.national.com/environment/momentum/location05.html;
    www.tsmc.com.tw/Image/iso14001e.html

15.6 **Summary**

Changes in how and where US semiconductor firms make chips outstrip the present ability of government institutions to track and monitor potential threats to humans and the environment. Mechanisms that could help to improve information about the industry, such as the TRI, are increasingly inadequate owing to complicated reconfigurations in how and where chips are produced.

Although new chip-making regions such as Taiwan's Hsin-chu have recently enacted environmental laws with standards that are comparable to those in the United States or Japan, these countries often lack both the resources and the political will to conduct inspections and enforcement.

It is too early to assess how well voluntary initiatives such as ISO 14001 improve environmental performance among suppliers. However, US semiconductor companies that rely on foreign foundries may find it in their interest to require their suppliers to adopt ISO 14001 or some similar voluntary standard if poor environmental performance is linked to low output and to production delays.

MICROPOWER
Electrifying the digital economy

Seth Dunn
Worldwatch Institute, USA

Utility stocks have long been thought of as stable, unexciting and suitable for 'widows and orphans'. But a handful of power industry newcomers have behaved rather out of character since the beginning of the new millennium. As of mid-May 2001, share prices in solar cell manufacturers Astropower and Energy Conversion Devices have roughly tripled and doubled. Fuel cell firms Fuel Cell Energy and Ballard Power Systems have seen their stocks roughly quadruple and double, respectively.

Far from a temporary day-trading trend, these recent stock surges in 'micropower' technology companies are symptomatic of systemic change in the electricity business. A 'triple power shock' of technological, economic and environmental trends is reviving Thomas Alva Edison's original vision of small-scale, localised electric generation, as new technologies as small as one-millionth the size of a large nuclear plant begin to enter the market. Now, as then, entrepreneurialism and investment capital are feeding off each other, bringing a long-dormant dynamism to the power sector.

The resurgence of smaller, more localised power has spawned a diverse nomenclature: distributed generation, on-site generation, personal power, small-scale generation, self-generation. But the underlying premise is simple: the growing economic value, and viability, of using decentralised, modular power that is closer to the site and scale of actual use. Parallels are being drawn with the recent revolutions in the telecommunications industry, which has been transformed by new technology and competition, and in the computer industry, which has been completely realigned by the rapid shift from mainframe to personal computers.

Cleaner, quieter and more efficient than their ancestors of a century ago, the new micropower technologies are more closely scaled to the electrical needs of today's world (see Table 16.1). Power use in residential and commercial buildings significantly outweighs industrial power use in most countries. And, while conventional power plants generate approximately 1 million kW, actual scales of use are far smaller: US residential

Plant type	Average scale (kilowatts)
Nuclear plant, 1980	1,100,000
Coal plant, 1985	600,000
Gas turbine, combined-cycle plant, 1990–2000	250,000
Industrial cogeneration plant, 2000	50,000
Wind turbine, 2000	1,000
Microturbine, 2000	50
Residential fuel cell, 2000	7
Household solar panel, 2000	3

Table 16.1 **Typical power plant scales, United States, 1980–2000**

Source: Lovins and Lehmann 2001; Cler *et al.* 1999

consumers use power at an average rate of no more than 1.5 kW, and commercial consumers 10 kW. Providing electrical services at these sizes, and nearer the user, avoids a whole range of economic and environmental costs associated with generating power from large, centralised thermal plants and delivering it over long distances.

In particular, rapid deployment of small-scale power would foreshorten the central model's long legacy of environmental damage by facilitating the broader energy transition to a clean, efficient renewable–hydrogen economy. For the two billion people who remain without access to electricity, micropower may represent the last best hope of joining the electrified world. As societies move towards more open, competitive electricity systems, the advantages of small-scale power will become increasingly apparent.

The merits of micropower may perhaps become most evident with the advent of the information or digital economy, whose growing need for reliable power is proving increasingly incompatible with the large, central system. As with political systems, structural change can occur with surprising speed when people stop taking the existing paradigm for granted. And, not unlike Soviet-style planning a decade ago, the large-scale electrical model is beginning to collapse under its own economic and ecological weight.

16.1 Hot little numbers

The leading edge of the micropower technologies—defined here as systems of 10 MW and below—is the 'genset', or reciprocating internal combustion (IC) engine, which is closely related to those found in trucks and buses and has for decades provided power for off-grid applications. Even as these traditional markets expand, a growing number of these systems are now being installed as backup generators for many commercial and even residential buildings. Since these engines are already mass-produced (for transport) by manufacturers around the world, they are relatively low-cost (as low as US$600/kW) and have a well-developed sales and maintenance infrastructure in some countries (see Table 16.2).

	Reciprocating engine	*Microturbine*	*Stirling engine*
Current size range (kilowatts)	5–10,000	30–200	0.3–25
Electrical efficiency (%)	20–45	27–30	15–30
Current installed cost ($ per kilowatt)	600–1,000	600–1,100	1,500
Expected installed cost with mass production ($ per kilowatt)	<500	200–400	200–300

Table 16.2 **Combustion-based micropower options**

Source: Cler *et al.* 1999

Their efficiencies range from 20% to 45%, but can reach more than 80% through the use of waste heat, or 'cogeneration', for water or space heating or industrial process heat. At least 20 companies already produce these systems, most based in Europe and North America; Waukesha and Caterpillar, for example, offer 25 kW units suitable for small commercial applications such as fast-food restaurants. The global market for these engines has more than doubled since 1990. The genset's immediate small-scale challenger is the microturbine, a tiny engine that uses heat released by combustion to spin a single shaft at high speed that in turn spins a high-speed generator. Microturbines are derived from commercial jet engines and the gas turbines now dominating the power market. Ranging in size from 15 to 300 kW, they are expected to be more efficient than IC engines, particularly if waste heat is re-used.

The chief advantage of microturbines is their expected low cost: with just two moving parts, they are easy to manufacture. They are also longer-lived, produce fewer local pollutants and are adaptable to a wide array of fuels, including natural gas, propane and biogas. Capstone Turbine has shipped several hundred of its 28 kW units and begun offering a 75 kW system that it has tested at restaurants, factories and bakeries. Company President Ake Almgren estimates that annual mass production of 100,000 units would bring the cost of 30 kW and 100 kW turbines to US$400 and US$200 per kilowatt, respectively: less than that of large gas turbines. He predicts that a US$1 billion microturbine industry will emerge within five years.

Another 'newcomer' to the small power market is Scottish engineer Robert Stirling's engine, invented in 1816, unable to find a commercial market in the 20th century, but renewed by modern advances in piston efficiency. These pistons are driven by a gas that is heated by 'external combustion', a cycle that allows the engine to be made at very small scales and run by natural gas, most combustible materials, including agricultural and forestry residues, and solar concentrators. Current versions have efficiencies of 10%–30%, are simple and highly durable, and require minimal maintenance.

Stirling engines are quieter and have lower emissions than IC engines. Their initial commercialisation will probably be at sizes of 30 W and below, useful for portable off-grid applications. A number of these engines have been installed in remote regions, and several companies are beginning to market packaged systems suitable for home use. The UK's BG Technology is testing a 1 kW cogenerating system that runs on natural gas and is small enough to fit into a kitchen cabinet.

16.2 Cool power

The most revolutionary micropower devices require no combustion or moving parts (see Table 16.3). The fuel cell, invented by British physicist William R. Grove in 1839, is an electrochemical device that splits hydrogen into ions that either run along an electrode or combine with oxygen, producing electricity and water. Deployed extensively in the US space programme, fuel cells are now—thanks to dramatic technical improvements—being explored as viable replacements for stationary power plants, the internal combustion engine and portable electronics.

	Fuel cell	Solar cell	Wind turbine
Size range (kilowatts)	<1–10,000	<1–1,000	<1–3,000
Electrical efficiency (%)	35–50	–	–
Current installed cost ($ per kilowatt)	2,000–3,500	5,000–10,000	900–1,000
Expected installed cost with mass production ($ per kilowatt)	100–300	1,000–2,000	500

Table 16.3 **Non-combustion-based micropower options**

Source: Cler *et al.* 1999

Initially running on hydrogen derived from natural gas or other hydrocarbons, fuel cells will eventually use pure hydrogen, with water as its only by-product. They also have no moving parts, high efficiency with cogeneration, and high reliability. Those attracting the most attention are phosphoric acid fuel cells (PAFCs), already available commercially, and proton-exchange membrane (PEM) fuel cells, which several companies plan to market in the next few years. An estimated 85 organisations are undertaking research on PEM fuel cells, including all of the world's major auto-makers. DaimlerChrysler, Honda and Toyota all aim to have fuel cell cars on the road by 2003–2004. Transport-driven improvements in fuel cells will benefit the stationary market, which is also receiving major attention. Ballard Power Systems and FuelCell Energy plan to deliver their first commercial 250 kW systems in 2001.

Other emerging micropower technologies run on renewable energy. Wind power is the world's fastest-growing energy source, with a 24% average annual growth rate during the 1990s. The generating cost of wind power has dropped eightfold since 1980: at 5 cents/kW, it is competitive with coal and natural gas. A US$4 billion annual global market, wind power is taking off most dramatically in Europe, which boasts seven of the top ten producers. The US, which is experiencing a resurgence, is second in new installations. By one estimate, wind power could supply 10% of global electricity by 2020 if recent growth rates are sustained. Promising regions include inland areas, such as the US Midwest and China's Inner Mongolia, and the offshore resource. Shell Renewables, which has invested US$500 million over five years in renewable energy, is exploring projects in the North and Baltic Seas.

Solar cells or photovoltaics (PVs), made of semiconductor chips that convert sunlight into electricity, held an average annual growth rate of 17% during the 1990s. Solar PVs have seen a fourfold cost decline since 1980, and are now a US$2.2 billion global industry. The leading manufacturer, BP Solar, reports annual revenues of US$2.2 billion and has cells in use in more than 150 countries. The fastest-growing sector is the grid-connected market, due to ambitious government solar rooftop programmes in Japan, Germany and the United States and the growing economic viability of building-integrated solar cells. Also poised for growth is the off-grid rural market, which is forecast to expand more than fivefold over the next ten years. Already, some 500,000 PV cells have been deployed in the developing world.

Hydropower, geothermal power and biomass energy have experienced slower growth over the past decade, ranging from 1% to 4%. These technologies are benefiting from modern advances that are increasingly orienting them towards small-scale applications, especially in the Americas and Asia. They, too, will contribute to a more downsized, decentralised and diversified power system

16.3 Is smaller greener?

Micropower carries several 'hidden benefits' over large-scale, central power generation; about 75 benefits, according to Amory Lovins and Andre Lehmann of the Rocky Mountain Institute (see Table 16.4 for a synthesis) (Lovins and Lehmann 2001). These relate largely to the 'diseconomies of scale' of building power plants at sizes as much as one million times the actual scale that is used. Including these benefits in comparisons of power sources, Lovins and Lehmann argue, would make wind farms more economical than natural gas-fired combined-cycle plants and make solar PVs broadly cost-competitive.

Some of the most significant benefits may be environmental. Tied to fossil fuel mining, extraction and combustion, nuclear fission and the construction of large hydro-electric dams, the large-scale generation, transmission and distribution of electricity is currently among the most ecologically disruptive of all human activities. Large-scale power generation is associated with several air pollutants, precursors to acid rain and the production of greenhouse gases that contribute to global climate change. US utility power plants, which rely on coal for 56% of their electricity, account for 64% of national

Benefit	Description
Modularity	Micropower system size can be adjusted, by adding or removing units, to match demand.
Short lead time	Small-scale power can be planned, sited and built more quickly than larger systems, reducing the risks of overshooting demand, longer construction periods and technological obsolescence.
Fuel diversity and reduced price volatility	Micropower's more diverse, renewables-based mix of energy sources lessens exposure to fossil fuel price fluctuations.
'Load-growth insurance' and load matching	Some types of small-scale power, such as cogeneration and end-use efficiency, expand with growing loads; the flow of other resources, such as solar and wind, can correlate closely with electricity demand.
Reliability and resilience	Small plants are unlikely to all fail simultaneously, have shorter outages, are easier to repair, and are more geographically dispersed.
Avoided plant and grid construction losses and connections	Small-scale power can displace construction of new plants, reduce grid losses, and delay or avoid adding new grid capacity or connections.
Local and community choice and control	Micropower provides local choice and control, and the option of relying on local fuels and spurring community economic development.
Avoided emissions and environmental impacts	Small-scale power generally emits lower amounts of particulates, sulphur and nitrogen oxides, and carbon dioxide, and has a lower cumulative environmental impact on land and water supply and quality.

Table 16.4 **Eight hidden benefits of micropower**

Source: Lovins and Lehmann 2001

sulphur dioxide emissions, 33% of mercury emissions, 26% of nitrogen oxide emissions and 36% of greenhouse gas emissions. Globally, electricity generation accounts for one-third of emissions of carbon dioxide, the most significant greenhouse gas. Large-scale power generation also imposes ecological burdens on land, water and wildlife through mining, the release of solid waste and heavy metals, and radiation risks.

Micropower systems will also entail certain 'life-cycle' environmental impacts. Those of solar PV will be the largest among non-combustion options, because of the energy needed to make silicon, but will be lower than those of combustion-based units. Life-cycle impacts will also vary according to the efficiency of the system and the fuel source. Those of combustion-based systems will depend on whether diesel, natural gas, biomass or solar thermal energy is used. Those of fuel cells will depend on the source of hydrogen: natural gas reformers will release air pollutants and carbon dioxide, but these levels can be halved through cogeneration. In the long term, hydrogen derived from renewable energy via electrolysis—the splitting of water by an electrical current—will almost eliminate life-cycle greenhouse gas emissions.

In general, the natural gas and renewable energy expected to run modern micropower units will have lower life-cycle emissions than the current mix. Combustion-based systems using waste heat can achieve overall efficiencies of 80%–90%, versus 30%–60% for a coal-fired power plant or 45%–80% for a large natural gas-fired turbine. Relying on natural gas or renewables and using cogeneration, micropower will on a per-kilowatt basis emit 50%–100% lower emissions of particulates, nitrogen and sulphur oxides, mercury and carbon dioxide.

Studies indicate that the United States could cut power plant carbon emissions by half or more by meeting new demand with microturbines, renewable energy and fuel cells. In the developing world, where half of new power generation over the next 20 years is to be built, power sector carbon emissions are projected to triple under business as usual. RAND Corporation reports suggest that widespread adoption of micropower would lower this trajectory by as much as 42% (Bernstein et al. 1999). These steps would also cut sulphur oxides by up to 72% and nitrogen oxides by up to 46%, while lowering electricity prices by 5%.

16.4 Digital demands

The summer heatwaves in the United States in 2000 offered a glimpse of the growing incompatibility between the 21st century's new information economy and the 20th century's ageing power system. Following a spate of power outages in California, publications as diverse as Internet Week Online and the New York Times ran headlines exclaiming 'E-commerce short on juice', 'Looming electricity shortages threaten Internet economy' and 'Digital economy's demand for steady power strains utilities'. At a Silicon Valley Energy Summit held in July, a spokesman for software giant Oracle proclaimed:

> The Internet changes everything, especially with electricity. A dependable, uninterrupted power supply is a top priority with the e-world . . . What we have worked fine for an economy that ran on motors and lights. There's a major disconnect with what's going on in the digital economy.

What is 'going on' in the digital economy is that growing dependence on computerised processes is heightening the need for high-quality, high-reliability power. With the rise of computerised transactions and manufacturing, users become more susceptible to momentary voltage fluctuations or outages. In the past, such glitches were less important, causing lights and motors to dim but not fail. But greater reliance on computers demands voltage stability; computer networks cannot withstand disruptions longer than eight-thousandths of a second, a time-span utilities do not consider long enough to be considered a failure. And these demands come at a time when the electricity system, because of old equipment and rising demand, is increasingly stressed and subject to outages or flickers, costing businesses US$50 billion in power quality breakdowns in 1999, according to the Electric Power Research Institute (EPRI) (Ginsburg and Aston 2000).

For businesses that already cite electricity as a critical lifeline service, the growing use of 'e-commerce'—which by one estimate may account for as much as 25% of total US electricity by 2010—is likely to further increase the need for reliable power. While US utilities can boast 99.9% reliability, EPRI's Mark Wilhelm argues, 'that is only good enough if you're running light bulbs and refrigerators. Any industry that is computer chip-based needs 99.999999% reliability.' The Silicon Valley Manufacturing Group's 175 mostly high-tech manufacturers lost millions of dollars in revenue from summer 2000 outages. While some of these firms have responded by installing backup diesel generators, the long-term micropower solution is beginning to be considered. The group held another energy summit in April 2001 focusing on the use of energy efficiency and micropower technology to guard against blackouts.

Micropower is especially valuable for high-tech industries such as computer chips, semiconductors, pharmaceuticals, chemicals and biotechnology, which rely on computerised manufacturing. Computer chip plants, for example, can employ fuel cells as a source of on-site power as well as of hot distilled water. Supermarkets, restaurants, insurance companies, hospitals and factories are now beginning to look to micropower—despite its current higher installation cost—to avoid costly interruptions. The US Postal Service in Anchorage, Alaska, now runs five fuel cells that protect its automatic mail-processing system against grid outages.

Micropower also represents insurance for computers at the heart of the financial system, vulnerable to costly power flickers. The First National Bank of Omaha, whose credit card operation loses US$6 million per hour of lost business, has now installed four fuel cells. According to Dennis Hughes, the bank's director of property management, fuel cells were over a 20-year life-span 'the cheapest way to go'.

16.5 The Internet, electricity and energy

While the rise of the digital or information economy will be an important initial niche for micropower, there is considerable debate about the overall implications of the Internet for electricity and overall energy consumption. The debate was launched, at least in the public eye, by a provocative piece published in *Forbes* in May 1999. The article, entitled 'Dig more coal: the PCs are coming', argued that the Internet-driven computer explosion was generating 'a stealth revolution in kilowatt-hour demand', signalling enormous growth prospects for the thermoelectric power industry (Huber and Mills 1999).

Calculating the electricity requirements of manufacturing and using 'digital boxes'—personal computers, office hubs and servers, routers and wireless handhelds—the *Forbes* article contended that the convergence of information and electrical systems was already beginning to affect power demand. Its authors, Peter Huber and Mark Mills, estimated that Internet usage accounts for 8% of total US electricity demand, with the number rising to 13% if power used to build and operate stand-alone chips and computers is included. The authors attributed half of the annual 3% growth in US electricity consumption to the rise of the microprocessor and predicted that within the next decade half of the electrical grid would be powering the digital-Internet economy.

The article immediately created a stir. Environmental groups quickly pointed out that the article was drawn from a report financed and published by Greening Earth Society, a lobbying group for the coal industry. Energy analysts from the Lawrence Berkeley National Laboratory and Rocky Mountain Institute took issue with the numbers employed in the article, arguing that they were inflated. Other experts observed that the article, while mentioning in passing the digital economy's growing need for reliable power, implicitly assumed that the current centralised infrastructure would be capable of keeping up with these new demands.

More recently, in the inaugural issue of their new *HuberMills Power Report*, the authors argue the opposite. They argue that:

> Hundreds of billions of dollars per year are going to be invested in new technologies to move, condition, store and distribute electrons for the Internet Economy . . . To accommodate this great energy shift, much of the sprawling infrastructure of the US power grid will have to be rebuilt (Huber and Mills 2000).

Also mentioned briefly in the *Forbes* article was the Internet economy's potential effect on overall energy consumption trends. Joseph Romm of the Center for Energy and Climate Solutions notes that US energy demand remained almost flat in 1997 and 1998 while the economy grew by 9%, and contends that efficiency gains from the emerging digital economy may be the reason. Romm projects that energy savings due to the Internet-related reduction of paper use, commercial building space, inventory size, shipping, and commuting and transportation could double the past decade's rate of energy intensity improvement over the next ten years (Romm *et al.* 1999).

As *The Economist* has pointed out, new technologies often generate optimistic claims for their ability to, for example, prevent war and reduce inequality (*Economist* 2000b). In the case of the Internet and energy, it remains unclear whether online activities will actually displace more energy-intensive ones, and the Internet's share of electricity will no doubt grow. Yet as Internet reliability issues increase the use of on-site power, this may in turn create an economic incentive to use electricity more efficiently. Romm's hypothesis cannot be proven, but neither can it be discarded.

16.6 Finding funders

The importance of reliable power to the new economy is beginning to dawn on the financial community. In January 2000, *Business Week* announced 'Don't look now, but utilities could be one of the hot new investment opportunities', while *Venture Capital Journal* declared the electricity industry 'The Next Big Thing'. The following months witnessed sharp rises in the shares of several micropower companies—particularly fuel cell and solar PV manufacturers—some by as much as sevenfold. Even after a subsequent decline, many remained well above pre-surge levels. Investment banks, meanwhile, scrambled to set up power technology divisions and to court the companies developing these technologies. Several companies went public in the summer of 2000 to a generally positive response, even as investors went sour on many 'dot.com' companies.

The recent investor interest in micropower companies reflects a deeper trend, paralleling that described in Thomas Hughes's *Networks of Power*, a survey of the development of electric power systems in Western society between 1880 and 1930. Initially, 'inventor-entrepreneurs' such as Edison were the key actors, presiding over the creation and application of their innovations. Later on, 'manager-entrepreneurs' and 'financier-entrepreneurs'—such as J.P. Morgan—began to take centre stage as the problems blocking the growth of the new system became more managerial and financial. Inventors and engineers still played an important role in the evolution of the system, but were complemented by players experienced in the complexities of organisations and financing (Hughes 1983).

The micropower system appears to be evolving in the same way. Echoing Hughes, equity analyst Hugh Holman explains that:

> one reason we take a more optimistic view toward the future of energy technology is that we see a new breed of entrepreneur appearing in the power industry—the financial, versus the techie, entrepreneur . . . Thus, from day one, the financial entrepreneur brings rigor to the management of a technology start-up and has an eye on the financial end game, the exit strategy.

Holman notes a growing number of investment funds, both venture capital (VC) and those funding companies at a later stage, that specifically target business opportunities created by energy deregulation, as well as venture funds that include energy-related investments in their diversified portfolios (Holman 1999).

One prominent energy VC firm, Nth Power Technologies, has fully invested its first venture fund of US$65 million and recently completed raising money for a second fund, totalling US$120.5 million. Current investments include micropower technology suppliers well as developers of technologies related to power quality. Its investors include large energy players—among them ABB, Electricité de France and Itochu International—that intend to use these technologies to attract customers in a competitive market.

Nth Power Managing Director Maurice Gunderson believes that industry restructuring will eventually bring a flood of investment capital into the energy sector, just as it has done in the telecommunications sector. Venture funding in the US utility industry has indeed begun to surge and Gunderson believes 'we're only at the beginning at the growth curve' (see Fig. 16.1). Overseas, meanwhile, similar energy VC funds are appearing in Europe and Australia. Given the track record of venture capital in spurring technological innovation in other sectors, its growing presence in the energy 'space' bodes well for the micropower industry.

16.7 Reworking rules

Even with growing economic viability and investor interest, micropower technologies require supportive public policies. Many of today's power markets carry the legacy of the state-granted monopoly: a slew of regulations, subsidies and other policies reinforcing large, central power and inhibiting use of smaller systems (see Box 16.1). As Walt

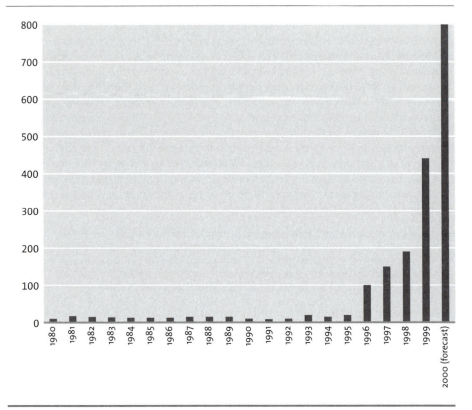

Figure 16.1 *Venture capital investment, US electric power industry, 1980–2000*

Source: Nth Power Technologies, Venture Economics

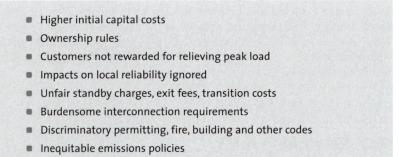

- Higher initial capital costs
- Ownership rules
- Customers not rewarded for relieving peak load
- Impacts on local reliability ignored
- Unfair standby charges, exit fees, transition costs
- Burdensome interconnection requirements
- Discriminatory permitting, fire, building and other codes
- Inequitable emissions policies

Box 16.1 *Eight barriers to micropower*

Source: Iannucci 1999

Patterson of the Royal Institute for International Affairs, puts it, 'all too often . . . inherently decentralised technologies find themselves "playing away", on the home terrain of the centralised system and according to its rules' (Patterson 1999). The creation of a fair playing field for micropower is a prerequisite for its spread.

The 'home rules' confronting small-scale power begin with the US$120 billion granted annually in subsidies for fossil fuel and nuclear energy production and consumption. Another barrier is that micropower developers are generally not reimbursed for the hidden economic and environmental benefits they provide. The 'in-feed laws' that have spurred wind power use in Europe are one way around the latter problem, requiring utilities to buy electricity from wind power developers at guaranteed prices. Micropower systems also have higher initial costs; to address this, the Japanese solar home programme allows customers to sell excess solar PV-generated power back to the grid. Similarly, 30 states in the United States have adopted 'net metering' programmes that permit PV system owners to, in effect, run their electricity meters backwards.

As policies such as net metering become more common, it will be important to standardise the requirements for safely and reliably interconnecting power systems with the distribution grid. Many of these standards are complicated and vary from utility to utility, making it difficult for a developer to plan for a larger market. In the United States, the Institute of Electrical and Electronics Engineers has approved standards designed to simplify the process for solar PV grid interconnection. Other barriers to fair competition include complex ownership rules, power purchase agreements and a host of standby, exit and transition costs that utilities impose on customers seeking to install micropower systems. Incentives for monopoly distribution utilities to support micropower and the standardisation or elimination of siting and permitting requirements and emissions policies—established when small-scale power was not an option—are among the needed changes.

Joseph Iannucci of Distributed Utility Associates has identified ten 'market accelerators' for micropower (see Box 16.2). He concludes that, if electric utilities do not take the lead in promoting distributed power, then customers, supported by aggressive new

- Simplified interconnection standards
- Modest or unpredictable growth in electricity demand
- Aggressive gas, energy service and distributed generation vendors
- More efficient electricity pricing schemes
- Saturation of electric transmission and distribution systems
- Siting difficulties for new central generation plants and transmission and distribution capacity
- Streamlined, standardised permitting procedures
- Dissatisfied electricity customers
- Distributed generation technology improvement
- Demand for green energy

Box 16.2 *Ten micropower market accelerators*

Source: Iannucci 1999

companies, will. Public interest in renewable energy has already spawned 'green power' programmes, which offer renewable power at a premium in unrestructured markets in Australia, Finland, Germany, the Netherlands, Sweden and the United States. The green power prospects in competitive markets are even bigger. In May 2000 BP Amoco and other investors announced that they would invest US$100 million in a leading marketer, Green Mountain Energy Company.

The restructuring of the power generation market provides an especially important opportunity to support micropower development. Available options include R&D, tax incentives, portfolio standards and government procurement. Stakeholders in a micropower system, such as the California Alliance for Distributed Power and the Distributed Power Coalition, are organising for the overhaul of discriminatory rules and advocating a range of new policies to address micropower in restructuring legislation.

16.8 A 'disruptive technology'?

A number of electricity industry-watchers have described micropower as a 'disruptive technology'. This phrase, coined by Harvard Business School professors Joseph Bower and Clayton Christensen, has been applied to a group of technologies—among them radial tyres, small copiers and personal computers—that leading companies neglected and customers virtually ignored at first. But these technologies gained small footholds in market niches, where they were to achieve technical improvements and cost reductions that enabled them to overtake the mainstream market. Small, hungry firms that had anticipated demand for these innovations overtook companies at the top: Goodyear, Xerox and IBM (Bower and Christensen 1995).

Companies were blindsided because they compared the new technologies with existing ones based on conventional criteria, rather than asking whether they could meet new market needs more effectively. Standard market research often misleads: marketers told Polaroid's president that only 100,000 instant cameras would ever be sold. Instead, millions were sold.

Micropower has many of the characteristics of a disruptive technology. It has important attributes that are not fully valued in today's marketplace, but is appearing in certain niches. Small companies developing the technologies are challenging the market dominance of utilities. Many analysts still evaluate micropower by conventional criteria— initial cost—instead of its ability to meet new market demands: clean, high-reliability, high-quality electricity. Thus they make conservative market projections of micropower penetration, exposing themselves to the risk of being caught flat-footed.

One common complaint is that small-scale power systems are too small to meet the electrical needs of a modern economy. This claim does not stand up against several simple calculations. The power rating, or maximum engine capacity, of the average American car is 124 kW; thus the US auto industry's annual production of roughly 6 million cars provides some 744 GW of capacity. This amount is comparable to the country's 1998 total installed capacity of 776 GW. The existing US car and truck fleet, meanwhile, represents more than 200 million reliable, self-generating power plants with a capital cost less than one-tenth of that of a large central generator.

Some market assessments suggest a substantial amount of micropower is coming. Studies by EPRI and others suggest that by 2010 small-scale power could be meeting 5%–40% of annual new US capacity, depending on how the details of restructuring are worked out. Allied Business Intelligence projects a US$10 billion fuel cell market by then, driven by power quality and reliability needs (ABI 1999). Like the first Polaroid surveys, however, these projections may underestimate the true potential. As the Arthur D. Little consultancy report observes, trends such as industry restructuring, growing capacity needs and technology are 'laying the groundwork for the possible widespread introduction of distributed generation' (ADL 1999).

New business models may evolve around the new micropower technologies, just as the vertically integrated utility developed in tandem with central-station power. Lest they repeat the mistakes of IBM, which initially underestimated the potential of PCs, utilities and firms vested in large-scale power face the challenge of 'cannibalising' themselves: creating businesses that may eventually displace their core operations. Tony Prophet, CEO of microturbine maker Honeywell Power Systems, frames it this way: 'At every point of evolutionary change, the survivors always adapt. Some of the dinosaurs turned into mammals. The others became fossils' (Golden 2000).

Appendix:
sampling of micropower developers and vendors

Reciprocating engines

Alstom Engines	www.engines.ind.alstom.com
Caterpillar	www.cat.com
Kohler Generators	www.kohlergenerators.com
SenerTec	www.senertec.de
Waukesha Engine	www.waukeshaengine.com

Microturbines

AeroVironment	www.aerovironment.com
Capstone Turbine	www.capstoneturbine.com
GE Power Systems	www.ge.com
Honeywell Power Systems	www.honeywell.com
Ingersoll-Rand Energy Systems	www.ingersoll-rand.com

Stirling engines

BG Technology	www.bgtech.co.uk
Sigma Elektroteknisk	www.sigma-el.com
Solo Kleinmotoren	www.solo-germany.com
Stirling Technology	www.stirling-tech.com
Whisper Tech	www.whispertech.co.nz

Fuel cells

Avista Labs . . . . www.avistalabs.com
Ballard Power Systems . . . . www.ballard.com
FuelCell Energy . . . . www.fce.com
Plug Power . . . . www.plugpower.com
Sanyo . . . . www.sanyo.co.jp

Solar photovoltaics

Astropower . . . . www.astropower.com
BP Solar . . . . www.bpsolar.com
Evergreen Solar . . . . www.evergreensolar.com
Kyocera . . . . www.kyocera.com
Shell Renewables . . . . www.shell.com

Wind turbines

Bonus Energy . . . . www.bonus.dk
Enron Wind . . . . www.wind.enron.com
NEG Micon . . . . www.neg-micon.de
Nordic Windpower . . . . www.nwp.se
Vestas . . . . www.vestas.com

EXTENDED PRODUCER RESPONSIBILITY AND THE EUROPEAN ELECTRONICS INDUSTRY

Lassi Linnanen
Helsinki University of Technology, Finland

The volume of electrical and electronic equipment waste is increasing rapidly in Europe and around the world due to rapid advances in information and communications technologies. Based on the recycling systems in Norway, the Netherlands and Sweden, this chapter examines the structural and operational changes in the electronics industry induced by the recent European Union (EU) draft proposal for a directive on waste electrical and electronic equipment.[1]

According to the proposed EU directive, the waste producers (i.e. the manufacturers and importers) are responsible for the organisation of the collection and recycling of electronic waste. Successful implementation of both collection and recycling schemes are going to require co-operation among several different operators. This chapter highlights the different ways the implementation of the electrical and electronic equipment waste take-back schemes can be designed and structured.

A key conclusion of this chapter is that alternative means of financing recycling schemes—which can be based on real costs, fixed costs or insurance fees—result in different organisational and co-operation structures, and consequently require varying incentives for pursuing product life-cycle management strategies.

---

1   The directive proposal can be found at http://europa.eu.int/comm/environment/docum/ 00347_en.htm; this and subsequent web links were valid as of 26 February 2001.

17.1 Assessment criteria: economic, technical and ecological

17.1.1 *Economic criteria*

In the economic assessment, the **costs** and **cost efficiency** of various implementation options are first examined. It is typically easiest to analyse the costs of the treatment, transport and recycling services. The costs of municipal waste management services are more difficult to assess since the treatment costs may vary from country to country, from product group to product group, and since the volumes and the possibilities for exploitation and re-use are different.

Cost efficiency in this context means that the environmental protection objectives stated in the draft directive are attained at the lowest possible cost to the producers. The recycling charges allocated to the producers are also affected by the **administrative efficiency** of the recycling system. The lower the administrative costs, the lower the share of the collected charges beyond the actual transport and treatment costs.

The costs of the recycling system and its cost efficiency are also affected by the **flexibility** of the selected implementation model. By **external flexibility** is meant how well the recycling system adapts to the changes in the external conditions such as the number of producers, the consumption of electrical and electronic equipment, and substantial changes in the costs of recycling.

The overall costs are also affected by **normative flexibility**. It should be possible to alter the recycling model in line with changing environmental protection objectives.

Finally, the economic criteria include **fairness** of the recycling system: that is, how equitably the recycling model treats the producers. For example, enterprises that have their own recycling systems for their equipment should not be discriminated against. If there is a fixed recycling charge on both imported equipment and domestically produced equipment, the producers may pay twice for the equipment recycling unless there is a refund system in the fixed-charge recycling system.

17.1.2 *Technical criteria*

There are important **technical requirements** on the collection and treatment of electrical and electronic equipment waste. First, tight regulations on the treatment of harmful substances, components and equipment increase the pressures for the adoption of new treatment techniques.

Second, a **dynamically efficient** recycling system encourages manufacturers to upgrade the environmental qualities of their products through a more eco-friendly product design and materials selection. Third, the recycling system and the relevant legislation on which the system is based must not select a **technologically inflexible** option.

17.1.3 *Ecological criteria*

The most important ecological criterion is how well the recycling system affects the detrimental environmental impacts of the electronic waste-stream. First, the collection system should be effectively managed. Second, the environmental impacts of waste treatment should be minimised. Third, the system should encourage producers to engage in environmentally friendly design.

Some of the important ecological principles from the EU's environmental policy include the proximity and the polluter-pays principles. The proximity principle recommends processing waste as close as possible to its source, while the idea of the polluter-pays principle mandates that the producer of the waste pays for its disposal cost.

The proposed EU directive on electronic waste allocates the cost of disposal to the producers, but it is the end-user's action at the end of the product life-cycle that remains crucial. The consumer cannot, under the threat of sanction, be required to return a discarded piece of equipment for appropriate treatment.

17.2 Evaluation of the recycling systems

The following recycling systems from Norway, the Netherlands and Sweden are analysed and evaluated according to the economic, technical and ecological criteria:

- Fixed recycling charge model

- Actual-cost invoicing model

- Recycling insurance model

17.2.1 Fixed recycling charge model

The basic principles of the fixed recycling charge model are:

- Items of equipment are assigned fixed recycling charges.

- The charge is collected on all equipment in the marketplace.

- The consumer pays the recycling charge in connection with the purchase of a new piece of equipment.

- The retailer pays the money to the producer organisation.

- The recycling charges are collected into a fund, from which the costs of the system are paid.

- The producer organisation agrees on and pays for the treatment and transport to the operations offering them.

- The administrative costs of the producer organisation are covered by the collected recycling charges.

- The costs incurred from non-brand equipment are paid from the funds collected by the producer organisation.

Examples of the fixed recycling charge system include the Norwegian producer organisation model[2] (decentralised for different product groups) and the electronic appliance recycling system in the Netherlands[3] (almost all consumer products). Figure 17.1 provides details on the recycling system of a Norwegian producer organisation.

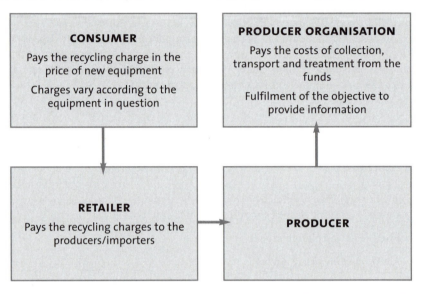

Figure 17.1 *Recycling system at a Norwegian producer organisation*

17.2.1.1 Economic criteria

One economic problem of this recycling system is that the charges are not based on the actual recycling costs; therefore, determining the product-specific charge is difficult. Due to its organisational structure and the fixed recycling charge, this model is not particularly **flexible.**

First, a number of factors such as development trends in the sector produce pressures for change in the recycling system. Changes in treatment techniques also have a direct impact on the actual treatment costs, while a substantial increase in the membership of the producer organisation will increase the cash flow of the producer organisation. If any changes need to be made in the cost of the recycling system to the producers, the recycling charge must be adjusted according to the jointly agreed-upon criteria.

Second, the collected fund of the producer organisation does not necessarily cover the recycling costs of the returned electronic equipment. The operation of the producer organisation needs to be transparent and controllable by the producer organisations.

Third, complying with the system's reporting requirements increases its overall financial costs and organisational burden. It requires its own multi-level reporting to and

2   www.elretur.no (in Norwegian only).
3   www.fme.nl

monitoring by the authorities, since the functions are centralised with the system administrator.

17.2.1.2 Technical criteria

The recycling system does not treat the producers in an **equitable manner**. A manufacturer that has invested in an environmentally friendly and recycling-oriented product design pays a fixed recycling charge on any equipment it launches in the market. Analysing the recycling costs of the product selection of even several dozen producers in a system such as this is complicated.

A recycling system based on a fixed recycling charge also does not encourage producers to use the most efficient recycling equipment, since the overall producer responsibility costs are tied to an agreed-upon fixed recycling charge. This recycling system does not therefore encourage firms or organisations that have their own recycling systems to join the producer organisation.

17.2.1.3 Ecological criteria

In this recycling model, environment-friendliness can be achieved only through the minimisation of the environmental impacts of the processing functions and logistics. This recycling model does not encourage environmentally friendly product design.

17.2.2 *Actual-cost invoicing model*

The basic principles of the actual-cost invoicing model are:

- Only one product group is included.

- The producers pay the actual collection, transport and treatment costs of their own equipment.

- The products are classified according to brand in connection with the collection.

- A contracted treatment operator invoices each producer separately for the above-mentioned costs and delivers a certificate of treatment.

- The system can be implemented at the level of a specific company or an entire industrial sector.

- A collective system means a pool of enterprises in a given sector.

- The pool negotiates the recycling service agreements and subjects the prices to competition.

- The pool agrees how the costs of non-branded products are to be divided among the producers.

- This recycling system is best suited for recycling similar product categories such as information technology (IT) equipment, large home appliances or professional electronics.

Equipment is returned to the contracted treatment operator from municipal collection points, from the producers' own collection containers and from the retailers of IT equipment. From customer enterprises the equipment is collected in connection with the purchase of new equipment. There are three enterprises engaged in contracted transport and two contracted treatment operators. What is essential in the model is the division of the final costs according to the actual treatment and transport costs. The costs are invoiced directly to the IT producers who have joined the pool.

In the recycling system, the equipment is channelled to contracted treatment operators or recycling services. However, the producers may direct desired batches of products to their own recycling systems. Transport can be organised by the recycling services, contracted transport enterprises or the producers themselves. For example, collection from a store selling the producers' equipment can be organised in part collectively through the recycling services and in part through the return transport of the retailers and producers themselves.

Figure 17.2 provides an outline of an IT equipment recycling system that uses the actual-cost invoicing model in the Netherlands.

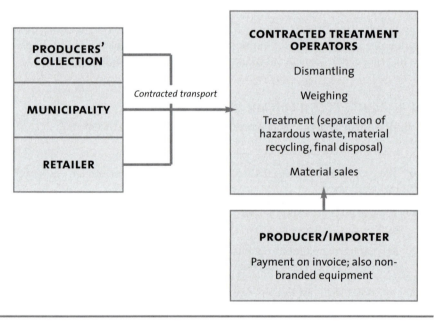

Figure 17.2 *Information technology recycling system in the Netherlands*

17.2.2.1 Economic criteria

This model is **economical** for the producers since the producers pay only the actual processing costs of their products. Since the members of the recycling system include the producers of only one product sector, in the case of the Netherlands example, the IT producers can negotiate the prices collectively with the contracted treatment operators.

The recycling model based on the actual treatment costs can be deemed to be **flexible** and **cost-efficient** for several reasons. First, the system has low **administration costs** compared to the fixed recycling charge model. The administrative costs are lower as the system does not have a complex organisational structure. The entire system can be easily established by a sector-specific voluntary agreement, while joining the system is relatively easy, since the invoicing corresponds to the accumulated equipment.

Changes in the prices of transport and treatment automatically affect the total recycling costs. The treatment costs can be strongly affected in the short term by the development of treatment techniques, and, in particular, the easier dismantling and better recyclability of the new equipment. The treatment operators and recycling services are also subjected to continual competition.

Second, another advantage of this recycling model is that business enterprises are able to **use their own recycling systems**. If a producer wishes to deliver equipment or if equipment is returned from a customer enterprise to the producer's own recycling system, there is enough flexibility in the recycling system to take this into account automatically. By contrast, in a fixed recycling charge model, the charge is paid for all equipment even if the producers were later able to channel their equipment to their own recycling systems. Whenever the recycling charges need to be refunded, there is a corresponding increase in the administrative bureaucracy.

Third, the recycling costs are divided **equitably** in this recycling system. All producers pay for the treatment of their own equipment with the price of the treatment being dependent on a number of factors, including the possibilities for the re-use of the materials as raw materials, the ease of dismantling of the equipment, and the volume of the waste. This system is particularly well suited to producers who wish to bear the collective responsibility for the appropriate recycling of their equipment according to agreed-upon rules and standards.

17.2.2.2 Technical criteria

The recycling system is also **efficient** with regard to technical criteria, since it encourages environmentally friendly and recycling-oriented product design, which is one of the most important objectives of the EU draft proposal on electronic waste. If the price of the treatment can be made lower for manufacturers who have made appropriate investments in product design, it will positively affect the price development of their equipment in the future.

The use of contracted treatment operators may enable the recycling of various materials, which may in the end lower the final price of the treatment. As a general rule, the larger the proportion of the recycled materials that can be sold in the marketplace, the lower the recycling cost of the equipment.

One potential drawback of this recycling system is the need to sort the equipment according to different brand types. The retailer, recycling service or treatment operator must separate the items of equipment of different manufacturers from one another. The model is therefore not appropriate for highly heterogeneous product groups or several product groups since the sorting costs will increase the total price.

17.2.2.3 Ecological criteria

A recycling system based on this model is likely to do the best job of encouraging and improving product recyclability. Producers can directly affect the price of the treatment costs through product design. The easier the equipment is to dismantle and the larger the proportion of the recyclable material content, the lower the overall treatment costs.

This recycling system does not solve the **free-rider problem**, but does offer an opportunity for the manufacturers of similar brands to organise the recycling of their own products. This model also enables materials to be more effectively used through treatment operators or recycling services. The producers may re-use recycled material or use in their production spare parts from dismantled equipment, which raises the degree of utilisation.

The most significant environmental quality of this system is that it encourages environmentally friendly and recycling-oriented product design. The most ecological transport options for various situations can be used in the system and the producers can continuously ensure the appropriateness of the treatment.

17.2.3 Recycling insurance model

The main components of the recycling insurance model include:

- The producer takes out a recycling insurance policy for every product launched in the market.

- The recycling costs of equipment of the insured (the producer) are compensated for with the income accumulated from the insurance premiums.

- The insurance company organises, on behalf of the insured, the delivery of discarded equipment for appropriate treatment.

- The producer must attach to the equipment an information label, which can be used by the insurance company to calculate the amount of compensation.

- A contracted treatment operator reports to the insurance company on the treatment of each producer's equipment and its costs.

- The insurance company adjusts the price of the insurance policy according to the actual treatment costs.

- The insurance premium is in other respects formed on the insurance company's normal pricing bases.

- The insurance company reinsures its own risk.

- The system does not cover historical waste.

Figure 17.3 describes the recycling insurance product of Swedish Länförsäkringar Miljö. The company operates the insurance programme in co-operation with a Swedish treatment operation, Ragn-Sells Elektronikåtervinning AB.[4]

---

4   www.ragnsells.se/english/index.htm.

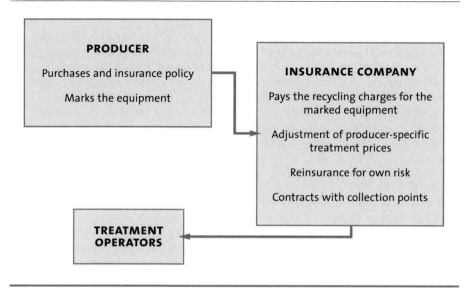

Figure 17.3 **A recycling insurance system in Sweden**

17.2.3.1 Economic criteria

The basic economic principles of this recycling insurance model are similar to those of the actual-cost invoicing model. The difference is that the pool or the organisation established by the producers is replaced by an insurance company, while the recycling insurance premium for the particular product is paid before the actual treatment costs.

The **economic efficiency** of the recycling insurance—as compared with a pool organised by the producers themselves—depends on the insurance premium. If the price of the insurance corresponds as closely as possible to the actual treatment and transport costs, one can say that the two models are almost the same.

The pricing of the recycling insurance of Swedish Länförsäkringar Miljö is based on the following factors:

- An estimate of what the treatment of a producer's equipment will cost, made on the basis of the treatment of a trial batch

- The estimated useful life of a piece of equipment

- The insurance company's conventional risk estimate

The **administrative efficiency** of the recycling insurance model may be higher than the actual-cost invoicing model. The existing administrative structure of an insurance company is likely to have better economies of scale and administrative capacity than a new company built from scratch.

In terms of **flexibility**, the recycling insurance model ranks somewhere in between the two recycling models described above. The insurance company may adjust the insurance premium to correspond to changes in the treatment and transport prices. But this assumes some kind of co-operation with at least one recycling operator, as is the case in Sweden where, for example, producer-specific treatment price differences can be observed.

In addition, the insurance company may subject treatment operators, recycling services and transport companies to competition. Insurance premiums may not react as quickly to price changes due to environmentally friendly product design or treatment techniques as the actual cost invoicing model.

The recycling insurance model is also **flexible** when a producer, manufacturer or importer goes bankrupt. The insurance will cover the recycling of equipment launched by the producer until the end of the insurance term.

17.2.3.2 Ecological criteria

Recycling insurance is an alternative programme to the above-mentioned recycling systems for implementing producer responsibility. This model emphasises minimising the environmental impacts of treatment and logistics. If the insurance premium in co-operation with the treatment operator can be adjusted to reflect the actual costs of processing the equipment, the recycling insurance model may aid in the promotion of environmentally friendly product design. For example, some of the treatment operators in Germany take in used computers free of charge as long as they carry the 'Blue Angel' certification.

17.3 **Conclusion**

As the analysis of the three recycling models shows, there are a number of different ways to design and organise the incentives to improve the life-cycle management of electronic products. Table 17.1 is a summary of the comparison between the three recycling models.

Based on this analysis, the optimal product responsibility solution for a company appears to be the actual-cost invoicing model. This model also holds the most promise in promoting environmentally friendly product design and management activities in the electronics industry. It also seems to offer the best cost-effectiveness and most incentives to further reduce the recycling costs.

	Fixed recycling charge	*Actual-cost invoicing*	*Recycling insurance*
Cost-effectiveness	Low	High	Low
Flexibility	Low	High	Moderate
Encourages product design	No	Yes	Possibly
Equitable treatment of producers	No	Yes	Yes
Suitable for several product groups	Yes	No	Yes

Table 17.1 **Comparison of the different recycling models**

However, it should be kept in mind that the EU directive on electronic waste encompasses numerous different products and not just a single product group. As not all product groups lend themselves to a manageable end-of-life material flow system, the parameters of circular material flow management should take into account:

- Physical point of the collection which is often not the point or even the country of sale or origin

- Time-span of the products in use, which has a significant influence on the stability of the closed-loop system

- Technical quality of the products reaching the end of their usage, which influences the possibilities for homogenous (and less costly) re-use and treatment solutions

- The weight of the product is one of the most important factors in the formation of actual treatment costs. Heavy electric appliances, such as refrigerators, will be more affected than products with lower mass per price ratio (e.g. mobile phones).

It can be argued that no universal rules can be drawn from the EU directive that is going to satisfy all the companies in the electronics industry. Any recycling schemes—whether on a national or the international level—are likely be a combinations of the three different models analysed in this chapter.

The electronics industry is only starting to face the kinds of environmental pressure that have already been encountered by petroleum, mining, forestry and other resource-intensive sectors. One important advantage the electronics industry might have with its environmental- and product-responsibility concerns is that they still have the opportunity to influence the establishment of rules and guidelines. There is a first-mover advantage with early adopters of recycling schemes since they are in a good position to influence the overall operations and the long-term structure of this emerging recycling industry.

This chapter does not take any position on the proposed EU directive on waste electrical and electronic equipment. However, a clear policy implication is that there should be enough space and flexibility given to companies and industry sectors to establish their own recycling schemes, which may also be a good goal for the electronics industry as a group to lobby for.

SUSTAINABLE TRADE IN ELECTRONICS
The case of the Indian components sector

Mohammed Saqib, Yashika Singh and Ritu Kumar
Rajiv Gandhi Foundation, India

As the pace of globalisation of the world economy increases, trade as an economic growth strategy is becoming ever more important for developing countries. Whereas this is a welcome trend, it has raised concerns that the pursuit of unlimited 'trade for growth' strategies brings with it not only the threat of greater environmental and ecological burdens, but also the exploitation of workers and human resources in the form of less-than-minimum wage levels, child labour, sub-standard working conditions and so on. This in turn raises a host of questions and issues related to how this sustainability burden can be managed. Which agents along the supply chain are responsible for ensuring that the production of traded goods is undertaken in an environmentally sustainable and socially responsible manner? How can this be done in the most effective and efficient manner?

This chapter examines some of these issues and questions in the context of the Indian electronics industry, which is characterised by complex supply chains and high levels of international sourcing. An important aim of this chapter is to provide a comprehensive analysis of the sustainability issues surrounding the electronic components trade between India and the European Union, and to identify the measures and actions needed to integrate sustainability factors into an economically sustainable export strategy.

Section 18.1 explores the critical sustainability challenges facing the electronics industry and reviews the implications of EU regulations such as the directive on Waste from Electrical and Electronic Equipment (WEEE) for developing-country suppliers. Section 18.2 provides a brief description of the electronics economy, the major sub-sectors and the key dynamics relating to the role of multinationals, contract manufacturing, international sourcing and system integration. Section 18.3 focuses on the ability and readiness of the Indian electronic components sector to adapt to the emerging sustainability challenges. Finally, Section 18.4 closes with some conclusions and policy recommendations.

18.1 Sustainability challenges: an overview

Not only has the electronics industry emerged as one of the fastest-growing manufacturing sectors, it is also characterised by rapid changes in production technology and output as well as by increasingly complex supply chains. The outsourcing of manufacturing operations from the industrialised to developing countries and the transformation of manufacturing chains into specialised subcontract assemblies has added even greater complexity to the supply chain of electronic products. However, as a study by the mobile telephone manufacturer Nokia[1] suggests, 'a good supply chain must not have a single weak link and all players must be able to rely on each other in the short and long term', despite the constant price pressures.

Moreover, environmental requirements of forthcoming EU regulations such as WEEE and other national directives are necessary to enable the supply chains to be sustainable. It is important to establish strategic alliances along the chain at the early stages of component development. But how such conditions can exist in the complex supply chains of the electronics sector has not yet been determined, and we hope that our work will highlight issues that can facilitate the sustainable management of supply chains.

The general perception about the electronics industry is that it is relatively clean and non-polluting. However, this perception is rapidly changing as the industry grows in size and importance and the environment hazards associated with the industry become more significant. There are two primary environmental dangers emanating from this industry: first, from the production process and, second, from the product itself. Typically, the production of electronic components involves the use of chemicals, metals and glass parts and emits a number of hazardous waste emissions in the form of solids, liquids and gases. The other environmental threat comes from the product itself. The waste-stream of electronic products is large and is continually growing as technology places more products in the marketplace and increases the rate of product obsolescence.

Moreover, the disposal of used electronic products in an environmentally friendly manner has emerged as a major challenge in this sector. Traditionally, disposal is done through landfills. But the bulk of electronic goods and the number of hazardous constituents associated with them have led to the examination of other alternatives. Recycling, therefore, has become an important area of enquiry. There are other options as well: reverse distribution (product take-back), third-party product collection and disposal (public or private) and outright disposal restrictions. A significant number of these options have already been adopted or are likely to be in the near future.

The drivers for sustainable production can come from the marketplace or regulatory pressures. Market pressures can take the form of business-to-business requirements embodied in company codes of practice and public procurement schemes, as well as

1   Telecom Supply and Subcontract Chains, 1998, Nokia Finland and Nokia, India.

consumer/NGO (non-governmental organisation) pressures. Many multinational companies have developed their own codes and corporate policies on environmental issues, but to what extent these requirements cover the entire supply chain of large electronics multinationals is still an open question.

A recent and important policy development that is expected to have wide implications for developing-country suppliers is the EU directive on WEEE and a proposal for a directive on the restriction of the use of certain hazardous substances in electrical and electronic equipment (ROS). European companies that are subject to this legislation will inevitably require their suppliers in developing countries to comply with the directives. This will, in many cases, mean a redesign in the manufacturing process of components. To understand the implications, a case study of Philips Electronics has been provided in Box 18.1.

18.2 Mapping the electronics industry in India

The electronics industry is one of the fastest-growing industries in India today and has emerged as one of the country's major export sectors in recent years. Despite the growth in exports, India's share of global electronics production is still less than 2.2% (source: Electronic Association of Japan, 1999) with 89% of production being consumed domestically. The Indian electronics industry has five major sectors: telecommunications, computers, industrial electronics, consumer electronics and semiconductors. These sectors are interdependent and share common manufacturing processes. The size of the domestic electronics workforce for electrical and electronics was estimated to be 2.39 million in 1998. In addition, the electronics/computer industry supports four million additional jobs in ancillary technology support and service sectors.

The industry has not, however, experienced growth in domestic employment for the past three years and is typically made up of very small household enterprises Fewer than 50% of semiconductor and printed wiring board manufacturing facilities in India have more than 20 employees. Electronics represented the fastest-growing sector of the Indian industry for most of the 1990s, but there has been a decline in overall production and in exports towards the end of the decade. From 1993 to 1998, the electronics industry achieved a cumulative annual growth of 20% in production and over 40% in exports. The sector-based production figures are shown in Table 18.1.

Table 18.2 gives India's annual total electronics hardware and computer software growth figures with 1993–94 as the base year, while the production of major consumer electronic products is noted in Table 18.3. Table 18.4 shows the sector breakdown of exported electronic products. The table illustrates that exports have been growing slowly over the past few years. 11,080 million rupees of electronics hardware was exported in 1993–94 and it increased to 18,000 million rupees in 1998–99 before declining to 14,000 million rupees in 1999–2000.

Although the growth in electronics production was impressive in the 1990s, the industry has been plagued with a number of structural problems. Some of these problems are described in more detail below.

PHILIPS ELECTRONICS IS ONE OF THE WORLD'S LARGEST ELECTRONICS companies, and the largest in Europe, and employs approximately 235,000 people in over 60 countries. The Amsterdam-based corporation manufactures a wide range of products from television sets and compact disc players to light bulbs, security systems and semi-conductors.

Corporate environmental policy

Philips's corporate environment and energy office co-ordinates the company's environmental policy, while overall policy implementation is entrusted to product division managers, country managers and factory managers. Environmental affairs are an integral part of the management's agenda, and the company carefully follows global and local standards for environmental and technical specifications. Monitoring of its global business operations is facilitated through a database that contains standards relating to technical specifications, manufacturing ability, price and quality performance, and environmental performance.

Supply chain compliance and monitoring

Philips's supply chain covers global and local suppliers. Semiconductors and key components are normally sourced globally, and suppliers are required to adhere to the global standards. If Philips starts exporting from its factories in India, the company's Indian business operations will need to follow all relevant global standards. Local suppliers provide materials and components, including packaging materials, resistors and so on, to local factories. All suppliers (local and global) are divided into three broad categories: key suppliers, suppliers of standard products, and jobbers.

Key suppliers have to comply with mandatory requirements for environmental and quality specifications based on customer demand: eco-efficient manufacturing including ISO 14000 procedures, efficient use of energy and water, pollution prevention and good housekeeping practices, and eco-design innovations as specified in Philips's Eco-Design Guidelines. **Suppliers of standardised products** are required to comply with the mandatory requirements and follow good housekeeping practices, but not necessarily comply with the implementation of eco-design guidelines.

Jobbers, both small and large, have to comply with mandatory requirements on quality and environmental specifications, but not necessarily with the other requirements. They are paid a fixed price for a certain quality standard, and if the quality standard is judged to be below expectations, their contracts are typically not renewed.

Box 18.1 **Supply chain management and WEEE/ROS: implications for Indian suppliers. The case of Philips Electronics**

18.2.1 *Fragmented industrial structure*

The Indian electronics sector is comprised a few large companies, a number of small and medium-sized enterprises (SMEs), and a large number of tiny and household enterprises. Most of the very small business enterprises are difficult to quantify or account for. Indian companies are facing an increasingly competitive business environment in large part due to the aggressive deregulation and privatisation policy of the Indian government in an effort to increase the openness, competitiveness and efficiency of the domestic electronics industry. Multinational companies from the United States, Europe and Japan are penetrating India's industrial, consumer and commodity electronics markets, and many

Products sector	1993–94	1997–98	1998–99
1. Consumer electronics	41,500	76,000	92,000
2. Industrial electronics	17,700	31,500	33,000
3. Computer systems	18,200	28,000	23,000
4. Communications and broadcast equipment	31,500	32,500	44,000
5. Strategic electronics	5,000	9,000	13,000
6. Components	26,800	44,000	47,500
Sub-total	140,700	221,000	252,500
7. Software for exports	10,200	65,000	109,400
8. Domestic software	6,950	34,700	49,500
Total	**157,850**	**320,700**	**411,400**

Table 18.1 *Production of electronic goods in India, by sector (cumulative; hardware and software)*

Source: Ministry of Information Technology, Government of India

Year	Production (rupees × 10 million)	Growth (%)
1995–96	22,340	18.6
1996–97	26,640	19.2
1997–98	32,070	20.4
1998–99	41,140	28.3

Table 18.2 *Growth in the Indian electronics industry (all electronics hardware and computer software)*

Source: Ministry of Information Technology, Government of India

Item	1997	1998	1999
Black-and-white TV	60	60	58
Colour TV	32	42	57
Radio receiver	70	70	70
Tape recorder	85	105	140
VCR/VCPs	3.7	3.9	3.6
Electronic watch	90	136	194
Electronic clocks	190	206	260

Table 18.3 *Production of major consumer electronics products (in 100,000s)*

Source: Ministry of Information Technology, Government of India

Item	1993–94	1998–99	1999–2000
1. Consumer electronics	2,500	4,000	3,000
2. Industrial electronics	1,150	1,600	2,000
3. Computers	4,200	4,000	2,400
4. Communications and broadcast equipment with strategic electronics	980	800	600
5. Components	2,250	7,600	6,000
Sub-total	11,080	18,000	14,000
6. Computer software	10,200	109,400	172,000
Total	21,280	117,400	186,000

Table 18.4 **Export of electronics products from India, by sector (in million rupees)**

Source: Ministry of Information Technology, Government of India

Indian companies are turning to joint venture/business alliances as part of their long-term business strategy. Although Indian electronics companies appear to recognise these challenges, it is not clear whether they fully appreciate the extent and potential impact of the changes currently under way.

18.2.2 Various pressures on subcontractors

Since most large companies want to subcontract as much of the production because of cost and labour factors, SMEs have to deal with diverse production tasks. Indian SMEs typically perform two or three levels of assembly before moving the goods to the next level of assembly. Companies that want good-quality products from these assemblers and suppliers have provided basic-quality standards and practices training. Components are purchased at competitive prices that fluctuate almost daily (10%–15% of base price). Most large companies prescribe quality and working standards requirements, with one company (Philips) issuing suggested but not mandatory environmental standards.

18.2.3 Excessive capacity and poor quality

Since India's electronics industry is highly fragmented, it frequently has excessive production capacity. Indian SMEs have expanded at a tremendous rate in the past 20 years, and they now make up the largest part of the assembly and manufacturing of components in the Indian electronics market. Most of the capacity problem stems from the exceptionally large number of companies that produce most electronic components and electronic goods. India has around 12,000 SMEs that manufacture electronic components and goods compared to only 1,900 in Europe, a market that is four times larger than India. Fragmentation and the desire to increase market share have generated substantial overcapacity problems in recent years.

Another important characteristic of the Indian electronics industry is the poor quality of its manufacturing and production technologies. With few companies actually making profits, most Indian producers cannot afford the investments that are required to keep pace with world-class standards. Other industry problems, such as bloated labour force, subscale assets and chronic managerial problems, explain why capacity utilisation is ironically low even for products such as CRTs (cathode-ray tubes), compressors, LCDs (liquid-crystal displays), capacitors and so on, whose demand outweighs the domestic supply. Moreover, competitively priced imports, some of which are smuggled (especially components), are flooding into the country to meet the unmet demand.

18.2.4 Weak domestic regulations

There is no specific domestic legislation that regulates the electronics sector in India nor is there any coherent national or state-level policy on recycling. Anti-dumping guidelines and metal recycling guidelines have been proposed by India's Ministry of Environment and Forests (MoEF). The only applicable domestic law and regulation is the Hazardous Waste Management Rules and Act (1989), which covers the management of hazardous metals, acids and solvents that are used in the manufacture, transport and assembly in the electronics industry. The act also specifies about 500 banned chemicals, a number of which apply to the electronics industry.

18.3 The Indian electronics sector and the sustainability challenge

To analyse the Indian electronics industry in addressing the wide range of sustainability issues, we decided to conduct a survey of 20 companies using questionnaires and personal interviews. The sample companies were selected according to size, structure, international exposure, trade intensity, regional diversity and so on; thus it was not a random sample. There were 3 large MNCs (multinational corporations), 3 large domestic companies and 14 small companies, almost all of which were vendors to large companies.[2]

The overall goal of the survey is to establish the status and future prospects of sustainability in the Indian electronics industry. We tried to find answers to some basic questions on sustainability and environmental issues, and determine the levels of awareness concerning sustainability issues, environmental legislation (domestic and international), and potential barriers to compliance. We also tried to gauge the technological awareness and the motivation or the limitations to adopting green technologies. If the economics of new technology is an obstacle, then is technical or financial assistance a viable option? Are the companies willing to view the environment as a social responsibility, green their supply chain and participate in waste management beyond their factory premises?

One of the reasons both small and large companies are included in the sample group is to see if there are any difference in production practices and environmental concerns

---

2 One of the large companies subsequently shed one of its units which made it a small company for all practical purposes during the course of the interviews. The breakdown of surveyed companies is therefore 5 large and 15 small.

between the selected companies. For example, one can expect that large companies, because of their market share, brand name, or the availability of funds, will use more environmentally friendly techniques than smaller firms. One can also expect that vertically integrated companies will have better environment management systems than horizontally integrated companies due to issues of economies of scale.

One can also hypothesise that companies with foreign business partners will do better environmentally due to more opportunities for training with and using advanced technologies. Similarly, export-oriented companies may exhibit better environmental practices because of pressures from foreign buyers. This survey covers four major issues: general environmental awareness; green technology and management systems; regulatory and standard compliance; and social and ethical concerns.

18.3.1 General environmental awareness

Table 18.5 covers the awareness of companies regarding issues related to sustainable production, environmentally friendly practices, green technologies, and national and international regulations. It is rather surprising that even small vendors are 'aware' of the details of the European electronics industry legislation. The large companies are also aware of domestic legislation of other countries, most likely their export destinations.

	Large companies (5)	*SMEs (15)*
Europe	5	15
Japan	3	–
USA	4	–

SMEs = small and medium-sized enterprises

Table 18.5 **Number of companies, of those surveyed, aware of environmental legislation in Europe, Japan and USA**

18.3.2 Green technology and management systems

Our survey explored the quality and the standards of environment technology and management systems among the sample companies. Out of a total of the 20 companies sampled, 8 companies have programmes that address quality issues. Of these 8 companies, 5 are large and 3 are SMEs (see Table 18.6). The quality system adopted by these large companies is the ISO 9000 series while SMEs use their own quality protocols. The results indicate that large companies do address quality issues and follow the internationally accepted management systems. However, the small firms do not really follow any quality issues, and, even if they do, they follow their own internal guidelines rather the international systems.

Table 18.7 shows that all 5 large companies state that they follow an environmental management system (EMS). The most popular EMS appears to be the ISO 14000 series. Of the 5 large companies, 4 have the ISO 14000 certification or are in the process of getting one. SMEs on the other hand do not have such certification. Our survey also suggests that

	Large companies (5)	SMEs (15)
Existence of such programmes	5	3
Certified to ISO 9000 series	5	1
Certified to company's own protocols	–	2
Stakeholder participation	5	–

SMEs = small and medium-sized enterprises

Table 18.6 **Programmes addressing quality issues**

	Large companies (5)	SMEs (15)
Existence of an EMS	5	1
ISO 14000 certification	4	–
Environmental management of supply chain	3	1

SMEs = small and medium-sized enterprises

Table 18.7 **Environmental management systems**

very few small companies have actually sought certification. Of the 1,200 companies in the Mumbai-Pune region of India, only 11 units are certified. Due to the high cost of certifying their operations to the ISO standard, very few small companies can afford to make this kind of investment.

Some of the survey respondents were aware of international quality standards issued by the Institute of Electrical and Electronic Engineers (IEEE) and other professional bodies, but not the environmental standards or policies. As highlighted in Table 18.8, the main motive behind ISO 14000 certification seems to be conforming to the standards of the company's foreign collaborator or joint-venture partner. Table 18.9 ranks the factors for accelerating greater involvement in environmental issues

Some large firms diffuse environmentally friendly methods of production through training and transfer of skills. However, this practice is not widespread. One important reason is the large number of suppliers with a very small size of operations. Although the operating cost of environmental programmes is only about 3%–5% of the total cost of

- To conform to global policy of headquarters/major partner

- To reduce economic costs on resources

- To meet increasing regulatory pressures

- To conform to global standards

Table 18.8 **Reasons for initiating an EMS (ranked most to least significant)**

- International market

- Large industry and/or industrial buyers

- International trade bodies

- Industrial associations

- Government and its agencies

- Domestic market

Table 18.9 ***Sources of change in environmental practices (ranked most to least important)***

production, the one-time investment tends to be high and beyond the financial means of many small companies. The trickling-down of good environmental practices does not get down to the last vendor in the supply chain. The size of the company plays an important role in determining the scope and quality of corporate environmental practices.

18.3.3 Regulatory and standard compliance

Complying with environmental standards and regulations is a major issue in the Indian electronics industry. First, there are no environmental regulations specifically designed for the electronics industry. Second, the application of existing anti-pollution regulations is very poor. Third, there are limited or no incentives for complying with the regulations, nor is there adequate punishment for non-compliance.

There are also internal and external factors that accelerate the adoption of environmentally friendly techniques. Internal factors include company leadership, changing technology and business competition; while external factors include regulations, customer demand and industry-wide voluntary measures. Which is the most important factor in motivating improved environmental practices? Table 18.10 analyses whether there are pressures from the buyers of the respective companies to follow environmental practices, while Table 18.11 outlines some of the assistance that had been offered to diffuse better environmental management practices.

There are a number of factors that motivate or force a company to adopt some form of an EMS. In the absence of social obligation or consciousness, the existence of relevant environmental regulations or standards assumes paramount importance. In India there

	Large companies (5)	*SMEs (15)*
Yes	5	1
No	–	14

SMEs = small and medium-sized enterprises

Table 18.10 ***Number of companies, of those surveyed, who had experienced pressure from buyers to follow environmental practices***

	Large companies (5)	SMEs (15)
Training	1	2
Transfer of skills	4	–
Transfer of technology	1	–

SMEs = small and medium-sized enterprises

Table 18.11 **Number of companies, of those surveyed, who had received various types of green technical assistance from the buyers**

are unfortunately no specific green regulations that govern the electronics industry. Even if this sector is covered by more general anti-pollution regulations, the implementation of the rules tends to be poor. Consequently, the most important driver for a firm to adopt an EMS is the market or the customer. Among SMEs, pressure from customers is the most important factor. For larger companies, changing technology and competition become important factors in deciding whether to adopt an EMS (see Table 18.12).

- Corporate customer demand

- Costs of resources and liabilities

- Regulations, particularly emerging policies

- Rapidly changing technologies

- Competition for global markets

- Internal company leadership

Table 18.12 **Drivers for adopting an environmental management system (ranked most to least influential)**

For the Indian electronics industry to adopt EMSs in a more widespread manner, a combination of factors is required, as no single option is likely to work very effectively by itself. As noted earlier, the most important determinants or motivators for adopting EMSs (government regulations or market forces) are not present in India. The larger companies do not really place any environmental conditions on their small suppliers. However, there are also other constraints as described in Table 18.13.

The EMS is rarely discussed as a corporate strategic planning issue. Even when the environment is discussed as a business concern, the co-ordination between the different units of a company is so poor that nothing really gets implemented. The other area of concern is the almost complete lack of awareness on issues of sustainability, product obsolescence and technology for the industry as whole. Information exists in a piecemeal fashion and is restricted to a few large companies only

- Rapid obsolescence of products, technology, production equipment

- Environmental issues not addressed at strategic level

- Lack of strong customer relationships

- Little awareness of sustainability issues in partner companies and suppliers

- Lack of clear public environmental goals and policies

- Weak internal relationships between environmental and product development groups

- Primary focus of the companies is on reducing costs

- Multiple suppliers of components along the supply chain

- Large energy demands for transport in local and global supply chains

- Eco-efficiency gains may be offset by growth in production

Table 18.13 **Barriers to adopting an environmental management system (ranked most to least binding)**

18.3.4 *Social and ethical concerns*

Our survey also looked at the social and ethical issues in the electronics industry. The rationale was that any studies of the sector with a view to examining its sustainability would be inadequate without an examination of the social and ethical aspects. We were interested in the working environment of the industry, safeguards for workers involved with handling hazardous substances in terms of training and so on, use of child labour and other hiring practices. The questions about good workplace practices were aimed not only at getting an update on these practices but to assess whether there were any buyer pressures to maintain certain hygiene standards. The companies did maintain suitable levels of hygiene and safety, but did not really perceive that hygiene would become a barrier to sales.

While certain buyers did check the factory premises, they also did not issue any specific standards for workplace practices. Moreover, even when standards did exist, it does not appear as if they represented a very important factor in the decision to buy from a particular company. For a typical small or medium-sized company, the amount spent on workplace practices is less than 1% of the total operating costs. With many other costs more or less fixed, most companies feel that this is one area in their budget where they can reduce expenditure if necessary.

Most companies have an orientation programme and periodic refresher courses for workers whose jobs involve the use of hazardous substances. However, there is an impression that the legal guidelines overseeing workers' safety training and procedures were less than strictly enforced. For example, there is a law that obligates electronics manufacturers to make available a first-aid kit with a properly trained person at the factory premises. But a first-aid kit was rarely seen at the companies, nor was there any evidence that there was a trained person at the facility.

None of the companies has a hiring policy that discriminates on the basis of gender, but it was noticed that very few women were employed in the actual assembly-line areas. The electronics industry also does not employ any child labour but it is possible that the tiny and household segment of this industry would have a fair degree of child labour. This study is somewhat constrained in this aspect in that it did not probe the supply chain deeply enough to verify many of these pertinent issues. A significant amount of the electronics assembly occurs in the micro-enterprise sector, which is highly disorganised, and where issues such as wages, child labour and workers' safety are particularly significant. Samtel Color Limited was one of the large firms interviewed during the survey. A snapshot view of its environment-related practices is provided in Box 18.2.

18.4 Conclusions

The electronics industry in India currently has a reactive stance towards sustainability issues. While awareness does exist in most quarters, it seldom translates into better practices. However, one has to be careful in not turning the environmental issue into a potential trade barrier. Environmental and social issues should be viewed within the framework of supply chain management. The industrialised nations consequently have a huge responsibility in educating and training electronics suppliers in India. Transfer of technology, transfer of skills and of technical know-how are all areas where the expertise of the multinational electronics companies would be very useful.

Moreover, international organisations and professional bodies (e.g. the IEEE) need to work with and better inform Indian companies on a wide range of sustainability concerns. Special information networks could be developed that collect and disseminate relevant information. This is particularly important for small and medium-sized companies who do not have many linkages to global information networks.

Domestically, industrial associations have a major role to play in promoting environmentally sound business practices. They could be a catalyst in increasing the adoption of EMSs such as the ISO 14000 series by educating individual companies about potential benefits and aiding companies in getting the appropriate consulting service that such certification requires. Some of the assistance, at least in the case of SMEs, can be in the form of financial assistance to get the eco-certification

The government is another stakeholder that has a very important role to play in this process. Only the government has the necessary authority and legitimacy to address the regulatory and legislative vacuum that currently exists in India. Based on prevailing international standards, the government needs to draft and implement legislation specifically aimed at the environmental dimensions of the electronics sector. Using prevailing international standards also reduces the likelihood that a trade barrier will arise because of environmental standards.

The survey reveals that a number of options exist for the implementation of environmentally sound practices. Further thought and research is needed to investigate the economic feasibility as well as the ecological benefits of these options. Perhaps different options or a different mix of options would be applicable to different countries. Techniques not conducive or not adaptable to local conditions would find acceptance diffi-

SAMTEL IS THE LARGEST MANUFACTURER OF MONO CATHODE-RAY TUBES IN THE world, as well as a major producer of colour picture tubes. The company was awarded an ISO 9002 in 1993, and is currently working towards ISO 14001 certification. The company's main export markets are Italy, France, UK, Spain, Germany and Austria.

Samtel launched a corporate environmental programme in 1995–96. The programme consists of annual policy statements from which a specific set of activities is organised on a monthly basis. The company's plan seeks to address and resolve all issues related to environmental hazards in air, soil or water. The programme is implemented simultaneously in all departments and is co-ordinated by the Utilities Department.

Every worker, supervisor and manager is responsible for achieving the company's environment, health and safety objectives. Examples of specific environmental policy and management activities at Samtel include:

- *Water.* The company installed an effluent treatment plant to enable it to re-use production effluent. The company is currently recycling about 50% of its waste water, and hopes to recycle 100% in the near future.

- *Recycling.* The company is making efforts to recycle its packaging materials at both ends, both as a buyer from its vendors and also as a seller of colour picture tubes. Requests for such recycling have now started coming in from its buyers from the EU.

- *Chemicals.* Scrubbers have been installed to trap air emissions of ammonium bifluoride, and a recycling programme has been instituted for certain chemicals (such as phosphors).

- *Product design.* As part of a product recycling programme, the glass part of an obsolete colour picture tube is dismantled and melted down so as to enable its re-use. As far as easy dismantlability of obsolete products is concerned (under take-back obligations), the company has to date received specifications from only one of its EU buyers.

- *Supply chain.* In some instances, Samtel has tried to convince its vendors to adopt more ecologically efficient industrial processes.

The company has so far only faced environmental specifications from one of its buyers. In this case, Samtel had to provide an environmental certificate indicating that the components do not use the banned substance. Samtel does not perceive any form of trade barriers related to the environment, but the company does believe that an ISO 14001 certification will project a green image and make a difference to market access.

Samtel clearly has been exposed to international views on product take-back, recycling and disposal. Most importantly, the company leadership is particularly committed to best environmental practices, with emphasis on voluntary measures. The company has developed a long-term relationship with its vendors and is using this relationship to diffuse better business practices. Samtel has the resources and the will to install the latest technologies that have been developed for greener production.

However, the problem of low compliance remains even with Samtel at the operational level. Even with almost everything going for it, the implementation of its environmental programme is still not 100%. This is partly due to the lack of external forces such as an effective set of government regulations.

Box 18.2 *Samtel Color Limited: a case study of environmental initiatives*

cult. It is important that a reverse flow of data—i.e. from producers to policy-makers—is established because the former are the best judge of what works best. All end-of-life options such as disposal and recycling carry certain environmental burdens. It is important that a cost–benefit analysis be carried out in qualitative as well as quantitative terms to develop the most feasible and viable option.

Our research found that there is very little awareness among the Indian electronics manufacturers about WEEE/ROS policies and their policy and business implications. Indian electronics exporters need to monitor the development and policy trends related to this legislation. A lack of environmental consciousness or a lack of environmentally sound practices could well be disastrous for this industry, while a lack of information about the various requirements and standards in importing countries could pose very serious trade hurdles.

BIBLIOGRAPHY

ABB (Asea Brown Boveri) (2000) ABB Group Annual Sustainability Report: 2000 (www.abb.com).

ABI (Allied Business Intelligence) (1999) US and Global Stationary Fuel Cell Markets: The Next Decade Defined (Oyster Bay, NY: ABI, August 1999).

ADL (Arthur D. Little) (1999) Distributed Generation: Understanding the Economics, White Paper (Acorn Park, MA: ADL).

Agenda 21 (1992) Earth Summit '92: The United Nations Conference on Environment and Development (London: The Regency Press Corporation).

Ahbe, S., A. Braunschweig and R. Müller-Wenk (1990) Methodik für Ökobilanzen auf der Basis ökologischer Optimierung (Schriftenreihe Umwelt, 133; Bern: Federal Environmental Protection Agency [BUWAL]).

Aldefer, R.B., M.M. Eldridge and T.J. Starrs (2000) Making Connections: Case Studies in Interconnection Barriers and their Impacts on Distributed Power Projects (Golden, CO: National Renewable Energy Laboratory).

Allen, W.T. (1992) 'Our Schizophrenic Conception of the Business Corporation', Cardozo Law Review 14: 261-81.

Altman, B.W. (1998) 'Transformed Corporate Community Relations: A Management Tool for Achieving Corporate Citizenship', Business and Society Review 102/103: 43-51.

Amburg, B.V., and M.J. Gage (2001) 'The Green Index Survey: Do Clean Fuel Vehicles Contribute to Auto Makers' Environmental Images and Global Competitiveness?', www.calstart.org/greenindex/gievs.html, 16 February 2001.

AMD (Advanced Micro Devices) (1996) 'Manufacturing Facilities Overview', www.amd.com/html/locations/mfg.html.

American Electronics Association Europe (1998) American Electronics Association Europe 10 Basic Principles on the DG XI Working Paper on End-of-Life Electronics (American Electronics Association Europe, September 1998).

Anderson, B. (1983) Imagined Communities: Reflections on the Origin and Spread of Nationalism (London: Verso).

Angel, D.P. (1994) Restructuring for Innovation: The Remaking of the US Semiconductor Industry (New York: Guilford Publications).

Arnfalk, P. (1999) Information Technology in Pollution Prevention: Telework and Teleconferencing Used as Tools in the Reduction of Work-Related Travel (IIIEE Dissertation; Lund, Sweden: Lund University).

Arrigo, L.G., T. Luen and Y. Lin (1996) 'Environmental Conditions and Environmental Law in Taiwan', http://taiwanese.com/tw-env/about.htm.

AT&T (2001) 'EHS Articles', www.att.com/ehs/brad/articles, February 2001.

Atkinson, A., V.V. Chari and P.J. Kehoe (1999) 'Taxing Capital Income: A Bad Idea', Federal Reserve Bank of Minneapolis Quarterly Review 23: 3-18.

Austin, D., and M. Macauley (2001) 'Cutting through Environmental Issues: Technology as a Double-Edged Sword', *The Brookings Review* 19.1 (Winter 2001): 24-27.

Axelrod, R.A. (1998) 'Ten Years Later: The State of Environmental Performance Reports Today', *Environmental Quality Management*, Winter 1998.

Ayres, R.U. (1998) 'Towards a Zero Emissions Economy', *Environmental Science and Technology*, VIEWPOINT 32.15 (1 August 1999), http://pubs.acs.org/hotartcl/est/98/aug/zero.html.

Ayres, R.U., G. Ferrer and T. van Leynseele (1997) 'Eco-efficiency, Asset Recovery and Remanufacturing', *European Management Journal* 15: 557-74.

Babcock, C. (2000) 'Ethical Sourcing in a Wired Economy', in R. Thamotheram (ed.), *Visions of Ethical Sourcing* (London: Financial Times/Prentice Hall): 42.

Barnum, A. (2002) 'Finding Polluters Close to Home: Information on Toxics Just a Click Away', *San Francisco Chronicle*, February 2002 [21 April 1998], www.sfgate.com/cgi-bin/article.cgi?file=/chronicle/archive/1998/04/21/BU77246.DTL.

Bartlett, C.A., and G. Sumantra (1994) 'Changing the Role of Top Management: Beyond Strategy to Purpose', *Harvard Business Review* 72.6 (November/December 1994): 79-88.

Bauer, D. (2000) 'Cross-Cutting Applications', WTEC Workshop on Environmentally Benign Manufacturing (EBM) Technologies, Loyola College, MD, 13 July 2000.

Bauman, Z. (1998) *Globalisation* (Cambridge, UK: Cambridge University Press).

Baumgarten, H., and B. Arnold (2000) *Greening of Supply Chain: An Analysis of Ecological Potentials through Integrated Logistics and Supply Chain in the European Union* (Berlin: Technical University of Berlin, Department of Logistics).

Baxter Healthcare Corporation (2001) '1999 Sustainability Report: Moving Towards Sustainable Development', www.baxter.com/investors/citizenship/environmental/index.html, January 2001.

Bayles, D.L. (2001) *E-Commerce Logistics and Fulfillment* (Upper Saddle River, NJ: Prentice Hall).

Bayus, B.L. (1994) 'Are Product Life Cycles Really Getting Shorter?', *Journal of Product Innovation Management* 11.4: 300-309.

Bayus, B.L., and W.P. Putsis, Jr (1999) 'Product Proliferation: An Empirical Analysis of Product Line Determinants and Market Outcomes', *Marketing Science* 18.2: 137-53.

Beck, U. (2000) *What is Globalisation?* (Oxford, UK: Polity Press).

Bender, A.R., and Stephenson, F.B. (1996) 'Watershed: The Future of US Business Air Travel', *Transportation Journal* 35.3: 14-32.

Bennett, J.W. (1976) *The Ecological Transition: Cultural Anthropology and Human Adaptation* (New York: Pergamon Press).

Bennison, D.J. (1988) 'Transport/Telecommunication Interactions: Empirical Evidence from a Videoconferencing Field Trial in the United Kingdom', *Transportation Research* 22A.4: 291-300.

Benz, M. (1999) *Umweltverträglichkeit von Transportketten* (Berlin: Fachbereich Wirtschaft und Management der Technischen Universität Berlin).

Berkhout, F., and J. Hertin (2001) *Impacts of Information and Communications Technologies on Environmental Sustainability: Speculations and Evidence*, Report to the OECD, Brighton, UK, January 2001.

Berle, A.A. (1931) 'Corporate Powers as Powers in Trust', *Harvard Law Review* 44: 1049-74.

Bernstein, M., P. Brumley, J. Hagen, S. Hassell, R. Lempert, J. Munoz and D. Robalino (1999) *Developing Countries and Global Climate Change: Electric Power Options for Growth* (Arlington, VA: Pew Center on Global Climate Change, June 1999).

Bérubé, M.R. (1992) *Integrating Environment into Business Management: A Study of Supplier Relationships in the Computer Industry* (Cambridge, MA: MIT Technology, Business and Environment Research Group).

Bezos, J. (2000) Interview in *Red Herring*, August 2000: 80-88.

Blair, M.M. (1995) *Ownership and Control: Rethinking Corporate Governance for the Twenty-First Century* (Washington, DC: Brookings Institution).

Blum, W.J., and H. Kalven (1953) *The Uneasy Case for Progressive Taxation* (Chicago: University of Chicago Press).

Bolt, D.B., and R.A.K. Crawford (2000) *Digital Divide: Computers and our Children's Future* (New York: TV Books).

Bowen, H. (1953) *Social Responsibilities of the Businessman* (New York: Harper).

Bower, J.L., and C.M. Christensen (1995) 'Disruptive Technologies: Catching the Wave', *Harvard Business Review* 73.1: 43-53.

Braga, C.A., C. Kenney, C. Qiang, D. Crisafulli, D. Di Martino, R. Eskinazi, R. Schware and W. Kerr-Smith (2000) 'The Networking Revolution: Opportunities and Challenges for Developing Countries', InfoDev Working Paper Series, The World Bank Group, June 2000.

Brand, G., A. Braunschweig, A. Scheidegger and O. Schwank (1997) *Bewertung in Ökobilanzen mit der Methode der ökologischen Knappheit: Ökofaktoren 1997* (Schriftenreihe Umwelt, 297; Bern: Federal Environmental Protection Agency [BUWAL]).

Braunschweig, A., and R. Müller-Wenk (1993) *Ökobilanzen für Unternehmen: Eine Wegleitung für die Praxis* (Bern: Verlag Paul Haupt).

Brezet, H., and C.G. van Hemel (1997) *Ecodesign: A Promising Approach to Sustainable Production and Consumption* (Paris: United Nations Environment Programme).

Brezet, H., B. Houtzager, R. Overbeeke, C. Rocha and S. Silvester (2000) *Evaluation of 55 POEM Subsidy Projects* (Delft, Netherlands: Delft University of Technology, Design for Sustainability Program).

Bristol-Myers Squibb (2001) 'Environment, Health and Safety website', www.bms.com/ehs, February 2001.

British Airways (2001) 'British Airways: Community and Environment', www.britishairways.com/responsibility/, February 2001.

Brockmann, T. (1999) '21 Warehousing Trends in the 21st Century', *IIE Solutions* 21.7: 36-40.

Brown, D., J. Green, F. Hall, S. Rocchi, P. Rutter and A. Dearing (2000) *Building a Better Future: Innovation, Technology, and Sustainable Development* (Geneva: World Business Council for Sustainable Development).

Brown, L., et al. (1999) *State of the World: A Worldwatch Institute Report on Progress toward a Sustainable Society* (New York: W.W. Norton).

BSR (Business for Social Responsibility) (2000) *Greening the Supply Chain* (San Francisco: BSR, www.bsr.org).

BT (British Telecom) (1991) *Energy, Telecommunications and the Environment* (London: BT).

Business 2.0 (2001) 'Man bites dog.com', *Business 2.0*, 20 March 2001, www.business2.com/articles/mag/0,1640,14580,FF.html, accessed 8 February 2002.

Business Week (1997) 'Silicon Valley: How it really works', *Business Week*, 18–25 August 1997: 64-147.

—— (2000) 'The Big Picture: The Helping Hand', *Business Week*, 5 June 2000: 14 (data supplied by Edventure Partners based on Giving USA/Commerce Department sources).

—— (2001) 'Why the supply chain broke down', *Business Week*, 19 March 2001: 41.

Capria, A. (ed.) (1996) *A World Survey of Environmental Laws* (Milan: Giuffre Editore): 765-77.

Carnegie, A. (1900) *The Gospel of Wealth, and Other Timely Essays* (New York: Century).

Carroll, A.B. (1991) 'The Pyramid of Corporate Social Responsibility: Toward the Moral Management of Organizational Stakeholders', *Business Horizons* 34.4 (July/August 1991): 39-48.

—— (1998) 'The Four Faces of Corporate Citizenship', *Business and Society Review* 100/101: 1-7.

Case, D.W. (2000) 'Legal Considerations in Voluntary Corporate Environmental Reporting', *The Environmental Law Reporter*.

Caudill, R.J., et al. (2000) 'Exploring the Environmental Impact of eCommerce on Electronic Products: An Application of Fuzzy Decision Theory and Lifecycles Studies', in H. Reichl and H. Griese (eds.), *Electronics Goes Green 2000+: A Challenge for the Next Millennium. Proceedings. I. Technical Lectures* (Berlin: IZM): 877-86.

Celarier, M. (1999) 'Citibank Tackles the Problem of Global Sprawl', *Global Finance* 8.8 (August 1999): 49-54.

Center of Excellence for Sustainable Development (2001) Eco-Industrial Park, www.sustainable.doe.gov/business/ecoparks.shtml, 23 March 2001.

Chambers, N., and K. Lewis (2001) *Ecological Footprint Analysis: Towards a Sustainability Indicator for Business* (ACCA Research Report, 65; London: Association of Chartered Certified Accountants, www.bestfootforward.org).

Charnovitz, S. (2000) 'Current Development: World Trade and the Environment: A Review of the New WTO Report', *Georgetown International Environmental Law Review* 12: 523-42.

Charter, M., and I. Belmane (1997) 'Integrated Product Policy (IPP) and Eco-Product Development (EPD)', *Journal of Sustainable Product Design*, July 1997.

Chernow, R. (1999) 'Learning from Robber Barons', *Houston Chronicle*, 10 October 1999: 1C, 5C.

Chilton, K.W. (1999) *Are Economic Growth and a Sustainable Environment Compatible?* (Policy Study, 152; St Louis, MO: Center for the Study of American Business, Washington University, September 1999).

Christensen, C. (1997) *The Innovator's Dilemma* (Cambridge, MA: Harvard Business School Press, www.disruptivetechnologies.com).

Clark, J.M. (1916) 'The Changing Basis of Economic Responsibility', *Journal of Political Economy* 243 (March 1916): 209-29.

Cler, G., N. Lenssen and C. Manz (1999) *Residential Distributed Generation: Options and Prospects* (Boulder, CO: E Source).

Cohen, N. (1999) 'Greening the Internet: Ten Ways E-commerce Could Affect the Environment and What We Can Do', *iMP magazine*, October 1999, www.cisp.org/imp/october_99/10_99cohen.htm, accessed 8 February 2002.

—— (2000) 'E-commerce and the Environment', in *Environmental Perspectives*, Special Edition, 'Environment and the Information Age', April 2000 (www.tellus.org): 2-5.

ComEd (2001) '1998 Annual Report on the Environment: The Value of Environmental Leadership', www.ucm.com/comed/residential/display.asp?id=485, February 2001.

Conference Board (1995) *Corporate Giving Strategies that Add Business Value* (Report No. 1126; New York: Conference Board).

—— (1996) *Shaping a Superior Corporate Image* (Report No. 1156; New York: Conference Board).

—— (1998) *Using Technology to Strengthen Employee and Family Involvement in Technology* (Report No. 1223; funded by US Department of Education; New York: Conference Board).

—— (1999a) *Corporate Contributions: The View from Fifty Years* (Report No. 1249; New York: Conference Board).

—— (1999b) *The Expanding Parameters of Global Corporate Citizenship*, (Report No. 1246; New York: Conference Board).

—— (1999c) *The Future Organization: New Leadership and Employee Roles* (Report No. 1245; New York: Conference Board).

—— (1999d) *The Link between Corporate Citizenship and Financial Performance* (Report No. 1234; New York: Conference Board).

—— (2000a) *Corporate Environmental Governance: Benchmarks toward a World-Class System* (Report No. 1266; New York: Conference Board).

—— (2000b) *Does a Rising Tide Lift All Boats? America's Full-Time Working Poor Reap Limited Gains in the New Economy* (Report No. 1271; New York: Conference Board).

—— (2000c) *The Impact of Mergers and Acquisitions on Corporate Citizenship* (Report No. 1272; New York: Conference Board).

Cook, D. (2001) 'Managing e-Business: Top Ten Myths', IBM white paper, www-1.ibm.com/services/insights/ten_myths.html, January 2001.

Council on Foundations (1996) *Measuring the Value of Corporate Citizenship* (Washington, DC: Council on Foundations).

Couzin, J. (2000) 'Net Retailers Aren't All Losers', *The Industry Standard*, 20 October 2000, www.thestandard.com/article/0,1902,19770,00.html, accessed 8 February 2002.

Cowe, R., and S. Williams (2000) *Who Are the Ethical Consumers?* (Manchester, UK: The Co-operative Bank).

Cox, R. (1997) *Production, Power and World Order: Social Forces in the Making of History* (New York: Columbia University Press).

Cromie, W.J. (2000) 'Carbon Bits to Revolutionize Computer Construction', *Harvard University Gazette*, 21 September 2000, www.news.harvard.edu/gazette/2000/09.21/nanotubes.html; repr. as 'Future Computers: Smaller, Faster, More Wearable', *Harvard College Gazette*, November 2000: 5.

CSMINC (Chartered Semiconductor Manufacturing) (1997) 'Chartered Semiconductor Manufacturing named top fab by *Semiconductor International* magazine', www.csminc.com/ pr18.htm.

CSP (Chemical Strategies Partnership) (2001) 'CSP Manual: Tools for Optimizing Chemical Management', www.chemicalstrategies.org.

Cyrix Corporation (1996) *1995 Annual Report*, available at www.cyrix.com/corpor/annual.

Dataquest (1997) *Top 10 Worldwide Semiconductor Market Share Estimates: 1996* (San Jose, CA: Dataquest).

Davis, G.A., C.A. Wilt, P.S. Dillon and E.K. Fishbein (1997) *Extended Product Responsibility: A New Principle for Product Oriented Pollution Prevention* (Center for Clean Products and Clean Technologies, University of Tennessee, June 1997).

Davis, K. (1960) 'Can Business Afford to Ignore Social Responsibilities?', *California Management Review* 2.3 (Spring 1960): 70-76.

Day, G.S. (1994) 'The Capabilities of Market-Driven Organizations', *Journal of Marketing* 58: 37-52.

de Bakker, F.G.A. (2001) *Product-Oriented Environmental Management: A Study of Capability-Building, Stakeholder Orientation and Continuous Improvement Regarding Products' Environmental Characteristics in Firms* (Enschede, Netherlands: Twente University Press).

de Bakker, F.G.A., O.A.M. Fisscher and A.J.P. Brack (1999) 'Organizing Product-Oriented Environmental Management from a Resource-Based Perspective', paper presented at the 8th *Greening of Industry Network Conference*, Chapel Hill, NC, USA, 14–17 November 1999.

den Hond, F. (1996) *In Search of a Useful Theory Of Environmental Strategy: A Case Study on the Recycling of End-Of-Life Vehicles from the Capabilities Perspective* (PhD thesis; Vrije Universiteit, Amsterdam).

Deutscher Bundestag (1994) report of the Enquete-Kommission *Schutz des Menschen und der Umwelt*, Bonn.

—— (ed.) (1998) *Konzept Nachhaltigkeit: Vom Leitbild zur Umsetzung. Abschlußbericht der Enquete-Kommission 'Schutz des Menschen und der Umwelt' des 13. Deutschen Bundestages* (Bonn: Deutscher Bundestag).

Diamond, J. (1997) *Guns, Germs, and Steel: The Fates of Human Societies* (New York: W.W. Norton).

Dodd, E.M. (1932) 'For Whom Are Corporate Managers Trustees?', *Harvard Law Review* 45: 1145-63.

Drucker, P.F. (1999) *Management Challenges for the 21st Century* (New York: HarperBusiness).

DTI (UK Department of Trade and Industry) (1998) *Our Competitive Future: Building the Knowledge Driven Economy* (London: DTI).

Duany, A., E. Plater-Zyberk and J. Speck (2000) *Suburban Nation: The Rise of Sprawl and the Decline of the American Dream* (New York: North Point Press).

Dun & Bradstreet (2001) '19th Annual D&B Small Business Survey', sbs.dnb.com, February 2001.

Dunham, R.S. (1999) 'Across America, a Troubling "Digital Divide" ', *Business Week* 3640 (2 August 1999): 40.

Dunn, S. (2000) *Micropower: The Next Electrical Era* (Worldwatch Paper, 151; Washington, DC: Worldwatch Institute).

Dyer, J. (2000) *Collaborative Advantage: Winning through Extended Enterprise Supplier Networks* (Oxford, UK: Oxford University Press).

Dyllick, T. (1999) 'Environment and Competitiveness of Companies', in D. Hitchens, J. Clausen and K. Fichter (eds.), *International Environmental Management Benchmarks* (Berlin/Heidelberg/New York: Springer): 55-69.

Economist (1997a) 'Silicon Valley Survey', *The Economist*, 29 March 1997: 1-20.

—— (1997b) 'Deep in the Heart of Texas', *The Economist*, 29 March 1997: 14-15.

—— (2000a) 'The Dawn of Micropower', *The Economist*, 5 August 2000: 75-77.

—— (2000b) 'What the Internet Cannot Do', *The Economist*, 17 August 2000: 11-12.

EDB Singapore (Economic Development Board of Singapore) (1996a) 'More semiconductor companies doing multi-activities', www.sedb.com/what/index_search.html (search on 'semiconductor').

—— (1996b) 'Two new schemes to boost semiconductor industry', available at www.sedb.com/what/index_search.html (search on 'semiconductor').

EEA (European Environment Agency) (2000) *Are we Moving in the Right Direction? Indicators on Transport and Environment Integration in the EU* (Copenhagen: EEA).

Ehrlich, P., and J.P. Holdren (1971) 'Impact of Population Growth', *Science* 171: 1212-17.

EIAJ (Electronic Industries Association of Japan) (not dated a) *EIAJ Standard*, prescribed by the Japanese Standard Association (JSA) based on article 4.4.1 of the WTO/TBT (World Trade Organisation Technical Barriers to Trade) Agreement.

—— (not dated b) *Standards Information under the WTO/TBT (World Trade Organisation Technical Barriers to Trade Agreement) Code of Good Practice for Electronics* (Electronic Industries Association of Japan *et al.*)

ELCINA (Electronics Components Industry Association) (1999) *Electronics Outlook* (New Delhi: ELCINA).

—— (2000) *Electronics Outlook* (New Delhi: ELCINA).

Electrolux (2001) 'Eco Savings', www.corporate.electrolux.com/node338.asp, February 2001.

Elkington, J. (1998) *Cannibals with Forks: The Triple Bottom Line of 21st Century Business* (Gabriola Creek, BC: New Society Publishers).

eMarketer (2001) 'Comparative Assessments: Worldwide B2B Commerce', eMarketer, www.emarketer.com.

Environics International Limited (1999) 'The Millennium Poll on Social Responsibility', www.environics.net; www.mori.com/polls/1999/millpoll.shtml.

Environment97.org (2001) 'Environmental Reporting: A Vital Corporate Communications Tool or an Unnecessary Business Risk?', www.environment97.org/text/reception/r/techpapers/papers/g55.htm, January 2001.

EPA (US Environmental Protection Agency) (1990) *Toxics in the Community: National and Local Perspectives* (1989 Toxics Release Inventory National Report; Office of Pollution Prevention and Toxics; Washington, DC: Government Printing Office).

—— (1995) *Federal Environmental Regulations Affecting the Electronics Industry* (EPA 744-B-95-001; Washington, DC: Design for the Environment Program, Economics, Exposure and Technology Division, Office of Pollution Prevention and Toxics, EPA, September 1995).

—— (1997) *Toxics Release Inventory: Public Data Release* (Office of Pollution, Prevention and Toxics; Washington, DC: Government Printing Office).

—— (1999) *Substitutes in Electronics Cleaning as prescribed by US EPA as of 8 June 1999* (Washington, DC: EPA).

EPRI (Electric Power Research Institute) (1999) *Electricity Technology Roadmap: Powering Progress* (Palo Alto, CA: EPRI).

Ericsson (1998) *Environmental Report 1997* (Stockholm: Ericsson).

EURESCOM (European Institute for Research and Strategic Studies in Telecommunications) (1996) *Calling for a Better Tomorrow: Environmental Improvement through the Use of Telecommunication Services* (Heidelberg, Germany: EURESCOM).

Europa (2000) 'Commission Tackles Growing Problem of Electrical and Electronic Waste', Brussels, 13 June 2000 (http://europa.eu.int/comm/environment/docum/00347_en.htm).

European Commission (1997a) 'Working Paper on the Management of Waste from Electrical and Electronic Equipment', European Commission Directorate General XI, 9 October 1997.

—— 'Comments on the Commission "Working Paper on the Management of Waste from Electrical and Electronic Equipment" ', European Commission Directorate General XI, December 1997, ECTEL (Association of the European Telecommunications and Professional Electronics Industry).

—— (1997c) *Environmental Quick Scan*, August 1997, European Commission.

—— (1998) *Eco Trade Manual: Environmental Challenges for Exporting to the EU*, August 1998, European Commission.

Evans, P., and T.S. Wurster (1999) *Blown to Bits: How the New Economics of Information Transforms Strategy* (Boston, MA: Harvard Business School Press).

Fattah, H. (2000) 'The Digital Divide: Politics or a Real Problem?', *Mc Technology Marketing Intelligence* 20.9 (September 2000): 82-88.

FEE (Fédération des Experts Comptables Européens) (2000) *Towards a Generally Accepted Framework for Environmental Reporting* (Brussels: FEE).

Feldman, J.M. (1993) 'Bane of Business Travel? (Videoconferencing)', *Air Transport World* 30.9 (September 1993): 44-46, 48, 51.

Fichter, K. (2001) *Environmental Effects of E-business and Internet Economy: First Insights and Conclusions for Environmental Politics* (Berlin: available as PDF, www.borderstep.de).

Fineman, S., and K. Clarke (1996) 'Green Stakeholders: Industry Interpretations and Response', *Journal of Management Studies* 33: 715-30.

Foley, D., C. France, I. Maslennikova, K. McIntyre and R. Royall (2000) 'Measuring "Sustainability" at a Corporate Level: The Environmental Space Approach', Proceedings of the Engineering Doctorate in Environmental Technology Annual Conference, 2000.

Fombrun, C.J. (1997) 'Three Pillars of Corporate Citizenship: Ethics, Social Benefit, Profitability', in N.M. Tichy, A.R. McGillis and L. St Clair (eds.), *Corporate Global Citizenship: Doing Business in the Public Eye* (San Francisco: New Lexington Press): 27-42.

Frederick, W.C. (1994) 'From CSR1 to CSR2', *Business and Society* 33.2 (August 1994): 150-64.

Friedman, M. (1962) *Capitalism and Freedom* (Chicago: University of Chicago Press).

—— (1970) 'The social responsibility of business is to increase its profits', *New York Times Magazine*, 13 September 1970: 32-33, 122, 124, 126.

Frischknecht, R., P. Hofstetter, I. Knoepfl, R. Dones and E. Zollinger (1994) *Ökoninventare für Energiesysteme* (ESU-Reihe, 1/94; Laboratorium für Energiesysteme, Zurich: ETH Zürich/PSI Villingen).

Galster, G., R. Hanson, H. Wolman, S. Coleman and J. Freihage (2000) *Wrestling Sprawl to the Ground: Defining and Measuring an Elusive Concept* (Washington, DC: Fannie Mae Foundation).

Gandhi, G.P. (1998) 'Export Prospects of Electronics and Computer Software', *Saket News Digest*, July–September 1998: 133-39.

GEMI (Global Environmental Management Initiative) (2000) Workgroup on Web-Based Technologies Benchmarking Survey, *How GEMI Companies are Managing HS&E Information on the Web*, January 2000: 14.

—— (2001) *New Paths to Business Value: Strategic Sourcing—Environment, Health, and Safety* (Washington, DC: GEMI, www.gemi.org).

Gensch, C.-O., and D. Quack (2000) *Orientierende ökologische Betrachtung der T-NetBox* (Freiburg: Oeko-Institut, September 2000).

Geoffrion, A., and R. Krishnan (2001), 'Prospects for Operations Research in the E-Business Era', *Interfaces* 30.2 (March/April 2001): 6-36.

Gibbs, H.K. (2000) 'Expense Checks (and Balances)', *Export Today's Global Business* 16.11: 48-54.

Gilbert, A. (2000) 'E-procurement: Problems behind the Promise', *InformationWeek* 813: 48-62.

Gilder, G. (2000) *Telecosm: How Infinite Bandwidth Will Revolutionize our World* (New York: The Free Press).

Ginsburg, J., and A. Aston (2000) 'Green power is gaining ground', *Business Week*, 9 October 2000: 45.

Global Reach (2001) 'Global Internet Statistics', www.glreach.com/globstats/, February 2001.

Goedkoep M. (1995) *The Ecoindicator 95: Final Report* (National Reuse of Waste Research Program; NOH report, 9523; Amersfoort, Netherlands: PRé Consultants).

Goedkoop M., and R. Spriensma (2000) *The Eco-indicator 99: A Damage Oriented Method for Life Cycle Impact Assessment. Methodology Report* (www.pre.nl/eco-indicator99/ei99-reports.htm).

Golden, M. (2000) 'Power points: electricity industries, Wall Street clash on fuel cells', *Dow Jones Energy Service*, 21 January 2000: 1.

Gooley, T.B. (1998) 'Reverse Logistics: Five Steps to Success', *Logistics Management and Distribution Report* 37.6: 49-55.

Gordon, P., and H.W. Richardson (2000) *Critiquing Sprawl's Critics* (Washington, DC: Cato Institute).

Gossett, W.T. (1957) *Corporate Citizenship* (Lexington, VA: Washington and Lee University).

Green Business Letter (2001) 'Six Keys to Creating a Winning Environmental Report', www.greenbiz.com/toolbox/Howto.cfm, February 2001.

Greusing, I., and S. Zangl (2000) 'Vergleich von Print- und Online-Katalogen: Akzeptanz, ökologische und ökonomische Analyse', *IZT-Werkstattbericht* (Berlin) 44.

GRI (Gas Research Institute) (1999) *The Role of Distributed Generation in Competitive Energy Markets* (Chicago: GRI).

Grießhammer, R. (1997) *Umweltschutz im Cyberspace* (Freiburg: Oeko-Institut Freiburg).

Griffin, A. (1997) 'The Effect of Project and Process Characteristics on Product Development Cycle Time', *Journal of Marketing Research* 34: 24-35.

Grove-White, R. (1996) 'Environmental Knowledge and Public Policy Needs: On Humanising the Research Agenda', in S. Lash, B. Szerszuynski and B. Wynne (eds.), *Risk, Environment and Modernity: Towards a New Ecology* (London: Sage).

Gulati, R., and J. Garino (2000) 'Get the Right Mix of Bricks and Clicks', *Harvard Business Review*, May/June 2000: 107-14.

Habersatter, K., and I. Fecker (1998) *Ökoinventare für Verpackungen* (Schriftenreihe Umwelt, 250; Bern: Federal Environmental Protection Agency [BUWAL]).

Halme, M., Z. Fadeeva and P. Arnfalk (2001) 'Is There a Better Option to Corporate Travel Management?', paper presented at the Ninth International Greening of Industry Network Conference, *Sustainability at the Millennium: Globalization, Competitiveness, and the Public Trust*, Bangkok, Thailand.

Hamilton, M.M. (1996) 'The economy gets a new taxonomy: Analysts welcome a SIC transit to '90s realities', *Washington Post*, 28 June 1996.

Handy, C. (1997) 'The Citizen Corporation', *Harvard Business Review* 75.5 (September/October 1997): 26-28.

Hansell, S. (2001) 'Some Hard Lessons for Online Grocers', *New York Times*, 19 February 2001: C1.

Harris Interactive (2001) 'Reputation Quotient, RQ Gold 2000', www.harrisinteractive.com/pop_up/rq/index.asp, February 2001.

Hart, S., and C.K. Prahalad (2000) 'Strategies for the Bottom of the Pyramid: Creating a Sustainable World', briefing paper for the conference *Creating Digital Dividends*, Seattle, WA, October 2000, www.digitaldividends.org.

Hart, S.L. (1995) 'A Natural-Resource-Based View of the Firm', *Academy of Management Review* 20: 986-1014.

—— (1997) 'Beyond Greening: Strategies for a Sustainable World', *Harvard Business Review*, January/February 1997: 66-76.

Harvey, R. (1995) *The Return of the Strong: The Drift to Global Disorder* (London: Macmillan).

Hawken, P., A. Lovins and L.H. Lovins (1999) *Natural Capitalism: Creating the Next Industrial Revolution* (New York: Little Brown & Co.; www.natcap.org).

Heald, M. (1970) *The Social Responsibilities of Business: Company and Community, 1900–1960* (Cleveland, OH: Press of Case Western Reserve University; New Brunswick, NJ: Transaction Books, repr. 1988).

Heijungs, R., J.B. Guinée, G. Huppes, R.M. Lankreijer, H.A. Udo de Haes and A. Wegener Sleeswijk (1992) *Environmental Life Cycle Assessment of Products: Guide and Background* (Leiden, Netherlands: Centrum voor Milieukunde).

Held, D., A.G. McGrew, D. Goldblatt and J. Perraton (1999) *Global Transformations: Politics, Economics and Culture* (Stanford, CA: Stanford University Press).

Heller, L. (2000) 'Reversing a Costly Trend', *Chain Store Age* 76.6: 70-72.

Hendrickson, C.T., H.S. Matthews and D.L. Soh (2001) 'Environmental and Economic Effects of E-commerce: A Case Study of Book Publishing and Retail Logistics', in *Proceedings of the Transportation Research Board Annual Meeting, Transportation Research Record (January 2001)* (Washington, DC: National Academy of Sciences).

Henig, P. (2000) 'Revenge of the Bricks', *Red Herring*, August 2000: 164-72.

Henriques, I., and P. Sadorsky (1999) 'The Relationship between Environmental Commitment and Managerial Perception of Stakeholder Importance', *Academy of Management Journal* 42: 87-99.

Hicks, L. (1996) 'Caterpillar flunks corporate citizenship test', *The York Dispatch* (Pennsylvania), 8 May 1996; repr. in *UAW CAT Update* 1.2 (August 1996).

Hirsh, R. (1999) *Power Loss: The Origins of Deregulation and Restructuring in the American Electric Utility System* (Cambridge, MA: The MIT Press).

Hofstadter, R. (1963) *The Progressive Movement 1900–1915* (Englewood Cliffs, NJ: Prentice Hall).

Holman, H. (1999) *Energy Technology: Oxymoron? Or Moxie Home Run?* (New York: Robertson Stephens): 2-3.

Huber, P. (2000) 'Wealth is not the enemy of the environment: Big business prevents urban sprawl', *Vital Speeches of the Day* 66.12 (1 April 2000): 380-83.

Huber, P., and M.P. Mills (1999) 'Dig more coal: the PCs are coming', *Forbes*, 31 May 1999, 37-40.

—— (2000) 'The PowerChip Paradigm', *HuberMills Power Report Inaugural Issue* (Summer 2000): 1.

Hughes, T.P. (1983) *Networks of Power: Electrification in Western Society, 1880–1930* (Baltimore, MD: Johns Hopkins University Press).

Hutchinson, B. (2000) 'Return to Sender', *Logistics*, May 2000: 69-73.

Iannucci, J. (1999) 'Distributed Generation: Barriers to Market Entry' (Presentation to Board on Energy and Environmental Systems; Washington, DC: National Research Council).

Iansiti, M., and K.B. Clark (1994) 'Integration and Dynamic Capability: Evidence from Product Development in Automobiles and Mainframe Computers', *Industrial and Corporate Change* 3: 557-605.

IBC (International Botanical Congress) (1999) 'World's biodiversity becoming extinct at levels rivaling Earth's past "mass extinctions", International Botanical Congress president calls for seven-point plan to reverse alarming rates of plant species losses', XVI International Botanical Congress, www.burnessc.com/press/ibc/index.asp.

IBM Corporation (1996) *IBM and the Environment: Annual Environmental Report*, www.ibm.com/IBM/ Environment/annual/01Ger.htm.

ICER (Industry Council for Electronic Equipment Recycling) (2000) *UK Status Report on Waste from Electrical and Electronic Equipment* (London: ICER).

Infocom (1999) *Meetings in America: A Study of Trends, Costs and Attitudes towards Business Travel and Teleconferencing, and their Impact on Productivity* (Greenwich, CT: Infocom at NFO Worldwide).

International Paper (2001) 'Sustainable Forestry Challenge', www.internationalpaper.com/our_ world/sfi/sust_forestry1.html, February 2001.

IPG (Iwate Prefectural Government (1999) *Ihatov Land Area with an Affluent Future Environment in Harmony with Nature: Aiming to Create the Iwate Environmental Capital, Iwate Basic Environment Plan* (Morioka, Japan: IPG).

—— (1998) *Ihatov Information Forest Initiative* (Morioka, Japan: IPG).

IPPR (Institute for Public Policy Research) (2000) *Plane Trading: Policies for Reducing the Climate Change Effects of International Aviation* (London: IPPR).

ISO (International Organisation for Standardisation) (1995) *Environmental Management Systems: Specification with Guidance for Use* (draft International Standard ISO 14001; Geneva: ISO).

ITT Flygt (2001) 'ITT Flygt 1999 Sustainability Report', www.ittflygt.com/default.asp?sidnr=64, February 2001.

James, P. (1997) 'The Sustainability Cycle: A New Tool for Product Development and Design', *Journal of Sustainable Product Design*, July 1997.

Jarrett, I. (2000) 'Bridging the Digital Divide', *Asian Business* 36.1 (January 2000): 14.

Jelinski, L.W., T.E. Graedel, R.A. Laudise, D.W. McCall and K.N. Patel (2001) 'Industrial Ecology: Concepts and Approaches', AT&T Bell laboratories, Murray Hill, NJ 07974, www.sustainable. doe.gov/articles/indeccon.shtml, 23 March 2001.

Jenks, J.W. (1917) *Business and the Government* (New York: Alexander Hamilton Institute).

Jensen, R. (2000) 'In Moral Accounting, First World's the Debtor', *Houston Chronicle*, 16 April 2000: 5C.

Jones, H. (1999) 'Corporate Citizenship 2: When sponsors can really mean business', *Daily Telegraph*, 27 July 1999: 33.

Jones, K., T. Alabaster and K. Hetherington (1998) 'Virtual Environments for Environmental Reporting', *Greener Management International* 21 (Spring 1998): 121-37.

—— (1999) 'Internet-Based Environmental Reporting', *Greener Management International* 26 (Summer 1999): 69-90.

Jönson, G., and M. Johnsson (2000) Electronic Commerce and Distribution Systems (Lund, Sweden: Lund Institute of Technology; available as PDF, www.kfb.se/junikonf/upps/G_Jonsson.pdf).

Jungbluth, N., and R. Frischknecht (2000) *Empfehlungen zur Beschaffung von Computerbildschirmen: Energiebilanz und ökologische Aspekte von Flach- und Röhrenbildschirmen im Vergleich* (Uster, Switzerland: ESU-Services, unpublished).

Jupp, B., and T. Bentley (2001) 'Surfing Alone? E-commerce and Social Capital', in J. Wilsdon (ed.), *Digital Futures: Living in a Dot-Com World* (London: Earthscan Publications): 97-114.

Karlsson, M., and L. Sturesson (eds.) (1995) *Världens största maskin: Människan och det globala telekommunikationssystemet* (*The World's Largest Machine: Humankind and the Global Telecom System*) (Universitetet i Linköping, Tema Teknik och social förändring; Stockholm: Carlsson, Swedish language).

Kärnä, A. (1999) *Managing Environmental Issues from Design to Disposal: A Chain Reaction?* (licentiate thesis; Helsinki: Federation of Finnish Electrical and Electronics Industry).

Kates, R.W., and R.D. Torrie (1998) 'Global Change in Local Places', *Environment* 40.2: 5, 39-41.

Keidanren (1997) 'Keidanren Voluntary Action Plan on Environment', http://www.keidanren.or.jp/ english/policy/pol058/intro.html.

Keim, G.D. (1978) 'Managerial Behavior and the Social Responsibility Debate: Goals versus Constraints', *Academy of Management Journal* 21.1 (March 1978): 57-68.

Kelly, M. (ed.) (2000a) 'Misuse of pension fund is "breathtaking"', *Business Ethics: Corporate Social Responsibility Report* 14.4 (July/August 2000): 9.

—— (ed.) (2000b) 'Personal E-mail at Work: To Ban or Not to Ban', *Business Ethics: Corporate Social Responsibility Report* 14.4 (July/August 2000): 9 (citing Minnesota Employment Law Letter).

—— (ed.) (2000c) 'Should a code of conduct be mandatory?', *Business Ethics: Corporate Social Responsibility Report* 14.4 (July/August 2000): 9.

Kelly, M., and T. Klusmann (2000) 'Is IBM still socially responsible? Addressing the Deluge against Naming IBM the No. 1 Best Corporate Citizen', *Business Ethics: Corporate Social Responsibility Report* 14.4 (July/August 2000): 4-5.

Kempton, W., J. Boster and J. Hartley (1995) *Environmental Values in American Culture* (Cambridge, MA: The MIT Press).

Kerr, W., and C. Ryan (2001) 'Eco-efficiency Gains from Manufacturing. A Case Study of Photocopier Manufacturing at Fuji Xerox Australia', *Journal of Cleaner Production* 9: 75-81.

Kinsley, M. (1987) 'Companies as Citizens: Should they have a conscience?', *Wall Street Journal*, 19 February 1987: 29.

Knauer, N.J. (1994) 'The Paradox of Corporate Giving: Tax Expenditures, the Nature of the Corporation, and the Social Construction of Charity', *DePaul Law Review* 44 (Fall 1994): 1ff.

Kogg, B. (2000) *Optimal Meetings: Realising the Environmental and Economic Promise of Virtual Business Meetings. A Case Study of Telia Research AB* (IIIEE master's thesis; Lund, Sweden: Lund University).

Kolk, A. (1999) 'The Internet as a Green Management Tool', *Corporate Environmental Strategy* 6.3: 307-16.

Kortmann, J., and S. de Winter (1999) *On Line Applications in the Netherlands: Looking up Telephone Numbers by Internet* (Amsterdam: IVAM, Universiteit Amsterdam).

Kotabe, M. (1998) 'Efficiency vs Effectiveness Orientation of Global Sourcing Strategy: A Comparison of US and Japanese Multinational Companies', *Academy of Management Executive* 12.4: 107-19.

KPMG (2001) 'Beyond the Numbers', www.kpmg.com/search/index.asp?cid=416, February 2001.

Krasner, S.D. (ed.) (1983) *International Regimes* (Ithaca, NY: Cornell University Press).

Kratochwil, F.V. (1989) *Rules, Norms and Decisions: On the Conditions of Practical and Legal Reasoning in International Relations and Domestic Affairs* (New York: Cambridge University Press).

Kulkarni, S.P. (2000) 'Environmental Ethics and Information Asymmetry among Organizational Stakeholders', *Journal of Business Ethics* 27: 215-28.

Kumar, K., and S.L. Sarnot (1994) 'Advances in Electronic Board Cleaning: Alternatives to CFC (an Ozone Depleting Agent) Cleaning', *Electronic Information and Planning*, December 1994.

—— (1998) 'Is Lead (Pb) Usage in Electronics an Environmental Hazard?', paper presented at *Componex '98*, 3rd International Conference and Exhibition of Electronic Components, Materials and Production Equipments, Bangalore, India, January 1998.

Kurzweil, R. (1999) *The Age of Spiritual Machines: When Computers Exceed Human Intelligence* (Harmondsworth, UK: Penguin).

LaDou, J. (1986) 'Health Issues in the Microelectronics Industry', *Journal of Occupational Medicine* 1: 1-11.

Laitner, J.A., and J.G. Koomey (2000) 'Re-estimating the Annual Energy Outlook 2000: Forecast using Updated Assumptions about the Internet Economy', http://enduse.lbl.gov/Projects/InfoTech.html.

Lall, S. (1998) 'Exports of Manufactures by Developing Countries: Emerging Patterns of Trade and Location', *Oxford Review of Economic Policy* 14.2: 54-73.

Lang, J.C., and A.C. Ho (1998) 'Virtual Teams for Corporate Environmental Excellence', in J. Moxen and P.A. Strachan (eds.), *Managing Green Teams: Environmental Change in Organisations and Networks* (Sheffield, UK: Greenleaf Publishing): 237-50.

Lash, J. (2000) 'Radical Openness as a Winning Strategy', presentation at the World Resources Institute Sustainable Enterprise Summit, 19 September 2000.

Law, A. (2000) Interview in *Harvard Business Review*, September/October 2000.

Leadbeater, C. (1999) *Living on Thin Air* (London: Penguin).

Lenox, M.J., and J. Ehrenfeld (1997) 'Organizing for Effective Environmental Design', *Business Strategy and the Environment* 6: 187-96.

Lenssen, N., C. Hurley and L. Audin (1999) *How will distributed generation be deployed?* (Boulder, CO: E Source).

Lerner, N. (2000) 'Latin America and Mexico: A Change in Focus: Bridging the Digital Divide', *Telecommunications* 34.3 (March 2000): 59-66.

Levine, R., C. Locke, D. Searls and D. Weinberger (2000) *The Cluetrain Manifesto: The End of Business as Usual* (London: Financial Times).

Levine, S. (2000) 'Is the Digital Divide a Mirage?', *America's Network* 104.7 (May 2000): 41-44.

Levitt, T. (1958) 'The Dangers of Social Responsibility', *Harvard Business Review* 36.5 (September/ October 1958): 41-50.

Lifset, R. (1998) 'Introduction to the Roundtable on the Industrial Ecology of Pulp and Paper', *Journal of Industrial Ecology* 1.3: 13-14.

Lovins, A.B. (1997) 'Hypercar: The Next Industrial Revolution', Rocky Mountain Institute, www. hypercar.com.

—— (2001) 'Response: Etopia?', in J. Wilsdon, *Digital Futures, Living in a Dot-Com World* (London: Earthscan Publications, www.digitalfutures.org.uk): 69-71.

Lovins, A.B., and L.H. Lovins (2001) 'Frozen Assets? Alaskan Oil's Threat to National Energy Security', *RMI Solutions Newsletter*, Spring 2001, www.rmi.org.

Lovins, A.B., and A. Lehmann (2001) *Small is Profitable: The Hidden Benefits of Making Electrical Resources the Right Size* (Boulder, CO: Rocky Mountain Institute).

Lovins, A.B., and R. Sardinsky (1988) *The State of the Art: Lighting* (Snowmass, CO: COMPETITEK/ Rocky Mountain Institute, www.rmi.org).

Lovins, A.B., L.H. Lovins and P. Hawken (1999) 'A Road Map for Natural Capitalism', *Harvard Business Review* 77.3 (May/June 1999): 145-58.

Low, M., S. Nakayama and H. Yoshioka (1999) *Science, Technology and Society in Contemporary Japan* (Cambridge, UK: Cambridge University Press).

Luttwak, E. (1999) *Turbo-Capitalism: Winners and Losers in the Global Economy* (New York: Harper-Collins).

MacLean, R. (2000) 'Corporate Environmental Reports: Three Dimensions to Success', *Environmental Manager*, June 2000: 23-26.

Maibach, M., D. Peter and B. Seiler (1995) *Ökoinventar Transporte* (Zurich: Verlag INFRAS).

Mani, J. (1994) *Eine Ökobilanz von Glühlampe und Energiesparlampe* (Schriftenreihe des Bundesamtes für Energiewirtschaft, 53; Bern: Eidgenössische Drucksachen und Materialzentrale).

Marchand, P. (1998) *Marshall McLuhan: The Medium and the Messenger* (Cambridge, MA: The MIT Press).

Martin, J. (2000) *After the Internet, Alien Intelligence* (Los Angeles: Capital Press).

Maslennikova, I., and D. Foley (2000) 'Xerox's Approach to Sustainability', *Interfaces* 30: 226-33.

Matthews, H.S., C. Hendrickson and L. Lave (2000) 'Harry Potter and the Health of the Environment', *IEEE Spectrum*, November 2000: 20-22.

Mazurek, J.V. (1994) *How Fabulous Fablessness? Environmental Planning Implications of Economic Restructuring in the Silicon Valley Semiconductor Industry* (master's thesis; Los Angeles: University of California).

McIntosh, M., D. Leipziger, K. Jones and G. Coleman (1998) *Corporate Citizenship: Successful Strategies for Responsible Companies* (London: Financial Times/Pitman).

McKendrick, D.G., R.F. Doner and S. Haggard (2000) *From Silicon Valley to Singapore* (Stanford, CA: Stanford University Press).

McLaren, J., L. Wright, S. Parkinson and T. Jackson (2000) 'A Dynamic Life Cycle Energy Model of Mobile Phone Take-back and Recycling', *Journal of Industrial Ecology* 3 (1 November 2000).

McLuhan, M. (1962) *The Gutenberg Galaxy: The Making of Typographic Man* (Toronto: Toronto University Press).

McNealy, S. (2000) Interview in *Wired*, April 2000: 12.

McWilliams, A., and D. Siegel (2000) 'Corporate Social Responsibility and Financial Performance: Correlation or Misspecification?', *Strategic Management Journal* 21.5 (May 2000): 603-609.

—— (2001) 'Corporate Social Responsibility: A Theory of the Firm Perspective', *Academy of Management Review* 26.1 (January 2001): 117-27.

Meyer, H. (1999) 'Many Happy Returns', *Journal of Business Strategy* 30.2: 27-31.

Miller, A.S. (1968) *The Supreme Court and American Capitalism* (New York: The Free Press).

Milliman, K. (1995) *ISO 14000 and US Manufacturing* (Washington, DC: Center for Risk Management, Resources for the Future).

Mills, M.P. (2000) 'Kyoto and the Internet: The Energy Implications of the Digital Economy', Subcommittee on National Economic Growth, Natural Resources, and Regulatory Affairs, US House of Representatives, Washington, DC, 2 February 2000, www.house.gov/reform/neg/hearings/020200/mills.htm.

—— (2001) 'Energy Policy in the Electron Age', www.fossilfuels.org/Electric/electron.htm.

Ministry of Information Technology, Government of India (1999) *Guide to Electronics Industry in India 1999* (New Delhi: Government of India, Ministry of Information Technology [formerly Department of Electronics], Data Bank and Information Division).

Ministry of the Environment, Singapore (1997) www.gov.sg/etnet/inddevpl.htm.

MITI (Japan Ministry of International Trade and Industry) *Promotion of Electric and Electronic Apparatus Recycling (outline)* (not dated) (Tokyo: MITI Industrial Structure Council).

Mittleman, J. (1996) 'The Dynamics of Globalization', in J. Mittleman (ed.), *Globalization: Critical Reflections* (Boulder, CO: Lynne Rienner).

Mol, A.P.J., and D.A. Sonnenfeld (2000) *Ecological Modernisation Around the World: Perspectives and Critical Debates* (London: Frank Cass).

MPT (Ministry of Post and Telecommunications) (1998) *Addressing Global Environmental Preservation through Info-Communications Systems* (Tokyo: Government of Japan).

—— (2000) *Introducing Teleworking in the Asia-Pacific Region: A Reference Guide* (Tokyo: Government of Japan).

National Semiconductor (1995) *Annual Report*, www.national.com/annual_report/Management's_Discussion.html.

Negroponte, N. (1995) *Being Digital* (New York: Alfred A. Knopf/Vintage Books).

Novo Nordisk (2001) 'Environmental and Social Report', http://novo.dk/site/esroo/default.asp, February 2001.

Nunan, R. (1988) 'The Libertarian Conception of Corporate Property: A Critique of Milton Friedman's Views on the Social Responsibility of Business', *Journal of Business Ethics* 7.12 (December 1988): 891-906.

Oakley, K. (2000) 'The New Victorians', unpublished article.

OECD (Organisation for Economic Co-operation and Development) (1997) *OECD Policy Meeting on Sustainable Consumption and Individual Travel Behaviour* (Paris: OECD).

—— (1998) *Extended and Shared Producer Responsibility* (Phase 2, Framework report, ENV/EPOC/PPC (97)20/REV2; OECD, Environment Directorate, Group on Pollution Prevention and Control, www.oecd.org).

Orts, E.W. (1992) 'Beyond Shareholders: Interpreting Corporate Constituency Statutes', *George Washington Law Review* 61I.1 (November 1992): 14-135.

Östermark, U., and E. Eriksson (1999) *Livscykelanalys av en bildkonferens: En jämförelse med andra kommunikationssätt* (Gothenburg: CPM, Chalmers Institute of Technology).

Ottman, J. (2001) 'It's Not Just the Environment, Stupid', www.greenmarketing.com/index.html, January 2001.

Otto, T. (2000) *E-Commerce im Buchhandel: Eine vergleichende Betrachtung der Buchdistribution des stationären und Online-Buchhandels unter ökologischen Gesichtspunkten* (Darmstadt: Deutsche Telekom AG).

Patterson, W. (1999) *Transforming Electricity: The Coming Generation of Change* (London: Earthscan Publications).

—— (2000) 'Coming Full Circle', in G. Isherwood (ed.), *WorldPower 2000* (London: Isherwood Production): 19-21.

Pezzoli, K. (2000) 'Environmental Management Systems (EMSs) and Regulatory Innovation', *California Western Law Review* 36: 335-64.

PIRC (Pensions Investment Research Consultants) (2000) *Environmental Reporting 2000* (London: PIRC).

Plätzer, E.T., and L. Göttsching (1998) 'Print Media in the Era of Information Technology: How Environmentally Sound are Electronic Newspapers?', *Das Papier* 2.98: 56-65.

Plazola, C. (1997) *The Globalisation of High Tech: Environmental Injustices Plague Industry* (San Jose, CA: SVTC).

Pogorelec, J. (2000) 'Reverse Logistics Is Doable, Important', *Frontline Solutions* 1.10: 68-69.

Pohlen, T.L., and M.T. Farris (1992) 'Reverse Logistics in Plastics Recycling', *International Journal of Physical Distribution and Logistics Management* 22.7: 35-47.

Porter, M.E., and C. van der Linde (1995a) 'Green and Competitive: Ending the Stalemate', *Harvard Business Review* 73.5 (September/October 1995): 120-33.

—— (1995b) 'Toward a New Conception of the Environment–Competitiveness Relationship', *Journal of Economic Perspectives* 9.4 (Fall 1995): 97-118.

Preston, L.E., and D. Windsor (1997) *The Rules of the Game in the Global Economy: Policy Regimes for International Business* (Dordrecht, Netherlands: Kluwer Academic Publishers, 2nd edn [1991]).

Prince, W., and D. Nelson (1996) 'Developing an Environmental Model: Piecing Together the Growing Diversity of International Environmental Standards and Agendas Affecting Mining Companies', *Colorado Journal of International Law and Policy* 7: 247-316.

Proddow, L. (2000) *Heroes.com: The Names and Faces behind the Dot Com Era* (London: Hodder & Stoughton).

PSI Global (1999) 'More small firms are now online', *Atlanta Business Chronicle*, 30 April 1999.

Putnam, R. (2000) *Bowling Alone: The Collapse and Revival of American Community* (New York: Simon & Schuster).

Quack, D., and C.-O. Gensch (2000) *Orientierender ökologischer Vergleich von Videokonferenzen mit Face-to-Face Besprechungen* (Freiburg: Oeko-Institut Freiburg).

—— (2001) Potential for Reducing Environmental Impacts by Means of Dematerialization, Exemplified by Deutsche's Virtual Telephone-Call Manager, the "T-Net Box" ', in L.M. Hilty and P.W. Gilgen (eds.), *Sustainability in the Information Society: 15th International Symposium Informatics for Environmental Protection, Zurich 2001* (Marburg, Germany: Metropolis Verlag): 143-50.

Radermacher, F.-J. (1999) 'Chancen der digitalen Revolution', www.ixmagazin.de/tp/deutsch/inhalt/co/2738/1.html, 12 April 1999.

Rainie, L., and D. Packel (2001) 'More Online Doing More', *Pew Internet Tracking Report* (Pew Internet and American Life Project), 18 February 2001, www.pewinternet.org/reports/toc.asp?Report=30, accessed 8 February 2002.

Rastogi, R. (1998) 'Indian Electronics Industry: An Overview', *Saket Industrial Digest*, October 1998: 23-31.

Regner, S. (2000) *Telekommunikation im ökologischen Fokus: Ermittlung und Bewertung des Ressourceneinsatzes für die Festnetzbestandteile der Netzinfrastruktur* (Darmstadt/Rüsselsheim: Deutsche Telekom).

Reichart, I., and R. Hischier (2001) 'Environmental Impact of Electronic and Print Media: Television, Internet Newspaper and Printed Daily Newspaper', in L.M. Hilty and P.W. Gilgen (eds.), *Sustainability in the Information Society: 15th International Symposium Informatics for Environmental Protection, Zurich 2001* (Marburg, Germany: Metropolis Verlag): 91-98.

Reichart, I., R. Hischier, H. Schefer and M. Zurkirch (2001) *Vergleich der Umweltbelastungen bei Benutzung elektronischer und gedruckter Medien* (St Gallen, Switzerland: EMPA St Gallen).

Reichl, H., and H. Griese (eds.) (2000) *Electronics Goes Green 2000+: Proceedings Volume 1. Technical Lectures of the Joint International Congress and Exhibition, September 11–13, 2000* (Berlin: VDE Verlag).

Rejeski, D. (1999) 'Electronic Impact', *The Environmental Forum* 16.4 (July/August 1999): 32-38; www.cisp.org/imp/october_99/10_99contents.htm.

Repetto, R., and D. Austin (2000a) *Coming Clean: Corporate Disclosure of Financially Significant Environmental Risks* (Washington, DC: World Resources Institute).

—— (2000b) *Pure Profit: The Financial Implications of Environmental Performance* (Washington, DC: World Resources Institute).

Report from the Clinton–Gore Administration (2000) *Building Livable Communities: Sustainability Prosperity, Improving Quality of Life, Building a Sense of Community* (Washington, DC: US Government Publications Office, June, revised).

Rheingold, H. (1994) *The Virtual Community: Homesteading on the Electronic Frontier* (Reading, MA: Addison–Wesley).

Robertson, R. (1992) *Globalisation: Social Theory and Global Culture* (London: Sage).

Robins, N., and S. Roberts (eds.) (2000) *The Reality of Sustainable Trade* (London: International Institute for Environment and Development).

Rogers, D.S., and R.S. Tibben-Lembke (1999) 'Going Backwards: Reverse Logistics Trends and Practices', Reverse Logistics Executive Council, www.rlec.org.

Romm, J. (2000) 'Kyoto and the Internet: The Energy Implications of Digital Economy', testimony given at United States House of Representatives, www.house.gov/reform/neg/hearings/020200/romm.htm.

Romm, J , A Rosenfeld and S. Herrmann (1999) *The Internet Economy and Global Warming* (Version 1, December 1999, www.cool-companies.org/energy/; Arlington, VA: Center for Energy and Climate Solutions): 5-8.

Roome, N.J. (1998a) 'Globalization and Sustainable Development: Toward a Transatlantic Agenda', paper given at the *Colloquium on Globalization and the Environment*, SPEA, Indiana University. In C. Bonser (ed.), *Security, Trade, and Environmental Policy: A US/European Union Transatlantic Agenda* (Dordrecht, Netherlands: Kluwer Academic Publishers, 2000).

—— (1998b) 'Conclusion: Implications for Management Practice, Education, and Research', in N.J. Roome (ed.), *Sustainability Strategies for Industry: The Future of Corporate Practice* (Washington, DC: Island Press): 259-76.

—— (2001) 'Metatextual Organizations: Innovation and Adaptation for Global Change', inaugural address, Erasmus University, Rotterdam,

Rosenau, M.D. (1988) 'Faster New Product Development', *Journal of Product Innovation Management* 6: 150-63.

Rowledge, L., R. Barton and K. Brady (1999) *Mapping the Journey: Case Studies in Strategy and Action toward Sustainable Development* (Sheffield, UK: Greenleaf Publishing).

Rowley, J. (2000) 'The Reverse Supply-Chain Impact of Current Trends', *Logistics and Transport Focus* 2.6: 27-31.

Roy, R. (1994) 'The Evolution of Ecodesign', *Technovation* 14: 363-80.

Royal Dutch/Shell (2001) 'The Shell Forum', www.shell.com/royal-en/directory/0,5029,25423,00.html, February 2001.

Salzman, J. (1999) 'Beyond the Smokestack: Environmental Protection in the Service Economy', *UCLA Law Review* 47: 411-89.

Sarkis, J. (2002) 'How Green is my Supply Chain: Theory and Practice', *Journal of Industrial Ecology*, forthcoming.

Sarkis, J., N.M. Darnall, G.I. Nehman and J.W. Priest (1995) 'The Role of Supply Chain Management within the Industrial Ecosystem', paper presented at IEEE International Symposium on Electronics and the Environment, Orlando, FL, May 1995.

Saurin, J. (1993) 'Global Environmental Degradation, Modernity and Environmental Knowledge', *Environmental Politics* 2.4: 46-64.

Schlesinger, A.M. (1986) *The Cycles of American History* (Boston: Houghton Mifflin).

Schwartz, B. (2000) 'Reverse Logistics Strengthens Supply Chain', *Transportation and Distribution* 41.5: 95-100.

Schwartz, P., P. Leyden and J. Hyatt (1999) *The Long Boom: A Vision for the Coming Age of Prosperity* (New York: Perseus Publishing, www.thelongboom.org).

Scott, P. (2001) 'Wired reports carry barbs', *Environmental Finance*, June 2000, www.environmental-finance.com/2000/featjun.htm (February 2001).

SEC (US Securities and Exchange Commission) (1997) *Edgar database 10K Reports* (Washington, DC: Government Printing Office, www.sec.gov/cgi-bin/srch-edgar?).

SEEQ Technology Incorporated (1991) *Annual Report* (Fremont, CA: SEEQ Technology Incorporated).

—— (1996) *Corporate Fact Sheet* (Fremont, CA: SEEQ Technology Incorporated, www.seeq.com).

—— (1997) *1996 Annual Report* (Fremont, CA: SEEQ Technology Incorporated).

Selbourne, D. (1999) '[Professor] Tony [Giddens], You're Talking Globaloney', *The Times* (London), 28 April 1999: Features Section.

Selekman, B.M. (1958) 'Is Management Creating a Class Society?', *Harvard Business Review* 36.1 (January/February 1958): 37-46.

Sennett, R. (2000) 'Street and Office: Two Sources of Identity', in W. Hutton and A. Giddens (eds.), *On the Edge* (London: Jonathan Cape): 181-83.

Sharma, S., and H. Vredenburg (1998) 'Proactive Corporate Environmental Strategy and the Development of Competitively Valuable Organizational Capabilities', *Strategic Management Journal* 19: 729-53.

Sheats, J.R. (2001) 'Information Technology in Sustainable Development', in R. Dorf (ed.), *Technology, Humans, and Society* (San Diego, CA: Academic Press): 146-58.

Shrivastava, P. (1995) 'The Role of Corporations in Achieving Ecological Sustainability', *Academy of Management Review* 20.4 (October 1995): 936-60.

SIA (Semiconductor Industry Association) (1994) *The National Technology Roadmap for Semiconductors* (San Jose, CA: SIA).

—— (1997a) *Chip Stats* (San Jose, CA: SIA, www.semichips.org).

—— (1997b) 'Worker Safety and Environment', www.semichips.org.

Simchi-Levi, D., P. Kaminsky and E. Simchi-Levi (2000) *Designing and Managing the Supply Chain* (Boston, MA: McGraw–Hill).

Slywotzky, A.J. (2000) 'The Age of the Choiceboard', *Harvard Business Review*, January/February 2000: 40-41.

Slywotzky, A.J. and D. Morrison (2000) *How Digital is your Business?* (New York: Crown Business, www.howdigitalisyourbusiness.com).

Socialfunds.com (2001) 'Introduction to Socially Responsible Investing', www.socialfunds.com/page.cgi/article1.html, February 2001.

Soldera, M. (1995) *Öko-Computer: Vergleich eines Öko-PC mit einem herkömmlichen PC anhand Lebenszyklusanalysen* (Gebenstorf, Switzerland: Soldera).

Spaargaren, G., A.P.J. Mol and F.H. Buttel (eds.) (2000) *Environment and Global Modernity* (London: Sage Studies in International Sociology).

Stevels, A. (2000) 'Green Marketing of Consumer Electronics', in H. Reichl and H. Griese (eds.), *Electronics Goes Green 2000+: Proceedings Volume 1. Technical Lectures of the Joint International Congress and Exhibition, September 11–13, 2000* (Berlin: VDE Verlag): 539-44.

Stock, J.R. (1998), *Development and Implementation of Reverse Logistics Programs* (Oak Brook, IL: Council of Logistics Management).

Strubel, V., C.-O.Gensch, M. Buchert, D. Bunke, F. Ebinger, E. Heber, C. Hochfeld, R. Grießhammer, D. Quack, I. Reichart and H.-G. Viereck (1999) *Verbundvorhaben: Beiträge zur Entwicklung einer Kreislaufwirtschaft am Beispiel des komplexen Massenkonsumproduktes TV-Gerät. Teilvorhaben 1. Ökologische und ökonomische Begleitforschung 'Grüner Fernseher' (Hauptphase). Endbericht* (Freiburg/Darmstadt: Oeko-Institut).

SustainAbility (1997) *The 1997 Benchmark Survey* (London: SustainAbility/United Nations Environment Programme).

—— (1999) *The Internet Reporting Report* (London: SustainAbility/United Nations Environment Programme).

—— (2000) *The Global Reporters* (London: SustainAbility/United Nations Environment Programme).

Szwajkowski, E. (2000) 'Simplifying the Principles of Stakeholder Management: The Three Most Important Principles', *Business and Society* 39.4 (December 2000): 379-97.

Tankha, S. (1999) *Corporate Sustainability: Reconciling Wealth Creation with Global Sustainability* (Houston, TX: Center for Global Change, Houston Advanced Research Center).

Tapscott, D. (1995) *The Digital Economy: Promise and Peril in the Age of Networked Intelligence* (New York: McGraw–Hill).

—— (1998) *Growing up Digital: The Rise of the Net Generation* (New York: McGraw–Hill).

Tapscott, D., D. Ticoll and A. Lowy (2000) *Digital Capital: Harnessing the Power of Business Webs* (Cambridge, MA: Harvard Business Press).

Thierry, M., M. Salomon, J. van Nunen and L. van Wassenhove (1995) 'Strategic Issues in Product Recovery Management', *California Management Review* 37.2: 114-35.

Thompson, B. (2000) *e-Mutualism or the Tragedy of the Dot-commons* (London: The Co-operative Party).

Tibben-Lembke, R.S., and D.S. Rogers (1998) 'Going Backwards: Reverse Logistics Trends and Practices', www.rlec.org/reverse.pdf.

Toop, C. (2000) *The US eConsumer Profile. II. Online Purchasing Patterns* (London: Datamonitor PLC).

Totten, M. (1993) The Power of Collaborative Global Communication Technologies to Promote Sustainable Architectural Design and Development, interactive multimedia presentation to the AIA and ACSA, Joint Council on Architectural Research.

—— (1998) Electronic Uses to foster USES (Universal Sustainable Energy Services), global assessment report prepared for the Rockefeller Foundation.

—— (1999) Business Plan for the Creation of SafeClimate.net, a Web Enterprise to Promote Institutional and Individual Commitments to Achieving Zero Net Carbon Emissions (Washington, DC: World Resources Institute).

UNCTAD (United Nations Conference on Trade and Development) (1995) Recent Developments in International Investments and TNC: Trends in FDI (Geneva: UNCTAD).

—— (1999) Profiting from Green Consumerism in Germany: Analytical Studies on Trade Environment and Development (UNCTAD).

UNEP (United Nations Environment Programme) (1992) Protecting the Ozone Layer. II. Solvents, Coatings and Adhesives (Paris: UNEP IE/PAC).

UNEP (United Nations Environment Programme)/UNIDO (United Nations Industrial Development Organisation) (1999) Environmental Management in the Electronics Industry: Semiconductor Manufacture and Assembly (Technical Report 23; UNEP/UNIDO).

US Department of Commerce (DOC) (1994) County Business Patterns (US Summary Data, Bureau of the Census; Washington, DC: Government Printing Office, www.census.gov/prod/www/abs/cbptotal.html).

—— (1997) Current Industrial Reports (MA36 Series, Bureau of the Census; Washington, DC: Government Printing Office).

US Department of Energy (2000) Report of the US Department of Energy's Power Outage Study (Washington, DC: US Department of Energy).

Vesey, J.T. (1992) 'Time-to-Market: Put Speed in Product Development', Industrial Marketing Management 21.2: 151-58.

von Moltke, K., et al. (1998) 'Global Product Chains: Northern Consumers, Southern Producers and Sustainability', Environment and Trade 15.

Wall Street Journal (2001) 'Solectron Sharply Lowered Financial Targets', Wall Street Journal, 20 March 2001: 1-3.

Wasserstrom, R., and S. Reider (1999) 'Here's a Side to Big Oil's Story that Needs Better Telling', Houston Chronicle, 24 January 1999: 4C.

WBCSD (World Business Council for Sustainable Development) (ed.) (2000) Eco-efficiency: Creating More Value with Less Impact (Geneva: WBCSD).

—— (ed.) (2001) The Business Case for Sustainable Development: Making a Difference. Toward the Johannesburg Summit 2002 and Beyond (Geneva: WBCSD).

WCED (World Commission on Environment and Development) (1987) Our Common Future ('The Brundtland Report'; Oxford, UK: Oxford University Press).

Weaver, P.M., L. Jansen, G. van Grootveld, E. van Spiegel and P. Vergragt (2000) Sustainable Technology Development (Sheffield, UK: Greenleaf Publishing).

Weterings, R.A.P.M. (1998) 'Product Innovation and Public Involvement', in J.E.M. Klostermann and A. Tukker (eds.), Product-Innovation and Eco-Efficiency (Dordrecht, Netherlands: Kluwer): 187-95.

White, A. (2000) 'Environment and the Information Age', Environmental Perspectives 16 (April 2000): 1.

Williams, R.H., E. Larson, and M. Ross (1987) Materials, Affluence, and Industrial Energy Use (Report 214; Princeton, NJ: Princeton University, Center for Energy and Environmental Studies).

Williamson, O. (1985) The Economic Institutions of Capitalism (New York: The Free Press).

Wilsdon, J. (2001) Digital Futures: Living in a Dot-Com World (London: Earthscan Publications, www.digitalfutures. org.uk).

Windsor, D. (1979) 'A Critique of "The Costs of Sprawl"', Journal of the American Planning Association 45.3 (July 1979): 279-92.

—— (1992) 'Stakeholder Management in Multinational Enterprises', Proceedings of the International Association for Business and Society, June 1992: 121-27.

—— (2000a) 'International Virtual Teams: Opportunities and Issues', presentation at 8th *Annual Individual, Team, and Organizational Effectiveness Symposium: Team Based Organizations for the 21st Century*, Center for the Study of Work Teams, University of North Texas, Denton, TX, May 2000.

—— (2000b) 'The Development Consequences of Virtual Knowledge Management Networks', presentation at 4th *International Conference on Technology Policy and Innovation*, Curitiba, Brazil, August 2000.

—— (forthcoming) 'The Global Regime for Intellectual Property Rights', in P. Conceicao, D.V. Gibson, M.V. Heitor and C. Stolp (eds.), *Systems and Policies for the Globalized Learning Economy* (Westport, CT: Greenwood).

Windsor, D., and K.A. Getz (1999) 'Regional Market Integration and the Development of Global Norms for Enterprise Conduct: The Case of International Bribery', *Business and Society* 38.4 (December 1999): 415-49.

Winter-Watson, B., and W.B. Weil (2001) 'The Internet and Environmental Reporting: Improving Communication with Stakeholders', www.erm.com/erm/adhocweb.nsf/(Page_Name_Web)/WebPage_Soc.resp.exe.sum, February 2001.

Witt, N. (2000) 'Mandela thanks Labour faithful', *The Guardian*, 29 September 2000: 9.

Wood, D.J. (1986) *Strategic Uses of Public Policy: Business and Government in the Progressive Era* (Boston, MA: Pitman).

—— (1991) 'Corporate Social Performance Revisited', *Academy of Management Review* 16.4 (October 1991): 691-718.

World Bank (2000) *Greening Industry: New Roles, for Communities, Markets and Governments* (Oxford, UK: Oxford University Press, www.worldbank.org/nipr/greening).

World Economic Forum (2000) *Pilot Environmental Sustainability Index*, WEF, Yale Center for Environmental Law and Policy, Center for International Earth Science Information Network, www.ciesin.org/indicators/ESI/pilot_esi.html; www.yale.edu/envirocenter; www.weforum.com/pdf/glt/glt_esi_2000.pdf.

WRI (World Resources Institute) (1998–99) *A Guide to the Global Environment* (WRI, UNDP, UNEP, World Bank; London: Oxford University Press).

—— (1999) *World Resources 1998–99: A Guide to the Global Environment* (Oxford, UK: Oxford University Press).

—— (2000) *The Weight of Nations: Material Outflows from Industrial Economies* (Washington, DC: WRI, www.wri.org/).

WRI (World Resources Institute) and Aspen Institute (Initiative for Social Innovation through Business) (1999) *Beyond Grey Pinstripes: Preparing MBAs for Social and Environmental Stewardship* (Washington, DC: World Resources Institute and Aspen Institute, www.wri.org/wri/bschools).

WTO (World Tourism Organisation) (2000) *Tourism Highlights 2000* (Madrid: WTO, 2nd edn).

Xerox (2000) 'Xerox Europe plans paperless future for 50 million documents', Xerox Industry Solutions and Services, www.xps.com/what/what.htm.

Zhang, H.C., T.C. Kuo, H. Lu and S.H. Huang (1997) 'Environmentally Conscious Design and Manufacturing: A State-of-the-Art Survey', *Journal of Manufacturing Systems* 16: 352-71.

Zint, M., and R. Frederick (2001) 'Marketing and Advertising a "Deep Green" Company: The Case of Patagonia, Inc.', *Journal of Corporate Citizenship* 1 (Spring 2001): 93-113.

ABBREVIATIONS

ABB	Asea Brown Boveri
ABI	Allied Business Intelligence
ADL	Arthur D. Little
AIDS	acquired immuno-deficiency syndrome
AMD	Advanced Micro Devices
AMeDAS	Automated Meteorological Data Acquisition System
AMI	American Microsystems Inc.
AOL	America Online
ASN	advance ship notice
AT&T	American Telephone & Telegraph Co.
B2B	business-to-business
B2C	business-to-consumer
BP	British Petroleum
BSR	Business for Social Responsibility
BT	British Telecom
BTU	British thermal unit
Cat	Caterpillar
CCD	charge-coupled device
CCI	corporate community investment
CD	compact disc
CD-ROM	compact disc–read-only memory
CEFIC	European Chemical Industry Council
CEO	chief executive officer
CEU	cumulated energy use
CFC	chlorofluorocarbon
CFL	compact fluorescent lamp
CIBC	Canadian Imperial Bank of Commerce
CML	Centre for Environmental Science, Leiden University, Netherlands
CO_2	carbon dioxide
CRT	cathode-ray tube
CSP	corporate social performance
CSR1	corporate social responsibility
CSR2	corporate social responsiveness
CSR	corporate sustainability report
DC	distribution centre
DEC	Digital Equipment Corporation

DfE	design for environment
DNA	deoxyribonucleic acid
DNV	Det Norske Veritas
DTI	Department of Trade and Industry, UK
ED	environmental declaration
EDI	electronic data interchange
EEA	European Environment Agency
EEOC	Equal Employment Opportunity Commission
EHS	environment, health and safety
EIP	eco-industrial park
EMAS	Eco-management and Audit Scheme
EMPA	Eidgenosse Materialprüfungs- und Forschungsanstalt (Swiss Federal Laboratories for Materials Testing and Research)
EMS	environmental management system
ENIAC	Electronic Numerical Integrator and Computer
EP	ecopoint
EPA	Environmental Protection Agency
EPCRA	Emergency Planning and Community Right to Know Act
EPD	environmental product declaration
EPRI	Electric Power Research Institute
ERM	Environmental Resources Management
ETNO	European Telecommunications Public Network Operators Association
EU	European Union
EURESCOM	European Institute for Research and Strategic Studies in Telecommunications
FEE	Fédération des Experts Comptables Européens
FTSE	*Financial Times* Stock Exchange
GDP	gross domestic product
GE	General Electric
GEMI	Global Environmental Management Initiative
GHG	greenhouse gas
GIS	geographic information system
GJ	gigajoule
GM	General Motors
GPS	global positioning system
GRI	Global Reporting Initiative
GW	gigawatt
GWh	gigawatt-hour
HP	Hewlett-Packard
hp	horsepower
IAS	Institute of Advanced Studies
IBC	International Botanical Congress
IBM	International Business Machines
IC	internal combustion
ICCE	information, communication, computing and electronic
ICT	information and communications technology
IEEE	Institute of Electrical and Electronic Engineers
IEN	Iwate Environment Network
IMP	International Microelectronic Products
IP	Internet Protocol
IPG	Iwate Prefectural Government
IPO	Initial Public Offering
IPPR	Institute for Public Policy Research
ISDN	integrated services digital network
ISO	International Organisation for Standardisation

IST	information society technology
IT	information technology
ITU	International Telecommunication Union
kg	kilogram
km	kilometre
kW	kilowatt
kWh	kilowatt-hour
LAN	local area network
LCA	life-cycle analysis/assessment
LCD	liquid-crystal display
lm	lumen
m	metre
Mbyte	megabyte
MEXT	Japanese Ministry of Education, Culture, Sports, Science and Technology
MHz	megahertz
MJ	megajoule
MNC	multinational corporation
MNE	multinational enterprise
MoEF	Ministry of Environment and Forests, India
mpg	miles per gallon
MPT	Ministry of Post and Telecommunications, Japan
MW	megawatt
MWh	megawatt-hour
Nasdaq	National Association of Securities Dealers Automated Quotations
NGO	non-governmental organisation
NHK	Japan Broadcasting Corporation
NIOSH	National Institute of Occupational Safety and Health, USA
NLRB	National Labor Relations Board, USA
NO_2	nitrogen dioxide
NO_x	nitrogen oxides
NRDC	Natural Resources Defense Council, USA
NTT	Nippon Telegraph and Telephone Corporation
OECD	Organisation for Economic Co-operation and Development
OEM	original equipment manufacturer
OPI	operational performance indicator
OSHA	Occupational Safety and Health Administration
PAFC	phosphoric acid fuel cell
PC	personal computer
PCB	polychlorinated biphenyl
PDF	portable document format
PEM	proton-exchange membrane
PERI	Public Environmental Reporting Initiative
PIRC	Pensions Investment Research Consultants Ltd
POEM	product-oriented environmental management
POTS	plain old telephone system
PV	photovoltaic
R&D	research and development
RICO	Racketeer Influenced and Corrupt Organisations
ROS	Restriction of the Use of Certain Hazardous Substances in Electrical and Electronic Equipment
SAM	Sustainable Asset Management
SARA	Superfund Amendments and Reauthorisation Act
SEC	Securities and Exchange Commission, USA
SIA	Semiconductor Industry Association

SIC	standard industrial classification
SME	small or medium-sized enterprise
SO_2	sulphur dioxide
TJ	terajoule
TQEM	total quality environmental management
TRI	Toxics Release Inventory
TSMC	Taiwan Semiconductor Manufacturing Corporation
TTM	time-to-market
TV	television
UAW	United Auto Workers
UN	United Nations
UNCTAD	United Nations Conference on Trade and Development
UNEP	United Nations Environment Programme
UNU	United Nations University
UPS	United Parcel Service, Inc.
USTA	United States Telecom Association
VC	venture capital
VCP	video cassette player
VCR	video cassette recorder
W	watt
WBCSD	World Business Council for Sustainable Development
WCED	World Commission on Environment and Development
WEEE	Waste from Electrical and Electronic Equipment
WNN	World Nature Network
WRI	World Resources Institute
WTDC	World Telecommunication and Development Conference
WTO	World Tourism Organisation
WTO	World Trade Organisation
WWW	World Wide Web
XML	Extensible Markup Language
XMM	Xerox Management Model

BIOGRAPHIES

Peter Arnfalk, MSc in Chemical Engineering and Licentiate in Industrial Environmental Economics, is an associate professor at the International Institute for Industrial Environmental Economics, Lund University, Sweden. He has experience of conducting research and working with environmental issues in Sweden, as well as in the US and Japan. He presented his licentiate dissertation 'Information Technology in Pollution Prevention' in October 1999.
peter.arnfalk@iiiee.lu.se

Brendan Barrett is a Fellow at the United Nations University/Institute of Advanced Studies. Educated in the UK with a doctorate from Oxford Brookes University, he is an environmental planner by training with 18 years' experience in international government, academic research and private-sector consultancy. He has published extensively on national and local environmental issues in Japan and has considerable practical experience in environmental impact assessment, environmental auditing and technology transfer.
barrett@ias.unu.edu

Frank de Bakker is an assistant professor at the Faculty of Social-Cultural Sciences of the Vrije Universiteit, Amsterdam, the Netherlands. He obtained a PhD degree at the Faculty of Technology and Management of the University of Twente, Enschede, the Netherlands, where he focused on organisational aspects of product-oriented environmental management. Capabilities, stakeholders and environmental management are important elements of his research, which has been published in the *Journal of Industrial Ecology* and in *Business Strategy and the Environment*.
fga.d_bakker@scw.vu.nl

Seth Dunn is a research associate at Worldwatch Institute, where he investigates energy and climate issues. He is the author of two Worldwatch Papers, 'Micropower: the Next Electrical Era' (No. 151), 'Rising Sun, Gathering Winds: Policies to Stabilise the Climate and Strengthen Economies' (No. 138), and four chapters in the Institute's annual *State of the World* books. Seth Dunn holds a BA in history and studies in the environment from Yale University.
sdunn@worldwatch.org

Klaus Fichter, PhD, is the director of the Borderstep Institute for Innovation and Sustainability, a Berlin-based, not-for-profit research institute. One major focus of Borderstep's research agenda is on the digital economy and its impacts on the environment.
fichter@borderstep.de

David Foley has been the environmental co-ordinator of Xerox Europe for two and a half years. He is sponsored by Xerox Europe for the Engineering Doctorate in Environmental Technology at the University of Surrey, UK, and co-sponsored by the EPSRC (Engineering and Physical Sciences Research Council, UK). He previously studied at the Universities of Nottingham and Birmingham.
david.foley@gbr.xerox.com

Chris Galea teaches at the Gerald Schwartz School of Business and Information Systems at St Francis Xavier University in Nova Scotia, Canada, in the areas of management and sustainability. His active research focuses on the process of experiential management learning as it relates to sustainable development.
cgalea@stfx.com

Ritu Kumar is an environmental economist experienced in dealing with issues related to sustainable production, trade and climate change. She is currently working on a number of projects aimed at enhancing the capacity of developing-country producers and exporters to meet sustainability requirements, either through the supply chain or those inherent in legislative measures. She is presently working as a consultant with the Commonwealth Science Council in London and is also the Director of the TERI-Europe office in London.
ritukumar@aol.com

Josephine Chinying Lang is an assistant professor at the Nanyang Technological University, Singapore, where she teaches organisational behaviour and strategic management. She received her Doctorate in Business Administration from Boston University, USA. Her current research interests include knowledge management, innovation and creativity, as well as government–business relations. She has taught graduate, undergraduate and executive courses in New Zealand and Malaysia, and has also consulted widely in both private and public sectors.
acylang@ntu.edu.sg

Lassi Linnanen is a Professor of Environmental and Quality Management at Helsinki University of Technology, Finland. He is also the founder and former CEO of Gaia Group, a leading sustainable development consultancy. His research interests include corporate environmental and social responsibility strategies, and system innovations for sustainable development.
lassi.linnanen@hut.fi

Jan Mazurek directs the Center for Innovation and Environment at the Progressive Policy Institute (PPI) in Washington, DC. She holds degrees in economics and regional planning from the University of California. Prior to PPI, Mazurek worked as a policy analyst at research organisations, including Resources for the Future, the National Academy of Public Administration and the Organisation for Economic Co-operation and Development. An expert on the use of voluntary environmental approaches, she has been a participant in the European Research Network on Voluntary Agreements (CAVA). Mazurek is the author of *Making Microchips: Policy, Restructuring and Globalisation in the Semiconductor Industry* (MIT Press, 1999) and the co-author of *Pollution Control in the US* (Johns Hopkins, 1998) with J. Clarence Davies.
mazurek@ppic.org

Laura M. Meade is an Assistant Professor of Logistics and Supply Chain Management at the University of Dallas, TX, USA. Her teaching and research interests include e-logistics and supply chain management.
lmeade@gsm.udallas.edu

Tim Otto has been with Deutsche Telekom since 1982. He is a telecommunications technician and studied at the University of Applied Sciences in Wilhelmshaven, Germany. Tim Otto has been working at the Central Environmental Affairs Office since 1996. Having developed an ecological

product evaluation system, his subsequent area of concern for the last three years has focused on the environmental impact of telecommunications services.
tim.otto@telekom.de

Jacob Park is a research scholar in the Harrison Program on the Future Global Agenda, University of Maryland, USA, and a senior research consultant specialising in Japanese and Asian equities for corporate governance and socially responsible investment, Friends Ivory & Sime. A fellow of the Environmental Leadership Program, a working interim group member of the Greening of Industry Network and a member of Center for Environmental Citizenship's board of directors, he will become an assistant professor in the business and economic department at Green Mountain College (Vermont, USA) in the fall of 2002.
sustainablebiz@alum.mit.edu

Inge Reichart is a scientist and head of life-cycle analysis (LCA) projects at the Swiss Federal Laboratories for Materials Testing and Research, St Gallen, Switzerland. Inge holds an MA in biology (University of Konstanz, Germany) and a postgraduate degree in business administration (Fern-Universität Hagen, Germany).
ingeborg.reichart@empa.ch

Markus Reichling has been with Deutsche Telekom's Central Environmental Affairs Office since 1996. He is a material sciences engineer and completed additional studies in environmental protection and quality management in 1995. His first two years at Deutsche Telekom were concerned with the implementation of environmental management systems according to ISO 14001. For over three years, he has been head of a group that analyses the environmental impacts of Deutsche Telekom's products and services.
markus.reichling@telekom.de

Nigel Roome is the Head of Department and Chair of Sustainable Enterprise and Transformation, Erasmus Centre for Sustainable Development and Management, Erasmus University Rotterdam. He is also the Chair of the Information and Communication Technologies Project, Industrial Transformation Programme, International Human Dimensions Programme on Global Environment Change.
roome@fsw.eur.nl

Mohammed Saqib is an economist working on trade and environmental issues. He is consultant to various international organisations such as the World Bank, the UN, Commonwealth and Indian Industry associations and the Government of India. He is presently working as a fellow with the Rajiv Gandhi Institute for Contemporary Studies, Rajiv Gandhi Foundation, New Delhi.
saqib@rgfindia.com

Joseph Sarkis is an Associate Professor of Environmental and Operations Management at Clark University, MA, USA. He received his PhD from the University of Buffalo and has published widely on environmental issues.
jsarkis@clarku.edu

James R. Sheats is currently a program manager in Hewlett-Packard Co.'s World e-Inclusion Initiative, with a variety of responsibilities involving technology assessment and product definition. A fellow of the American Association for the Advancement of Science, he holds a PhD in physical chemistry from Stanford University, and has worked on a wide variety of projects in thin film electronics during his 17 years as a technical staff member of HP Labs.
jim_sheats@hp.com

Yashika Singh is an economist working in the area of trade and environment, with emphasis on the impact of the environment on the multilateral trading system. She is currently involved in projects aimed at enhancing the sustainability of trade from developing countries. She is presently working

at the Rajiv Gandhi Institute for Contemporary Studies, Rajiv Gandhi Foundation, New Delhi.
yashikasingh@hotmail.com

Srinivas Talluri is an Associate Professor of Operations Management at Michigan State University, East Lansing, Michigan, USA. His research interests are in the areas of purchasing/supply chain management, technology management, business process improvement, and multi-criteria decision modelling.
talluri@msu.edu

Michael Totten is Senior Director in the Center for Environmental Leadership in Business (www. celb.org) at Conservation International, USA. He directs the 'Leaders on Climate, Biodiversity and Freshwater Project', involving corporations committed to shrinking their 'ecological footprints'. Totten received the 1999 Lewis Mumford Award for the Environment for his pioneering work in the use of the Internet and interactive multimedia software tools for promoting sustainable energy and resource development.
m.totten@conservation.org

Steve Walton has been Assistant Professor of Decision and Information Analysis at Goizueta Business School at Emory University, USA, since 1996. He earned his PhD from UNC–Chapel Hill in Operations Management in 1993.
steve_walton@bus.emory.edu

William B. Weil has degrees in Environmental Business Management in the Wharton School and Environmental Engineering from the University of Pennsylvania, USA. He is currently a consultant with Environmental Resources Management (ERM), where he has developed numerous paper- and Web-based corporate sustainability reports for *Fortune* 100 firms. Through ERM's Corporate Advisory Services group, he provides diagnostic strategy support on a broad range of corporate responsibility and sustainability concerns.
Bill_Weil@erm.com

James Wilsdon is Head of Strategy at Demos, the leading independent think-tank, where his research focuses on new technologies, sustainability and corporate responsibility. Prior to joining Demos, he was Senior Policy Adviser at Forum for the Future, where he co-ordinated the Digital Futures project, which explored the social and environmental impacts of e-commerce. He is editor of *Digital Futures: Living in a Dot-Com World* (Earthscan Publications, 2001).
james@demos.co.uk

Duane Windsor (BA, Rice University; PhD, Harvard University) is Lynette S. Autrey Professor at Rice University's Jesse H. Jones Graduate School of Management in Houston, TX, USA. His books include *The Rules of the Game in the Global Economy: Policy Regimes for International Business* (Kluwer Academic Publishers, 1992, 1997), *The Foreign Corrupt Practices Act: Anatomy of a Statute* (Lexington Books, 1982) and *The Changing Boardroom: Making and Policy and Profits in an Age of Corporate Citizenship* (Gulf Publishing Co., 1982).
odw@rice.edu

Barbara Winter-Watson has more than 15 years of experience at Environmental Resources Management (ERM) in environmental management consulting, specialising in communications; corporate strategic planning; workshop and meeting facilitation; environmental, health and safety business integration; product life-cycle studies; training; and management systems development. She managed the business integration practice for ERM Inc. and now leads the corporate reporting practice within ERM North America, playing an active role in all facets of printed and Web-based reporting since 1993. Ms Winter-Watson has worked with several clients to implement the Global

Reporting Initiative guidelines for sustainability reporting.
Barbara_Winter-Watson@erm.com

Ichiro Yamada is Director of the Lifestyle and Environmental Technology Laboratories, Nippon Telegraph and Telephone Corporation (NTT). He completed a master's degree in mechanical engineering at Tokyo University and joined the NTT Electrical Communications Laboratories in 1974. His early research and development activities related to motion control, optical disk memory storage and clean energy systems. He received his doctorate from Tokyo University in 1985. He is currently promoting research and development of environmental information technologies within NTT.
yamada@aecl.ntt.co.jp

Dr **Manfred Zurkirch** is the head of life-cycle analysis (LCA) projects at Swisscom Ltd. Manfred studied physics at the Federal Institute of Technology in Zurich, and is responsible for a research team at Swisscom that deals with electromagnetic and environmental issues.
manfred.zurkirch@swisscom.com

INDEX